S0-AXE-346

# healing with
# crystals and
## chakra energies

# healing with crystals and chakra energies

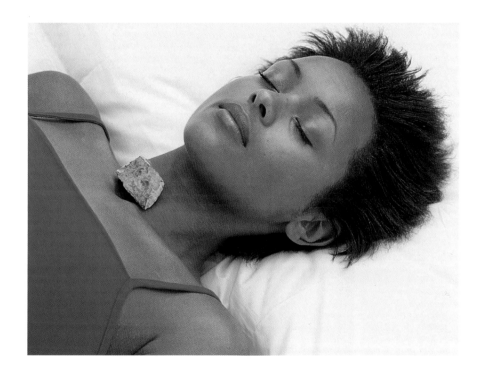

How to harness the transforming powers of colour,
crystals and your body's own subtle energies to
increase health and wellbeing

**SUE** and **SIMON LILLY**

HERMES
HOUSE

This edition is published by Hermes House, an imprint of Anness Publishing Ltd, Blaby Road, Wigston, Leicestershire LE18 4SE

Email: info@anness.com

Web: www.hermeshouse.com; www.annesspublishing.com

If you like the images in this book and would like to investigate using them for publishing, promotions or advertising, please visit our website www.practicalpictures.com for more information.

Publisher: Joanna Lorenz
Managing Editor: Helen Sudell
Senior Editor: Joanne Rippin
Photography: Michelle Garrett
Designer: Nigel Partridge
Production Controller: Wanda Burrows

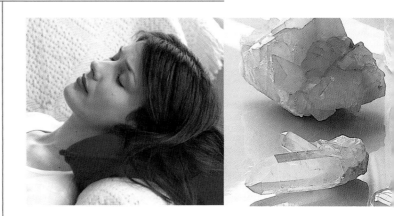

ETHICAL TRADING POLICY
At Anness Publishing we believe that business should be conducted in an ethical and ecologically sustainable way, with respect for the environment and a proper regard to the replacement of the natural resources we employ.
As a publisher, we use a lot of wood pulp in high-quality paper for printing, and that wood commonly comes from spruce trees. We are therefore currently growing more than 750,000 trees in three Scottish forest plantations: Berrymoss (130 hectares/320 acres), West Touxhill (125 hectares/305 acres) and Deveron Forest (75 hectares/185 acres). The forests we manage contain more than 3.5 times the number of trees employed each year in making paper for the books we manufacture.
Because of this ongoing ecological investment programme, you, as our customer, can have the pleasure and reassurance of knowing that a tree is being cultivated on your behalf to naturally replace the materials used to make the book you are holding.
Our forestry programme is run in accordance with the UK Woodland Assurance Scheme (UKWAS) and will be certified by the internationally recognized Forest Stewardship Council (FSC).
The FSC is a non-government organization dedicated to promoting responsible management of the world's forests. Certification ensures forests are managed in an environmentally sustainable and socially responsible way. For further information about this scheme, go to www.annesspublishing.com/trees

© Anness Publishing Ltd 2003, 2011

All rights reserved. No part of this publication may be reproduced, stored in a retrieval system, or transmitted in any way or by any means, electronic, mechanical, photocopying, recording or otherwise, without the prior written permission of the copyright holder.

A CIP catalogue record for this book is available from the British Library.

PUBLISHER'S NOTE
The reader should not regard the recommendations, ideas and techniques expressed and described in this book as substitutes for the advice of a qualified medical practitioner or other qualified professional. Any use to which the recommendations, ideas and techniques are put is at the reader's sole discretion and risk.

# Contents

# Introduction

Contemporary medical training is largely focused on the intricacies of the physical systems of the body and learning to recognize and treat states of disease. It often flounders where clear symptoms are absent. The techniques and exercises included here will help you to understand the power of the three natural therapies to work in harmony together, their capacities for healing and balancing, and how they can affect the subtle energy systems that exist within us all.

Our lives are influenced by many different energies that we cannot see, and yet they can profoundly affect our state of mind and our health. These therapies have all been shown to balance, heal, soothe and energize. Each therapy provides an effective series of simple techniques that can dramatically reduce levels of stress – one of the underlying causes of many types of disease – and enable us to harness the vital energies of nature to create balance and wellbeing of mind, body and spirit.

Crystal healing is aimed at attaining a level of wellbeing that is not simply freedom from illness, it also includes listening to our feelings, emotions and thoughts, and nurturing our spiritual lives. This section explores the power and beauty of crystals and how to unlock their capacity to strengthen and uplift.

Colour healing reveals the energetic reality of the world around us. What we perceive as colour is simply the brain's

▽ As ideal examples of the universe's pattern-making and orderly structural harmony, crystals naturally bring clarity to the mind.

way of recognizing the many different energy qualities of light. Every frequency of visible light, each colour, creates changes in us at many different levels: physically, emotionally and mentally. Learning to recognize and use colour with awareness can bring positive and powerful changes into our lives.

Chakra healing maintains the natural balance of the body and the flow of energy. We move within an invisible sea of electromagnetic energies, originating from the deepest regions of space and from the centre of our planet. Our personal space is also inhabited by invisible but nonetheless powerful energies that, by their interactions, create and maintain our health. Down the spinal column are seven great vortices – called 'chakras', meaning 'wheels' – which have been recognized by seers and healers for thousands of years as being essential to our wellbeing. Chakra healing seeks to understand the creative energies that each chakra centre can bring to our lives, and, by identifying imbalances, help to restore our health.

Why crystals placed on the body can have such a profound effect on our wellbeing is still not known. How colour can bring positive and powerful changes into our lives, and why chakras affect us on many different levels – physical, emotional, mental and spiritual – is not fully understood. However, experience is always more important than theory. This book brings together a range of complex and interrelated philosophies, and sets out to explain them in a simple and practical way so that everyone can benefit from the gentle power of these natural, healing therapies.

△ **Banging on a drum can help to restore balance to the throat chakra by dissipating excess energy.**

# The world of crystals

Crystals remind us of the structures upon which our universe is built. All matter, everything that is physical and solid, owes its existence to the organizing properties of crystals.

# In the beginning

In all parts of the world, and from the dawn of history, crystals have been regarded as belonging to the heavens, as gifts from the spirit worlds. Their colour and brilliance have set them apart from everything else on earth. Today we know that the story of crystals is indeed the story of the creation of the universe.

Astronomers believe that after the initial expansion of the universe from its original point, clouds of hydrogen, the simplest form of matter, began to cluster together. In time, within these vast balls of hydrogen, the pressures became so great that atoms began to fuse together, releasing a huge amount of energy. These glowing spheres became the first stars. Within these stars hydrogen continued to fuse to become helium and, as the burning continued, increasingly heavy elements were formed, such as nitrogen, oxygen, carbon, iron, lead and gold.

As the first stars eventually died, some exploded sending these new elements careering throughout space where gravity created new stars and planets from them. Our own solar system and the Milky Way formed in this way. Lighter gas clouds, the remains of countless stars, were drawn towards the young sun, while the heavier elements settled into orbits further away, gradually coalescing to become the planets.

## the earth

Earth formed at a distance from the sun that allowed both light and heavy elements to combine. The larger atoms sank downwards to create the planet's core of iron and nickel. The core is probably surrounded by a layer

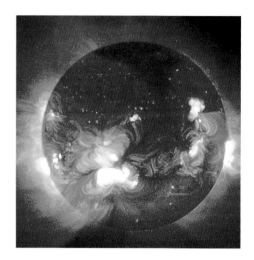

△ **Every element in the universe that makes up physical matter was formed within the stars.**

▽ **Throughout universal space the same raw materials come together to form crystals.**

△ **The apparent stability and continuity of the planet is in reality a constant cycle of erosion, deposition and metamorphosis.**

of molten metal. This layer, or mantle, around the planet comprises the greatest volume of the earth. It is 2,900km (1,800 miles) thick and composed of many layers of fluid, swirling rock. The outermost layer is the crust, a thin layer of rock that makes up the earth's continents.

The earth's crust forms less than 1 per cent of its total mass and is less than 40km (25 miles) thick over most of its surface. The distance from the surface of the planet to its centre is 6,391km (3,971 miles), yet the deepest humans have been able to drill is 8km (5 miles).

The earth's crust formed from super-heated rocks such as granite and basalt, that welled up through cracks in the surface layers either to spread out in vast domes called basoliths, or as volcanic eruptions. Rocks formed in this way are called igneous, meaning formed by fire. Millennia of erosion by wind and water wore these igneous rocks to dust. Carried downstream

by rivers, this dust was deposited at the bottom of the sea where it became compressed and eventually turned to rock again. This type of rock is called sedimentary, after the way it has been formed.

Wherever either igneous or sedimentary rock is subjected to extremes of heat or pressure by movements of the earth's crust,

its composition is altered. The change it undergoes gives it the name metamorphic rock. Crystals can be found in all types of rocks where conditions for their formation are right. As superheated gases and liquids rise to the surface, they begin to cool in the cracks and crevices of the surrounding rock, crystallizing into sparkling and coloured minerals. Harder minerals, such as diamonds and rubies, form at high temperatures in areas of volcanic activity. The crystals that form in sedimentary rock are usually much softer like gypsum and halite (common salt).

The same chemical elements appear throughout the whole of the universe. Given the right conditions, atoms of these different elements can come together to form new substances. Minerals are combinations of different elements that form the building blocks of all physical matter. All minerals, for example halite (sodium chloride – rock salt) and quartz (silicon dioxide – rock crystal), are composed of the same sorts of atoms in the same proportions.

▽ **Without the constant movement of the earth's crust many crystals would not be formed out of the sedimentary rock that lies beneath the sea.**

# The nature of crystals

All minerals will form crystals, though the conditions for their growth varies from mineral to mineral. Crystals begin to grow when the right amounts of their constituent atoms are present, usually in the form of a liquid or gas, but sometimes as a solid, in conditions that allow the atoms to move into those patterns where they are in the best possible state of equilibrium with each other. Heat and pressure ensure that the atoms have the maximum movement and energy to locate these positions before conditions change.

## CRYSTAL TOOLS

The first tools were made from stones such as flint and obsidian. Much later, once smelting techniques were discovered, tools and weapons were crafted from metals such as bronze and iron. Today's sophisticated technology makes use of some of the hardest elements on the planet – gemstones. Always valued as things of beauty, mystery and magic, crystals are now also prized as components in precision tools.

▽ In today's high-tech industries crystals are used in sophisticated automated tools.

## structure

Once the basic pattern has been taken up by a few atoms, called the 'unit cell' of a crystal, other atoms quickly repeat the arrangement and build up the crystal lattice, the characteristic pattern of atoms unique to each mineral.

A crystal will continue to grow in this way until the exterior conditions alter or the available raw material of atoms is used up. Once formed, crystals are the most stable and organized forms of matter in the

△ These crystals are used in industry. Clockwise from top left, ruby (corundum), two pieces of tourmaline, garnet, chalcopyrite and kunzite.

universe. Their 'ideal' structure means that they often display unique qualities that make them both useful and attractive. A crystal's physical form is the expression of its interior atomic arrangement. Crystals of any given mineral always display the same relationship of symmetrical faces, and each face will meet in flat planes at the same angle. Due

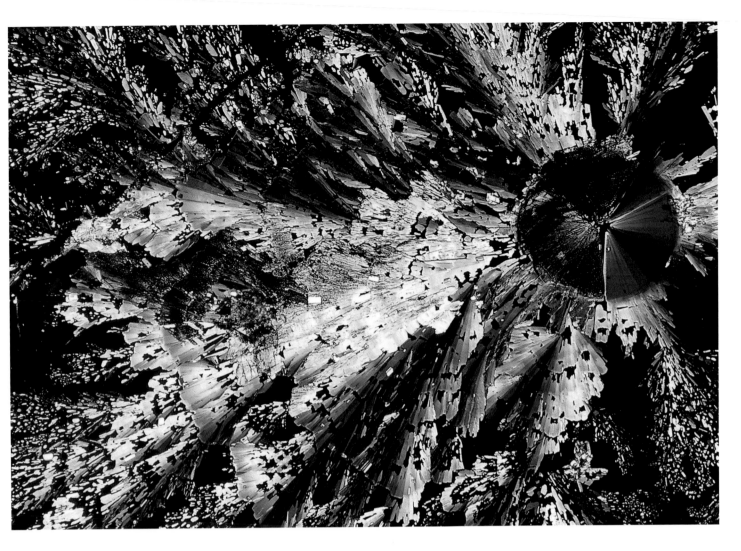

▽ **Every crystal is unique in size and shape, yet all crystals of the same mineral share an identical atomic lattice structure.**

to different growing circumstances no two crystals will be identical, but they will all show these characteristic features.

## colour

Although crystals are the most perfect arrangements of matter, small imperfections are present within the lattice structure of most crystals, and in fact these anomalies are often the very things that make them so useful to us. Crystals usually get their colour from the presence of a minute amount of another substance, which distorts the lattice and deflects or alters the light rays as they pass through it. Thus quartz, which is transparent, can appear violet coloured when iron atoms are present, and pink coloured with titanium or manganese. It becomes smoky brown when the lattice is subjected to natural radiation from radioactive elements such as uranium, or intense gamma rays from space and ultraviolet radiation from the sun. Internal fractures and dislocations within the lattice can also create wonderful plays of colour and light, which make some minerals valuable as gemstones.

△ **How light rays refract, reflect and move through crystal structures largely determines what colours a crystal will exhibit.**

▽ **Quartz crystal carries the properties of its elemental constituents: silicon and oxygen.**

# The power of crystals

Crystals are objects of beauty, fascination and mystery. They never lose their beauty so they can be treasured, hoarded and exchanged. They can become an expression of wealth. Fine examples of crystals are rare and difficult to find, which is why they have become symbols of high rank, royalty and even divinity.

## magical properties

The beauty of crystals makes them a natural choice in personal adornment or the decoration of precious objects. Their uniqueness imbues them with magical power: the power to protect, to enhance, to strengthen, to uplift. They have been used as amulets to ward off harm, as talismans to encourage virtues, as magical guardians to heal, and as tools to interpret messages from the spirit world. The attraction they hold transcends time and place. Many people are keen to own their birthstone, and to discover which stone will encourage love or wealth. With the much larger range of stones from all around the world available today everyone has a favourite, and is drawn to crystals for their particular qualities of warmth, subtlety or sparkle.

▽ **Many people simply collect crystals and gemstones for their visual appeal.**

## decoration and placement

Large crystal clusters are increasingly found in homes and offices. Their visual complexity and their wonderful colours make them ideal to gaze at while the mind relaxes a little. The beneficial energy that they may bring to the observer or the room they are in is an added bonus.

Crystals can be placed in the home according to feng shui, the traditional Chinese art of arranging objects, for the enhancement of positivity. The Chinese believe that they bring orderliness and clarity into life.

△ **Natural magic, in contrast to the complex rituals of ceremonial magic, has always used the unique properties of crystals.**

## the spiritual healing paradigm

Crystals and gemstones have a long tradition of being used for healing. In contemporary practice there are two main ways in which they are used, both of which have parallels in much older traditions across the world. The first method can be called the 'spiritual healing paradigm'. Here crystals, especially clear quartz stones, are used to channel,

are used. The second method of crystal healing can be called the 'resonance placement paradigm'.

## the resonance placement paradigm

This method doesn't require belief in the spirit worlds or in any kind of energy coming from elsewhere, but relies only on the power of the crystals themselves, and the healing intuition of an individual. Many different stones may be used, each one chosen for a particular beneficial effect on the patient. Placed on or around the body, the colour, shape and composition of the stones are thought to create a resonance that encourages healing to take place. This system parallels the magical, talismanic practices of carrying gemstones, as well as the Ayurvedic traditions of India in which stones are chosen to bring the most harmonious energy to each individual.

direct and amplify energy from the healer, or from the spiritual realms with which the healer works. Healing energy is mentally directed through the stone, which amplifies and clarifies the healing potential. Some North American Indian healers use quartz in this way to diagnose a problem and then remove it. In these instances the crystal may or may not come into contact with the patient. Very often only one or two crystals

△ **In all periods of history, crystals have been regarded as magical and otherworldly.**

▽ **As ideal examples of the universe's pattern-making and orderly structural harmony, crystals naturally bring clarity to the mind.**

▽ **The clarity of crystal can be felt to positively influence the space within which it is placed.**

# Getting to know your crystals

Each human being is completely unique, and we will all respond to a specific crystal's energy in a different way. Getting to know each crystal in your own collection is very important. It is more helpful to learn how to get to know the feel of an individual stone than to learn what other collectors or crystal experts have to say about it. What the body senses or knows, our intuition can be trained to access. The most effective healer uses information from a combination of sources, but the most important source is the physical and mental personal experience of healer and patient.

## learning a new stone

Once you have gathered together a small collection of crystals you need to begin to learn their potential. Cleanse all new stones well before working with them. Begin by holding a new stone in one hand for a

moment or two, then in the other. Notice how you are feeling. Remember that all the information you can get from the crystal's energy will be registered inside you. Get used to recognizing changes of feeling in your body, emotions and mind.

△ Lay out your entire collection on a neutral coloured background. Gazing quietly at a selection of stones will help identify the effect that each stone creates.

▽ Taking time to examine your crystals creates a strong intuitive energy link that will be useful in healing situations. It isn't necessary to always have new insights or experiences in this process.

After holding the stone for a moment, place it away from you and simply gaze at it. Pick it up once more and notice any changes within you. Close your eyes and simply sit with the stone, then, once more, place it away from you. By such processes you will gradually see a pattern emerging. Once you have established your own responses to a stone you will be able to begin by experience and experiment to find out whether your own response is shared by other people.

The next stage of getting to know your crystals is to place a stone at an energy sensitive spot such as a chakra. This can give you some further insight. Place the stone for a minute or two on each chakra in turn and take notes on your responses. You might find that some places, and some stones, are a lot more sensitive than others.

Keep a stone with you for a while to deepen your connection with it, especially if it is a new one. Putting one under your pillow or next to you when you sleep may produce significant dreams, particularly if you have a clear intention before you fall asleep that you wish to learn the properties of a stone. Again, make a note of these experiences. Carry a stone around with you for a few days and then leave it at home for a while. As you repeat this process you may notice changes in how you feel, or behave or in how others are behaving towards you.

▽ **Holding a stone to a chakra point will show you how it may modify the energy of that centre.**

## MEDITATION WITH THE SENSES

Sit quietly with the stone you wish to explore just in front of you. Close your eyes and quieten your mind by focusing your attention on your breathing for a minute or two.

**1** Pick up the crystal and hold it comfortably in your hands.

**2** Imagine your awareness spiralling down into the stone, as it opens up and lets you explore it.

**3** First see how, in your imagination, the inside of the stone feels. Is there a sense of texture, a change of temperature, a sense of space or restriction?

**4** Is there any sense of sound? If the energy within the crystal were expressed as sound, how would it seem to you?

**5** Breathe in the energy in your imagination. Does it remind you of anything? Is there a fragrance at all? Is there a quality of taste?

**6** Visualize that you open the eyes of your imagination and that you can see the energy of the crystal around you. This may take any form, pattern, landscape, or figure.

**7** When you have explored the stone enough simply close off your inner senses and bring your awareness back to your body and the sounds that are around you.

**8** Complete the grounding process by seeing all aspects of your awareness spiralling back out of the stone and into your body.

**9** Make a note of your experiences.

# Cleansing crystals

Crystals need to be protected from physical damage, but also from energetic imbalances. Crystals can register a wide range of vibrations, from electricity and magnetism, to sound, emotions and thoughts. The natural coherence of crystal can eventually dissipate imbalances within the lattice but the following cleansing techniques speed this process and ensure only positive energy is present in healing situations.

Every cleansing method has advantages and disadvantages. You will quickly learn to determine the most useful method for your situation. It is better to regularly cleanse the crystals you are working with rather than letting imbalances accumulate over time.

## cleansing with water and salt

With the exception of a few water-soluble minerals, each new crystal should be washed before you use it. Use a little soapy water to remove dust and fingerprints. Water will

▽ Use whichever cleansing techniques you find most effective and practical. You will soon learn to recognize the feel of a cleansed stone.

also cleanse your stones of energy imbalances. Another method is to hold the stones in cold running water and then leave them to dry naturally. Visualizing the flow of water drawing away all imbalances as you cleanse can speed up the process.

Salt water is often suggested as a medium for clearing crystal energies. Although effective, it can be difficult to remove all traces of salt from the tiny crevices in the crystal, and salt will damage the surface of many softer stones. Dry sea salt piled around each stone and left for a day is a good alternative. Either use small dishes for each stone or nestle each stone in its own little mound of salt on a large flat plate.

## cleansing with sound

Resonant sound from a tuning fork, metal bowl or bell rapidly vibrates the physical structure of the crystal allowing it quickly to 'shake off' any intrusive energies. Simply hold a struck bell or tuning fork close to your stones, or place one or two crystals in the bottom of a Tibetan singing bowl, and run the wooden handle around the rim.

△ Use a clear intention that your chosen method will cleanse your stones, to speed the process.

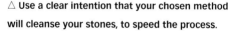

▽ Mineralogy reference books will tell you which stones can be placed in water.

◁ Dry sea salt, without any extra additives, draws out negative energies. Throw the salt away after use.

△ Surrounding a crystal with other cleansed stones, or placing the stone on a large cluster or bed of crystal, is an effective cleansing method.

▽ Incense cones or sticks make sufficient smoke for cleansing as well as grains, resins and herbs.

## enlivening crystals

To enliven a very tired crystal, it may be necessary to bury it in clay or the earth – but always be sure to mark the spot well! Leave in place for a day to a week before returning to check on progress.

## energy cleansing

After cleaning, it is important to remove any energy imbalances your crystal may have accumulated. Over time crystals can be affected by strong negative emotions or electromagnetic pollution. Such a stone will feel lifeless, dull or unpleasant in some way no matter what its appearance. Energy cleansing can be done in many ways. The simplest method is to use incense smoke or a smudge stick with traditional cleansing herbs and pass the stone through the smoke until you feel it clear.

Sandalwood, frankincense, juniper and sage have a long history of use simply because they were found to be powerful purifying herbs. Experiment to find those that work best for your stones.

Get into the habit of cleansing your healing stones before and after use – and don't forget to cleanse any large decorative crystals you may have around your home from time to time.

# Crystals and chakras

Gemstones were traditionally used to alleviate the physical symptoms of illness. Today, crystal healing focuses on removing the underlying energy imbalances that may eventually lead to physical problems. In modern complementary therapies, as well as many traditional forms of healing, the person is seen as a complex interaction of different sorts of energy systems. Though not so apparent as the physical body, these energy systems influence every aspect of our lives and they can be clearly felt by anyone trained to notice the subtle differences and states they produce.

△ **Tiger's Eye is a variety of quartz that works well at the solar plexus chakra.**

Ancient Indian seers perceived seven chakras – vortices of spinning energy along the spinal column, each with its own functions for maintaining health. They found exercises and meditations to regulate and enhance each chakra to promote spiritual wellbeing.

## chakras and colours

The chakra system was simplified in the West and a single rainbow colour was attributed to each of the seven chakras. The colour correspondences of the chakra system can be combined with the colour of

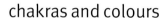

△ **Ruby, like all red stones, helps to energize and balance the first chakra at the base of the spine.**

▽ **Carnelian is coloured bright orange by iron particles. It helps balance the sacral chakra.**

△ **Moss agate is a green stone that works in harmony with the heart chakra.**

▽ **Turquoise is among the most-used light blue stones, which work with the throat chakra.**

△ **Sapphire is a deep blue crystal that works well at the brow chakra in the centre of the forehead.**

▽ **Purple stones, such as sugilite, can help to balance the crown chakra.**

crystals for a simple healing system. Through observation, intuition or dowsing, a crystal therapist can determine which of the chakras need re-balancing to restore equilibrium to the system as a whole. Appropriate crystals can be placed around the energy centre, and, by the colour or some other balancing aspect of the crystal, that chakra will be brought back to a healthier functioning. This is an effective way of releasing physical, emotional and mental stress.

## SIMPLE CHAKRA HEALING

Crystals that are the same colour as a chakra will enhance its natural qualities, whatever the situation. For a simple chakra balancing therapy, place one stone of the appropriate colour on each chakra area for a few minutes.

Use small tumbled stones or crystal points. Choose your stones and arrange them in sequence beside where you will be lying. When you are ready, you can easily pick up the stones and place them on your body without them falling off. If you prefer to sit, you will need small pieces of surgical tape to hold each stone in position on your body.

**1** The first or base chakra is at the base of the spine. Use a black or red stone between your legs to balance physical energy, motivation and practicality, and to promote a sense of reality.

**2** The second or sacral chakra is in the lower abdomen, below the navel. Use an orange stone here to balance creativity, and to release stress and blocks in your life that prevent enjoyment.

**3** The third or solar plexus chakra is close to the bottom of the ribcage. Use a yellow or gold stone in this position to

clear your thoughts, reduce anxiety and improve confidence.

**4** The fourth or heart chakra is in the centre of the chest. Use a green stone here to balance your relationship with others and the world, to increase calm and create a sense of direction in life.

**5** The fifth chakra is at the throat. Use a light blue stone here to ease communication difficulties, express yourself and bring peacefulness.

**6** The sixth is the brow chakra in the centre of the forehead. Use a dark blue or indigo stone here, to increase understanding, access ideas and promote intuitive skills and memory.

**7** The seventh chakra is the crown, situated just a little way above the top of the head. A violet stone placed in this position integrates and balances all aspects of the self – physical, mental, emotional and spiritual.

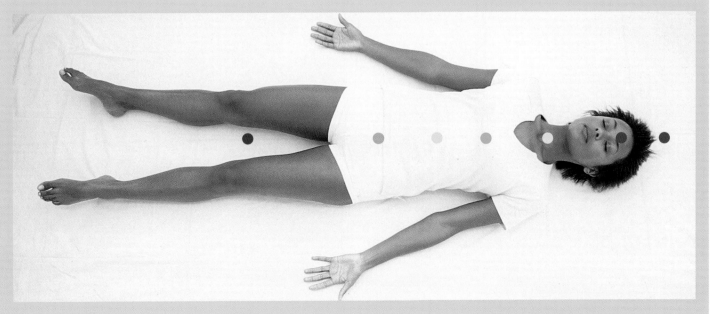

# Subtle bodies

The subtle bodies are non-physical aspects of each human being surrounding and interpenetrating the body. They constitute what is usually called the aura. Each level of the aura can be thought of as the individual seen from a slightly different energy vibration – like listening to the different instruments playing in an orchestra.

## different levels

Closest to the physical body in frequency is the etheric body, an exact double of the body and a template for the physical organs and systems. On a finer level is the emotional body, often perceived as a swirl of ever-changing colours that alters with our moods. The mental body contains thought processes, ideas and beliefs we hold about ourselves and the world. It usually appears as a yellow glow and can be bright around the head during concentration. The

▽ Dowsing can be used to choose the most appropriate crystal for healing. With the most useful stone or stones, the pendulum will rotate, while with others it will remain stationary.

finer vibrational subtle bodies contain the energy patterns of our spiritual natures and are less bound by rules of time and space.

Like the chakra system, the subtle bodies have a complex interaction and flow between them. When this is disrupted in some way it can create knock-on effects that may lead to the symptoms of stress and disease. Disruption in a subtle body can be likened to a storm that fails to dissipate and upsets the weather patterns for miles around – an El Niño in the body! The subtle bodies can also be imagined as many layers of glass letting light into a room. Dirt and dust accumulating on one layer will cast shadows on all the others and into the room itself. Crystals can be a very effective tool for removing these energy disruptions.

Subtle bodies are made up of fine energy frequencies so we need some way to detect them and then make accurate assessments of their condition. Using a crystal pendulum is the simplest method, amplifying the body's innate understanding of these subtle fields. Crystal pendulums will also help to restore most imbalances as they are located.

## PENDULUM HEALING

Learning to use a crystal pendulum can be one of the easiest ways to work with the subtle bodies.

1 Suspend the crystal pendulum. In your mind, intend that the pendulum will begin to swing away from its resting position when there is an energy imbalance in the subtle bodies that it is able to correct.
2 Allow the pendulum to move whichever way it wants until it comes to rest once more. When this happens it indicates the balance has been completed.

▽ Any crystal can be used for dowsing but it is best to start with a stone that has a broad healing ability such as clear quartz or amethyst.

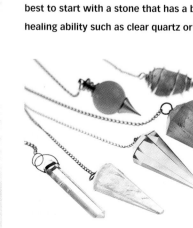

## FIVE-LINE CLEARING

This is a technique that can be used to restore balance to all the subtle bodies. It is not necessary to know what imbalances are being cleared where the pendulum begins to move away from the neutral swing. All subtle bodies interpenetrate and affect each other. An area of imbalance may be at only one level or it may move through many different layers. Simply focus on the pendulum movement and move steadily up the body on each line.

This technique is an excellent way to help others. A clear quartz or amethyst will give the best results because they act on very broad levels, and work as all-purpose healers. Stones such as garnet or lapis lazuli will focus their balancing abilities in more precise ways.

To help you to make the correct movements with the pendulum, imagine five lines running down your partner's body: one in the centre – the midline – and two either side, running parallel. The inner two lines should be within the outline of the body, the outer two lines are just outside the physical body.

**1** Put the crystal pendulum into a neutral backwards and forwards swing. With the patient lying down, suspend the pendulum a few centimetres above the body at the midline, in the centre of the body, just below the feet.

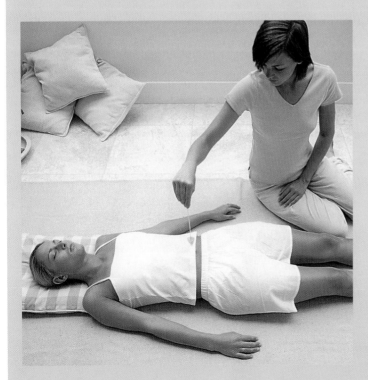

**2** Slowly move the swinging pendulum up the midline. Wherever there is a movement away from the neutral swing, stay there until the pendulum returns to normal. Move up the midline until you reach the top of the head.

**3** Start the process again, this time moving the pendulum up one side of the body, and then the other. Finally, move the pendulum up the fourth and fifth lines, just to the outside of the physical body.

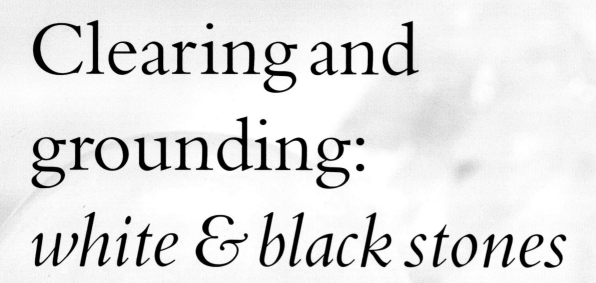

# Clearing and grounding:
## *white & black stones*

Stones that are clear or white in colour have the ability to bring clarity and purity to the aura. This makes them very useful healing tools. Black and other dark coloured stones help to integrate the healing that has taken place so that we can feel the practical effects of the process. They help to strengthen and stabilize our fundamental energies.

# Clear quartz – solidified light

Quartz (SiO$_2$) is the commonest and most widespread mineral in the earth's crust. It is a component of many types of rock and a constituent of many different minerals. The purest variety of quartz is known as rock crystal and has the clarity, transparency and coolness of ice.

Quartz can form as magnificent clusters of crystal, as gigantic single crystals and as massive aggregates. Impurities and inclusions of other minerals give the quartz family the greatest variety of any crystal. Quartz is very weather-resistant and with the erosion of bedrock it finds its way down rivers where it becomes the main component of river and seashore pebbles – as well as of sands and gravels.

△ **Clear quartz is completely transparent and colourless except for internal fractures and microscopic bubbles of gas or water that appear as milky areas.**

▽ **Quartz can form in a huge variety of beautiful clusters, aggregates and single stones.**

## DIRECTING ENERGY

A single quartz crystal anywhere within the aura will help to bring balance. It often helps to visualize the flow of energy you want and place the quartz appropriately. A quartz point above the head and another between the feet creates a useful flow up or down the body. Points facing downwards have a grounding effect. Points turned upwards give a feeling and quality of expansion. Another method is to hold pointed quartz in your hands. The left hand (in right-handed people) is receptive and absorbing, the right is projecting and energizing. It's the other way round for left-handed people.

**1** Hold a quartz point inwards with your absorbing hand and another with its point outwards in your energizing hand to create a flow through the body that balances and clears energy blocks.
**2** Change the direction of the crystals after a few minutes and see how you feel.

◁ Transparent, clear crystals have always held immense fascination. To hold solid matter and yet be able to see through it is a truly magical experience.

## types of clear quartz

Clear quartz normally grows long six-sided crystals, meeting at a natural point or termination. Opposite the termination, the base of the crystal grows from 'massive quartz', which consists of microscopic crystals, or a bedrock of some other mineral. Quartz with its point towards the body has a tendency to energize, whereas quartz with points away from the body releases or discharges excess or unwanted energy. Large flat crystals called tabular quartz also act as rapid transporters and transmuters of energy. Rough pieces, tumbled and smooth-polished quartz give a less directional, more diffuse effect that can be useful for gently infusing energy at one place.

Some quartz crystal shapes can focus or amplify energy many times above the usual. Laser wands are so called because they have slightly bent sides that narrow significantly towards a small termination. Energy

△ Herkimer diamonds, placed under a pillow at night, can help to encourage lucid dreaming.

entering the base becomes compressed and more energetic as it moves up the crystal towards the tip. These crystals can be powerful healing tools.

## Herkimer diamonds

The most brilliant quartz crystals are called Herkimer diamonds. First found in Herkimer County, New York State, USA they are particularly clear and bright. They are powerful cleansers renowned for their ability to enhance subtle perceptions. Herkimer diamonds encourage stabilization and a dynamic exchange of energy.

Clear quartz, of any shape, is very useful in crystal work because it amplifies and increases the harmony of all energies with which it is brought into contact. The coherence of rock crystal strengthens all the energy systems of the body, bringing stability and calmness to the mind. It can also direct energy from one site to another.

### THE SEAL OF SOLOMON

One of the simplest and most widely applicable layouts using clear quartz is called the Seal of Solomon. Some stones may need to be taped in place, some may be on and some off the body. This layout can also be used for localized healing – simply repeat the process with crystals placed around the area that you feel needs help.

1 Choose six natural crystals of equal size and arrange them, evenly spaced, in a hexagon shape around the body. Start off with the points facing outwards, this will help to release stresses and imbalances.

2 After a few minutes, turn the crystals round so the points face inwards. This re-energizes the body at every level.

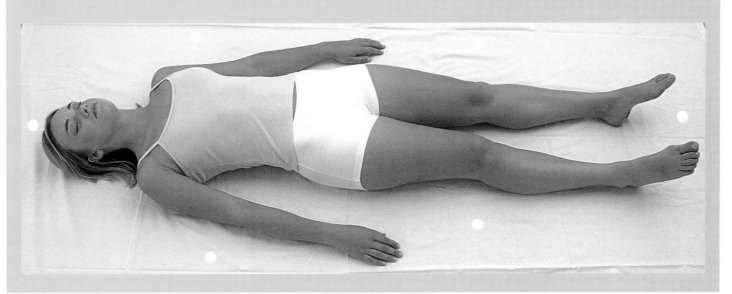

# Moonstone and selenite – moonlight and water

Moonstone and selenite each have a soft, luminescent quality and are associated with both moonlight and water because of the way the light plays on their surface.

## moonstone

A variety of the common mineral feldspar, moonstone ($KaSi_3O_8$) has a soft, lustrous translucence of white, yellow or pink. Moonstone can sometimes have a rich play of colour, in which case it is called rainbow moonstone. In India, moonstone has long been regarded as the perfect gemstone for women. It is well known for easing menstrual cramps and other constrictions

△ **Moonstone is recognized by its translucent sheen, no matter what colour it may be.**

▽ **Selenite is a very soft stone made up of thin layers of gypsum that diffuse the light.**

△ **Holding a piece of selenite helps to drain any negativity from the body.**

within the female reproductive system – carry a moonstone in your hip pocket to help relieve the symptoms of PMT. It is understood that emotional stress upsets the body's natural fluid balance. Moonstone helps to balance all fluid systems in the body, such as the lymphatic and digestive systems.

Emotional states are linked to the element of water, which is ruled by the moon. This is why the moon's gemstone is able to work so effectively in these areas.

Moonstone will gently stabilize all emotional states and help to release any stress and tension. These qualities link moonstone to the sacral chakra, which is a focus for emotional tension. Moonstone also works well at the solar plexus, where emotional stress can disrupt the nervous system and the digestion of food.

## MOON NET

To experience the soothing effects of moonstone, choose five pieces of about the same size.

**1** Place one moonstone on the front of each hipbone. You may need to tape the stones in place. Place another moonstone on the front in the dip of each shoulder.

**2** Place one just touching the top of the head.

**3** After a little while there will be a deep relaxation and a soothing energy washing through the body. After five to ten minutes, remove the stones and remain easy for a little while. Creativity and intuition may also be enhanced.

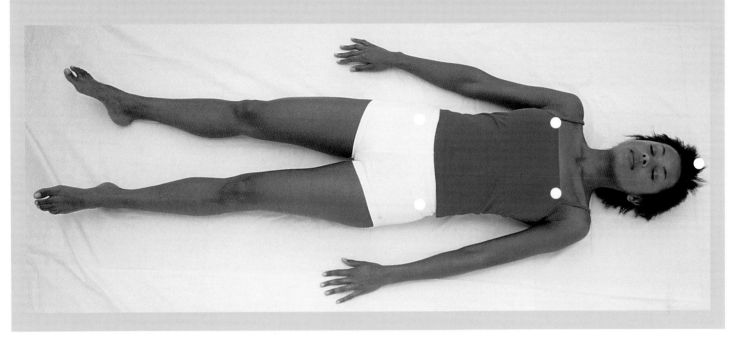

# selenite

A clear transparent form of gypsum, selenite ($CaSO_4.2H_2O$) is a very soft mineral easily scratched by a fingernail. Gypsum is so water-sensitive that even a change of humidity can make it bend. The thin layers or stripes visible in selenite create its moon-like luminescence. Such a delicate mineral needs careful care and handling, but it is well worth the effort. Few other crystals have the ability to effortlessly remove unwanted energies from the subtle bodies. Selenite combines the soothing effects of moonstone with the energy shifting properties of crystals with parallel striations (stripes). Whenever there are build-ups of energy, such as inflammation and pain, selenite brings a cooling release.

# clearing negativity

Selenite is a very common mineral that crystallizes in long blade-like shapes. Although it can be tumbled and shaped into wands or spheres, it is really so delicate that the finest quality stones should be collector's pieces rather than used in everyday healing.

When a stressful experience seems to be locked into the mind or the emotions, causing continual repetition of the same thoughts or feelings, selenite can be used to break that negative cycle.

Sit quietly for a moment and observe where the energy of the experience seems to be located. Somewhere in the body there will be an unusual sense of heaviness or dullness, or possibly an ache of some kind. Take a few minutes to see how sensations and thoughts revolve around the area. The selenite can now be used to drain the negative energy away. Either place the crystal on that spot and visualize the stone drawing away the source of stress, or hold the selenite in your hands and visualize the negative energy flowing and concentrating into the crystal and then rapidly streaming outwards to a place where it can be of use.

All soft minerals absorb imbalances rapidly and will need good cleaning after use. Do not use water with selenite. Sound or incense smoke cleansing will be effective.

▽ **Moonstone works where there is emotional or physical tension or blocks in energy flow.**

# Other white and clear stones

Transparent or clear stones exhibit the qualities of amplifying and clarifying. White stones can show the same characteristics, but they tend to be gentler in their actions. Milky quartz, for example, has the same structure as rock crystal, but the presence of many microscopic air bubbles reflects all light back from the interior. Milky quartz has a gentle energizing and soothing effect that radiates out into its surroundings.

Some agates, particularly Botswana agate, have a high proportion of white or light blue-grey banding. These are created by different sized quartz crystals, impurities and

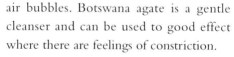

△ **Botswana agate is identified by its subtle bands of white and grey.**

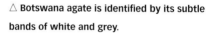

◁ **Milky quartz may seem less attractive than the clear variety but it is equally helpful as a healing tool.**

▽ **Agate slices show the formation of the crystal as different bands of coloured quartz.**

air bubbles. Botswana agate is a gentle cleanser and can be used to good effect where there are feelings of constriction.

## diamond

The strength and brilliance of diamond ($C_4$) has made it the world's most valuable gemstone. Diamonds are octahedral crystals of pure carbon found in many colours as well as clear. Most single diamonds are found in soil deposits along river banks. Large deposits of diamonds, found in hard igneous rock, are rare and difficult to work.

Diamonds were first mined in quantity in South Africa in the 19th century, and South African mines have produced more diamonds than any others throughout history. Most coloured diamonds are used in industry: less than a quarter of all finds are of the completely transparent quality that is required by the gem trade. This means that coloured diamond crystals are reasonably priced, though they are still quite difficult to obtain.

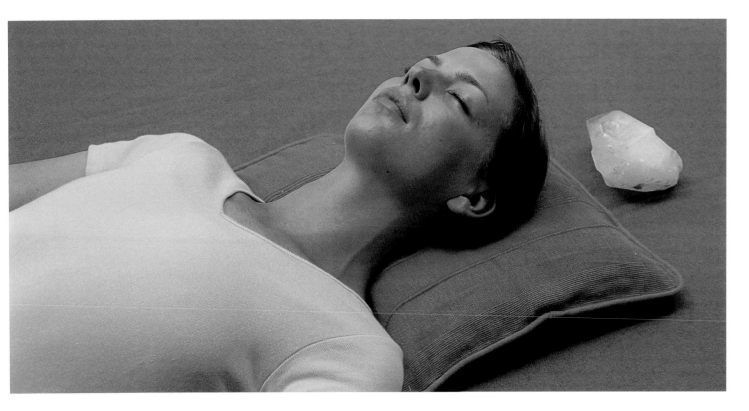

△ Clear stones have a natural affinity with the crown chakra. Both are able to reflect the whole spectrum of energy.

Diamond is primarily an amplifier of energy and is best used to enhance the properties of other stones. It is also a very effective detoxifying stone, effective at removing stagnant and inappropriate energies from the body. Diamond has a natural affinity with the crown chakra and has been found to help realign the bones of the head, the jaw and spine. It can be used to adjust small imbalances in the bones of the skull that may have been created after dental work, for example.

▽ Danburite is light and brilliant, amplifying the energy of stones around it.

## other transparent stones

Most crystals have a natural transparent form though this may be quite rare, as the impurities that enter a crystal lattice only need to be present in minute amounts to create colour. The clear form of any mineral can be used at the crown chakra above the top of the head. Simply placing the stone here will stimulate all the energy bodies and help remove imbalances.

Danburite ($CaB_2Si_2O_8$) is a brilliant clear stone that forms wedge-shaped crystals with parallel striations like those in topaz. It is light and fairly fragile, but is a useful activating and cleansing stone that amplifies and brightens the energies of other stones.

▽ Apophyllite is mined in Poona, western India. It can be brilliantly clear or translucent green.

Apophyllite ($KCa_4 Si_8O_{20}(F,OH). 8H_2O$) has greater brilliance than danburite but is even softer and lighter. The crystals tend to be cube-based or pyramidal with bright shiny surfaces. Apophyllite allows us to become more aware of subtle perceptions and can be an effective meditation crystal, expanding awareness while helping release blocks and stresses. The green variety encourages awareness of levels within nature.

Softer still is calcite ($CaCO_3$), a very common mineral that can sometimes be found as perfectly transparent crystals known as Iceland spar. All calcite is a good remover of stagnant energy and this too can be a useful meditation tool.

▽ Calcite, when perfectly clear, is called Iceland Spar. It commonly forms rhomboidal prisms.

# Smoky quartz – the solidifier

clearing and grounding

Smoky quartz ($SiO_2$) ranges from a light golden brown to deep black. Even when it is very dark, smoky quartz nearly always remains translucent. The colour is thought to be derived from natural sources of radioactivity close to where the crystals are formed. Smoky quartz carries the same basic energy as clear quartz but absorbs and stores it rather than radiating it. This gives the crystal a quietening and calming quality that makes it a help in focusing energy internally. The absorbing quality of smoky quartz makes it an excellent stone for meditation as it stabilizes the body and mind.

▷ **Smoky quartz is much less common than the clear, milky, or gem-quality varieties.**

## TO BRING CALM

Smoky quartz, with its quiet, calming energy is an effective grounding stone. As it draws energy towards itself it can remove imbalances from the subtle energy bodies, gently dissolving and transmuting negativity. This simple stone placement will help to collect all sorts of scattered and confused energies. It helps bring emotional calm and clarity of mind and allows any overabundance of energy to flow out into the earth.

**1** Use two smoky quartz crystals. If possible use crystals that have natural points (terminations). This helps to move the energy in the most appropriate direction. Place one with its point down the body at the base of the throat where the collarbones meet the breastbone.

**2** Place the other with its point downwards between the legs, either between the knees or between the feet. Stay like this for five minutes or until you feel fully grounded.

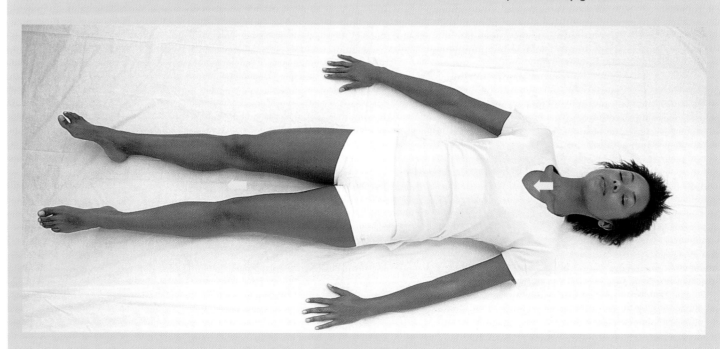

## GROUNDING STONES

The placement of a grounding stone during and after a crystal healing session, or holding one in your hand, really helps to integrate the changes into the physical body. Without proper grounding any benefits may disappear as soon as normal activity resumes. Grounding stones can be placed at any of the following locations:

1 At groin points on the front of the hips
2 At or near the base of the spine
3 Between the legs
4 By the insides of the knees
5 Between the feet
6 Below each foot

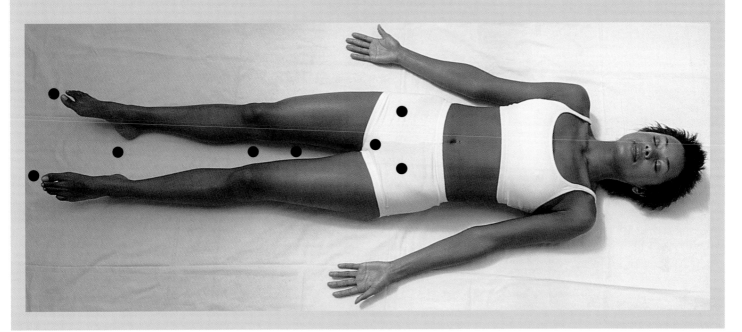

## achieving stability

Balance in life is essential. Outward, dynamic change needs to be countered by stability, focus and centredness. As most healing work is concerned with the removal of inappropriate energy it tends to initiate deep levels of energy adjustment throughout many subtle systems of the body. Any rearrangement of energy, no matter how beneficial eventually, can create turbulence in everyday life, bringing confusion, emotional instability and lack of focus. To avoid this discomfort, healers take care to emphasize grounding and centring techniques to act as an anchor, stabilizing and balancing the changes that healing creates. Grounding ensures a firm contact with the energies of the planet so that excess energy can be conducted away from the body. It focuses on the present moment, practicality and connectedness to reality.

Being centred suggests that the focus of awareness is balanced within the whole body – rather than just being in the head. There is awareness of the world outside, yet there is no confusion or distraction. It is not possible to be grounded effectively without being centred, and it is not possible to be centred unless our energies are grounded.

The first chakra at the base of the spine is concerned with centring and grounding. Techniques that direct energy and attention to this point and to points on the legs and feet are naturally grounding. Red, brown and black stones all help in directing and stabilizing energy in the body.

◁ **Confusion and anxiety can be rapidly reduced by holding a grounding stone.**

▷ **Red stones can also help to achieve stability, and can be used with black stones for grounding.**

# Black tourmaline – alignment

Extremely useful for protecting and grounding personal energy, tourmaline ($Na(Mg,Fe,Li,Mn,Al)_3Al_6(BO_3)_3Si_6O_{18}(OH,F)_4$) can be found in nearly every colour and the same crystal will often contain several different colours. Black tourmaline is known as schorl. It is easy to recognize with its long, thin striated sides with three

▷ **Tourmaline commonly crystallizes alongside quartz and often interpenetrates it. Tourmaline quartz (or tourmalated quartz) combines the qualities of both stones, clearing and grounding, energizing and protecting.**

## EARTH NET

A strong energy connection to the earth is a prerequisite for effective grounding and protective support. An energy net using eight black tourmalines can be used to reinforce this support, and can be particularly useful after moving house or travelling. Indeed, there have been reports that black tourmaline can reduce the effects of jetlag. One of the effects of tourmaline particularly emphasized in this layout is the ability to help the bones realign themselves. Tensions in bone and muscle are relaxed and physical balance improves. Tinnitus, the continuous ringing of the ears, has many causes, but misaligned skull bones can add to the problem. Wearing tourmaline earrings has been found to help this.

**1** Use a green cloth as a background to lie on, or a white sheet for second choice. If possible arrange it so that your head will be to the north.
**2** Put four tourmalines pointing inwards in a cross – one above the head, one between the feet and the others at either side, midway down the body.
**3** Place the remaining four tourmalines just to the right of the others at an angle of about 20 degrees, so all are aligned to the same imaginary point in the centre of the body.
**4** Remain in the energy net for five to ten minutes, then when you have removed the crystals spend at least 15 minutes resting before returning to normal activity.

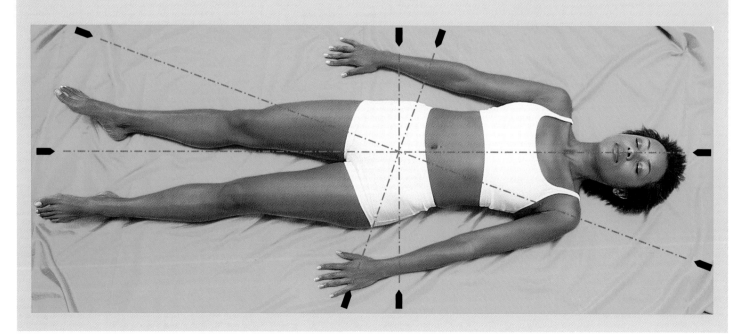

◁ Far left: tourmaline earrings can help in a wide range of situations, protecting the energy of the wearer. Tourmaline is thought to be able to help ease the symptoms of tinnitus.

◁ After using crystals for a healing session they should always be cleaned. Place tourmalines in a bowl of fresh water and leave for 2–3 hours.

faces giving it a triangular cross-section. When tourmaline is heated, it produces a positive electrical charge at one end and a negative charge at the other, making it a useful switching device in a lot of heat sensitive equipment.

## energy focus

As a grounding stone, black tourmaline can be used whenever energies are scattered and confused. It will very quickly bring the awareness back to the present moment. Because of this, the stone gives strong protection against negativity of all sorts. A negative influence is anything that superimposes itself and overrides the individual's own energy field to create imbalance. A crystal that reinforces personal energy will help against these disruptive effects. Black tourmaline deflects negativity back into the earth, rather than absorbing the energy into itself, where it would accumulate and interfere with its efficiency.

### TOURMALINE CIRCUIT

Crystals that have parallel striations running along their lengths tend to be very good at moving energy from one place to another, releasing blocks and tensions in the body. Sometimes the same problem resurfaces many times because a hidden, underlying block prevents effective healing. A pattern of black tourmaline crystals can clear away these deep levels of imbalance. Some stones in the pattern will be on the torso and hips, others will be put next to the head, shoulders, legs and feet. The number of crystals available to you will limit how and where they can be placed. Use dark tourmaline crystals – either black or very dark green. Alternatively, use smoky quartz.

**1** Place the stones, all pointing in the same direction, in a figure of eight over and around your partner's body.

**2** Emphasize the flow by tracing over the pattern with your hand, while holding another crystal.

**3** After a few minutes within the pattern, remove the stones. Use another grounding stone to settle the energies before ending the session.

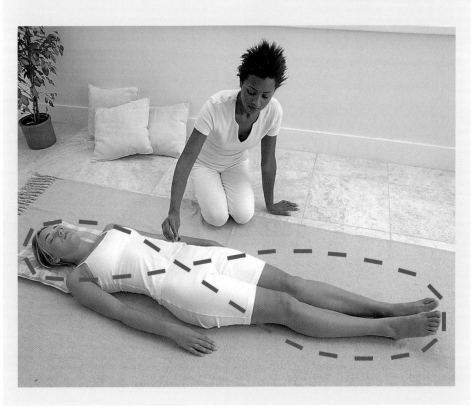

# Obsidian – delving deep

clearing and grounding

Obsidian is volcanic glass that solidifies so rapidly from lava that it does not have time to form crystals. Although non-crystalline, obsidian often contains very small crystals of other minerals, particularly quartz, feldspar and iron compounds. These microcrystals can create variations of colour and lustre as light is reflected off them. The random scattering of light rays makes most obsidian black in appearance. Clusters of feldspar crystals create white or grey patches in snowflake obsidian. Iron minerals give the red-brown colour to mahogany obsidian, while densely packed crystals create a rainbow lustre or iridescence.

Obsidian is an effective grounding stone, but its most useful attribute is the ability to draw hidden imbalances to the surface and

▷ **Obsidian is black volcanic glass – ideal for transforming energy patterns**.

## OBSIDIAN NET

This particular obsidian layout will allow the energies needed for cleansing and transformation to be gently integrated into the subtle bodies. Repeating this procedure regularly will bring about significant changes. You will need five obsidians and a red or black cloth to lie on.

**1** Place one obsidian above the top of the head; two level with the neck/shoulder area; and two at the feet.
**2** Lie within the net for three or four minutes. Then take as much time as you need before resuming normal activity, and sip a little water to help integration.

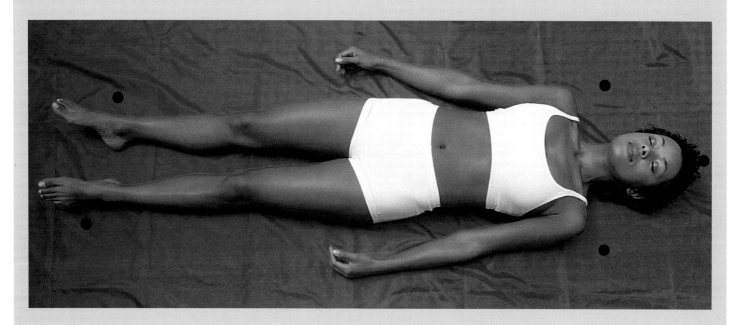

## HOW TO SCRY

You will need an obsidian sphere (the size of the crystal does not matter), a black or dark-coloured cloth and a candle. The surface and structure of obsidian quietens normal thought processes, enabling the scryer temporarily to leave behind the rules of time and space. Set your crystal sphere or obsidian at a comfortable viewing distance from you. Surrounding the back of the stone with a dark cloth will help to prevent visual distractions. Make sure there are no reflections to distract you – dim light is best – such as the light of a single candle. Scrying involves all the senses, so don't expect to see visual imagery in the ball.

**1** Gaze steadily at the sphere, without strain, looking through the crystal as if it were a window.

**2** Frame a clear intention of what it is you wish to discover, then relax. You will feel the answer as a thought rather than an image.

△ **Sipping a little water after any crystal healing will help to integrate the effects and ground and centre your energies.**

release them. This needs to be done with some care as most hidden things are buried because they are uncomfortable to face. There are times when outdated patterns need to be broken to release the energy that is being wasted in supporting them. Obsidian is ideal when a transformation is needed, bringing fiery energy from deep within the earth to purify and cleanse.

## scrying

Obsidian was one of the traditional materials used for scrying – seeing into the future. Scrying, or crystal gazing, is a worldwide practice that is used to reveal all sorts of information unknown to the conscious mind of the scryer. It has been known to reveal the causes and cures of illness, to explore and communicate with the spirit worlds and to foretell future events or disclose the truth of the past.

# Other black stones

Black stones have a solidifying and grounding effect on the human energy system. They increase our awareness of immediate reality and physicality.

## haematite

This stone is a very common oxide of iron ($Fe_2O_3$). Large crystalline masses of haematite have an attractive silver sheen and are often cut for use in jewellery, though the stone is very brittle. Haematite is the main source of iron for industry, but there is also a soft variety formed in sedimentary rocks known as red ochre. This is the most ancient of precious materials, regarded the world over as a symbol of life-energy – the blood of the earth – and it is much sought after as a pigment.

Haematite is an energizer of the physical body but its primary use is as a grounding stone. Wearing or holding a piece of haematite will bring most people's awareness back to the body and the present almost instantly. Some individuals, however, find

▽ **Haematite is one of the most effective grounding stones available.**

## RESTORING NATURAL BALANCE

We live in a very intense, artificially created electromagnetic environment. Treatment with a pendulum of lodestone or magnetite ensures that we do not suffer from the ill effects of strong electric fields. It is particularly useful for people who are over-sensitive to chemicals, who work with computers or other sources of electrical equipment or who are easily fatigued. Place a magnetite crystal or lodestone pendulum within a silver spiral on a length of cord or chain. Hold the stone a few centimetres above the body, and the pendulum will begin to rotate wherever there is an electromagnetic stress in the energy field. Hold the pendulum still until the rotation stops. The imbalance has now been removed.

Carrying a grounding stone will also help to prevent the unwanted accumulation of electromagnetic resonance. Holding the hands under cold running water, having a shower, wearing natural cloth and standing on the earth with bare feet are other ways of restoring natural balance.

▽ **A lodestone pendulum will rotate when it approaches electromagnetic imbalances.**

▽ **A build-up of electromagnetic stress can be dissipated by running water.**

that haematite has too energizing an effect and will need some less potent stone to ground them effectively.

## magnetite and lodestone

Another iron ore, magnetite ($Fe_3O_4$) has the highest proportion of iron to be found in any mineral, making it very important commercially. Magnetite forms metallic grey octahedral crystals. Lodestone is the name given to the magnetic iron ore in its massive (microcrystalline) form. Lodestone and magnetite are extremely useful healing tools. They can align the chakras and subtle bodies allowing rapid release of stress and tension.

Because of their composition (iron and oxygen) and because they have a strong magnetic field, magnetite and lodestone both help to align us with the earth's own electromagnetic fields. This has a very

▽ An octahedral crystal of magnetite (far left) with a piece of lodestone within a spring spiral ready for pendulum use.

△ Jet is found washed up on shorelines after it has been dislodged from ancient seabeds.

grounding effect and brings an increased sense of belonging and security. The many energies along the spine can be strengthened by placing a small lodestone near the base chakra and another at the base of the skull. When you are healing someone, move a single stone slowly along their back a few centimetres above the spine. Take time to hold the stone still over areas that feel particularly sensitive or are uncomfortable.

## jet

Like coal, jet is fossilized wood. Jet is formed when ancient waterlogged wood is compacted by vast pressure below the sea. It is found in several parts of the world. Like amber, jet produces static electricity when rubbed. This lightweight dark brown or black shiny gemstone exhibits grounding properties associated with its colour and the supportive, balancing qualities of the original source, trees. Valued for its protecting and comforting qualities in the 19th century, it was worn during mourning.

## USING JET TO ENERGIZE THE CHAKRAS

Jet placed by the lower spine energizes the base chakra. When placed higher up the body it can draw energy from the base into those areas. Jet is valuable in chakra balancing, particularly if the upper chakras are under-energized when compared to the lower centres. Indications of this sort of imbalance are: plenty of energy and drive, but inability to use it creatively; confusion; frustration.

1 Place grounding stones under the feet and between the legs. At the groin points, use two black or red stones to stabilize the base chakra.
2 Place jet on under-energized areas and check after a few minutes if the balance is better.
3 Repeating this regularly for five minutes at a time will help to alleviate imbalance.

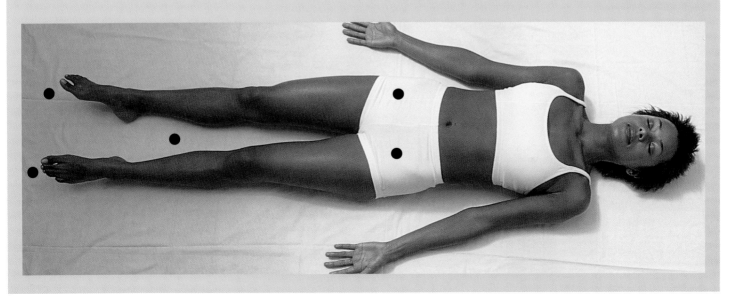

# Energizing and organizing: *red, orange & yellow stones*

Crystals from the warm end of the colour spectrum help to balance the first three chakras and release pent-up energy in the heart chakra. Stability, creativity and clear thinking, as well as the flow of life-energy through the physical body, are maintained by their properties.

# Garnet – stone of fire

A large and chemically diverse group of silicate minerals, garnets come in a variety of colours, a rich wine-red being the most familiar. All stones of this colour used to be known as carbuncles, from the Latin *carbunculus* meaning small, red-hot coal.

Garnets form at very high temperatures in many different rocks, often in those altered by close proximity to volcanic activity. As it is a hard mineral, garnet survives erosion and is found in riverbeds and gravels. Its hardness and durability makes garnet ideal for abrasives and polishing.

There are many green, orange and brown garnets but the red varieties are the most useful in crystal healing work. Garnet is the finest energizing stone for the body. Especially when cut, it can amplify and energize the properties of other stones. Cut faceted stones of most crystals increase the liveliness of the stone and can act like a lens, focusing light with more intensity.

The fiery garnet can be placed wherever a lack of energy exists. It can act as a 'starter motor' for the body's repair mechanisms, so

▽ Tumbled garnets can be so dark as almost to show no colour, but the dense weight gives a clue to their identity.

very often garnet needs to be in place for just a short while to do its work. Where there is an area of underactive or stagnant energy, place a garnet at the centre of the body and surround it with four clear quartz crystals, points facing outwards, to help increase energy and distribute it.

△ The name garnet derives from the Greek word for pomegranate. The small, bright red crystals resemble the seeds of that fruit.

▽ A garnet surrounded by clear quartz points, with points facing outwards, will rebalance a 'cool' spot in the aura.

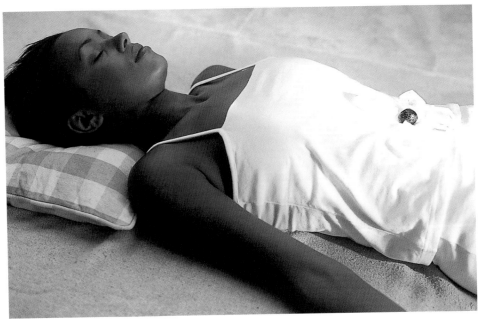

## BODY SCANNING

Identifying areas of poor energy flow is a useful skill to learn. It relies upon the healer's sensitivity to slight changes in the patient's aura. Everyone will have different ways of registering energy changes, so just be attentive. Low energy can often feel like a dip, hollow or emptiness in the aura. It may feel cool or somehow 'wrong'. You may sense the difference in your hand or arm or be struck by an intuitive thought or emotional impression. If you are not sure of your assessment, just repeat the body scan a few more times. Even without consciously registering it, the body scan will give you enough information at deeper levels of the mind to place healing stones appropriately. Learn to trust your intuition. Using grounding stones will help reduce any doubt.

**1** First sensitize your hands by rubbing them together or rolling a clear quartz crystal between your palms. Now bring your palms together slowly from a distance, and you should feel a tingling or a pressure as your hands come closer together. Gently 'bouncing' the space between your palms helps to

▽ **To increase your sensitivity in a scan, hold a clear quartz crystal in your scanning hand.**

build up your energy aura and your sensitivity to other energy fields.

**2** Starting from near the feet and moving upwards, use one hand to slowly sweep a few centimetres above the patient's body. Your intention is to locate areas of blocked energy or under-energy. Simply move your hand through the aura and be open to any changes you may feel.

**3** Where you have identified low energy, place a red, orange or yellow

stone, whichever feels most appropriate, for a few minutes. Then, remove the stones and repeat the body scan. There should now be an improvement in the energy field. If a few areas of imbalance remain make a note of them and then repeat the process after a few days.

▽ **Before beginning any kind of scan, sensitize your own hands, and centre and ground your energies.**

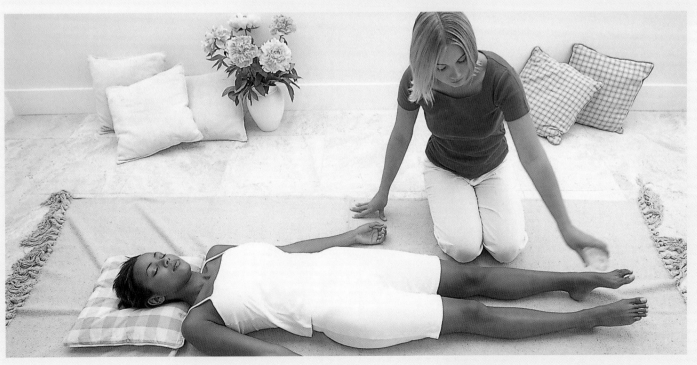

# Ruby – motivation and action

Ruby is the red variety of the very hard mineral corundum (aluminium oxide, $Al_2O_3$), which takes its colour from traces of chromium and forms characteristic barrel-shaped crystals. Ruby has a long history of use as a gemstone, though until recently, because of its hardness, the stone was not faceted but was always polished into a domed, cabochon shape. In Ayurvedic Indian healing traditions ruby is the stone of the sun.

## the heart

As the sun is the centre of the solar system so the heart is the centre of the physical body. Ruby balances the heart, enhancing its function and the circulation of the blood and improving the quality of thought and feeling associated with the heart – confidence, security, self-esteem and our relationship with others. Ruby acts by energizing us at the very centre of our being. It balances by reminding us of the

△ **Ruby has a hexagonal cross-section and usually forms barrel-shaped crystals.**

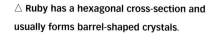

◁ **Polished ruby shows metal-like striations across its surface. Only the finest gem-quality rubies are translucent and deep red.**

vast reservoirs of energy within us that can enable us to succeed in any venture where we have full trust in our own abilities.

Red is the energy of gravity, pulling things together and establishing reality. Red is also the colour relating to the creation of matter and its manifestation. So it makes sense that a red stone such as ruby can help us to achieve our goals, particularly as ruby has such a connection with the heart, the seat of our desires.

### RELEASING THE HEART'S POTENTIAL

This net will help release pent-up energy in the heart, remove guilt and unworthiness, and reveal your true strengths and potential. If possible have a white sheet to lie on, this encourages a gentle cleansing of negative emotions. Place a small ruby crystal at the heart chakra in the middle of the chest. Place 12 clear quartz crystals, points outwards, equally spaced around the body. Lie in the net for about five minutes.

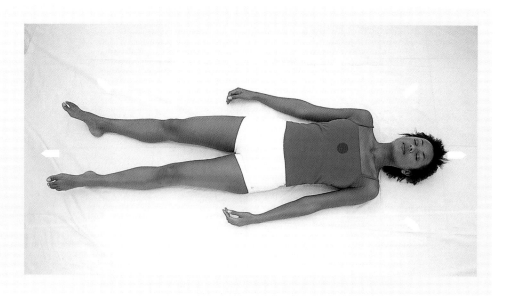

▷ **A ruby that has been polished into a traditional cabochon shape.**

Often in life the heart suffers pain because we feel unable to fulfil our wishes or desires. After pain such as this we often create barriers in an attempt to prevent future hurt. Unfortunately, what this really does is just separates us further from the source of our own power and courage.

Crystal healing techniques are ideal to help us solve such long-standing difficulties and barriers in our lives. Regular practice for five or ten minutes once or twice a week will begin to bring about positive change without having to revisit, and perhaps open, old wounds. In a situation where there is a loss of personal power, taking the initiative to help yourself is very important.

## SUN NET

When there is a fear of failure, the heart, whose natural energy needs to expand outwards and experience life, becomes restricted. Then there is a lack of security, which comes from having lost the sense of being centred in the self. This happens at a mental and emotional level, but can also manifest in physical symptoms such as poor circulation, cold hands and feet and other upsets to the temperature regulation of the body. Ruby can be an ideal healing stone in these circumstances. To amplify and integrate the energy of the sun net lie on a yellow cloth.

This net will be gently energizing, bringing focus and clarity to the mind and emotions. It can be useful to help regulate the circulatory system and usually produces a gentle warming sensation. Use six small ruby crystals – stones that are not of gem quality are inexpensive and fine to use.

**1** Place one ruby crystal above the head and one below the feet in the middle.

**2** Place one ruby crystal next to each arm and one next to each knee so that the six stones are all evenly spaced around the body. Stay in this position for five to ten minutes.

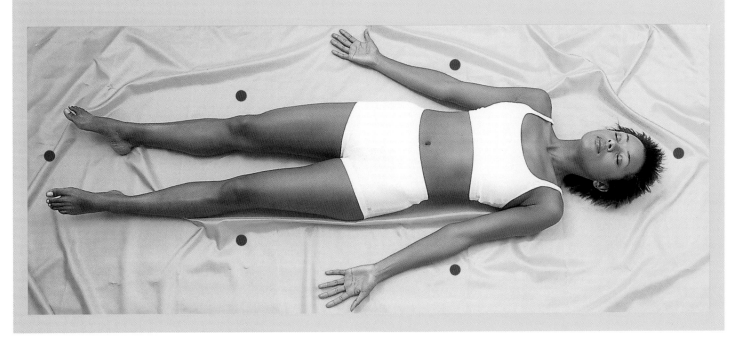

# Other red stones

Every red stone will give an energizing, activating and warming quality. Differences of crystal shape, quality of colour and chemical composition will affect the way each stone is experienced.

## red jasper

This stone is actually a form of quartz ($SiO_2$) that crystallizes from hot solutions and is changed several times by reheating. This process produces a wide range of internal colour and patterning that makes jasper a valuable gemstone. Unlike other microcrystalline quartzes, jasper has a strong permanent colour created by iron minerals.

As an opaque, massive variety of quartz, red jasper focuses on solidity and grounding. It is an ideal stone to balance the base chakra. Jasper will always emphasize practical, down-to-earth solutions, which, like each piece of the stone, are unique to the individual. Jasper can also be coloured by impurities that turn it yellow and green.

▽ **Red coral helps to balance the base chakra, regulating physical strength, and the skeletal and circulatory systems.**

## red coral

The earth's surviving natural growths of red coral ($CaCO_3$) are now largely protected from exploitation but this strikingly coloured organic secretion, the home of colonies of tiny sea creatures, has long been regarded as a precious gemstone. In Ayurvedic tradition red coral is the best stone for the energies of the planet Mars. In Asia and America turquoise and red coral have been put together in wonderful designs for ceremonial and decorative jewellery. Old red coral beads can still be found, though imitations are very common.

Coral primarily acts as a balance for the emotions – its watery origins suggest this function – and it will work well for the maintenance of energy levels, enthusiasm and practicality.

## fire opal

Opal ($SiO_2.nH_2O$) forms when hot silica-rich solutions fill the crevices of sedimentary rock. It is quartz with a high water content. All opals work well to balance the emotions. Fire opal is a deep orange-red, due to iron

△ **Each piece of jasper is unique in its patterning and colour. Fractures in older crystals are refilled with quartz of a slightly different colour.**

and manganese, which suggests a warming, activating quality. It is useful in emotional situations where there has been exhaustion, withdrawal and 'switching off'.

## spinel

Iron and chromium impurities often give spinel ($MgAl_2O_4$) a deep ruby red coloration. Many of the famous larger 'rubies' of the world are, in fact, spinels. Spinels commonly form spiky octahedral crystals, which give them their name – 'little thorns' in Italian. The brown or orange-red varieties encourage the energizing properties of the base chakra. Spinel may also help with detoxification as its red energy will focus on powerfully cleansing energy blocks.

## zircon

With a relatively recent history of use in jewellery making, zircon ($ZrSiO_4$) has clear varieties that can be cut and polished to the

◁ Red coral is useful for balancing the emotions and for maintaining enthusiasm.

▽ Like many red crystals, red calcite takes its colour from iron atoms in the surrounding rock. It has a smooth, energizing effect.

brilliance of diamond. The yellow-red variety is traditionally known as 'jacinth' or 'hyacinth' and has always been popular in the Far East. Today zircon is important for its constituent, the rare metal zirconium –

a hard, heat-resistant metal that is used in industry as an anticorrosive and abrasive.

As a healing stone, zircon exhibits some of the useful spiritual properties of red stones. Like red crystals, such as red calcite,

red zircon warms the subtle bodies, helping to prevent the stagnant conditions of listlessness, melancholy and depression. Zircon can also help to ground and clarify spiritual experiences and will ease any tensions that may have arisen in the mind from psychic or visionary experiences. Zircon reminds us that vibrations of red energy are needed to maintain stability at all levels. Red energy provides fuel for our mental, emotional and physical wellbeing.

▽ Fire opal is one of the less common varieties. It is unmistakable, with a dense orange-red glow.

▽ Spinel usually forms small crystals with a characteristic double pyramid shape.

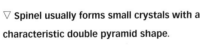

▽ Zircon crystals have a dull, red, metallic lustre and usually have clearly defined faces.

# Rose quartz – healing the emotions

Rose quartz ($SiO_2$) is an important crystal for removing blocked emotional stress. It is generally considered to encourage love and harmony. It is true that the vibration of pink does reduce aggression and promote understanding and empathy, but it is a mistake to think that because of this wearing a rose quartz will make you feel happier.

## emotional release

If there is suppression of barely controlled emotions, rose quartz will quite likely stir up a lot of turbulence. In such circumstances – and the majority of us have significant amounts of unresolved emotional stress – rose quartz can act like a safety valve, allowing a sudden release of emotional

▽ **Emotions are complex and many layered things. You may need to use a variety of different stones to effectively release emotional stresses.**

pressure. This can be an uncomfortable experience without understanding and guidance, and a little self-defeating if it creates further anxiety.

The guideline with rose quartz, as it should be with every crystal, is to explore the stone carefully and, if discomfort arises, change the approach. Our bodies are usually quite willing to correct imbalances gently, as long as they are provided with an appropriate stimulus. Stressful events tend to get frozen into repeating time-loops of memory in the body's muscles, as well as in the mind and emotional responses. Crystal healing is one of the most effective ways of allowing this trapped energy to release safely.

Emotional stress can become locked in any part of the body, and where it settles tension develops, restricting the local flow of energy. Starved of life-energy, these blocked areas become more susceptible to

## CALMING THE EMOTIONS

The heart chakra is the centre of many of the body's energies and this is where we feel emotional hurt. This simple layout of stones will relax and ease any unexpected emotional upsets. It is also beneficial when used on a regular basis to prevent stress building up.

**1** Place a small piece of rose quartz on the heart chakra in the centre of the chest.
**2** Surround the rose quartz with four clear quartz crystals with points initially facing outwards. This will help to release stress.
**3** Place a pointed citrine or smoky quartz over the second chakra below the navel, with its point downwards. This will have a gentle grounding and stabilizing effect and will also help to release any of the more long-term stresses that might be lodged in this centre.
**4** Place an amethyst quartz crystal in the centre of the forehead. This will help to calm the mind and will encourage a degree of mental detachment from any emotional recall.

Lie in this calming layout for five to ten minutes or until you become aware of a feeling of relaxation and balance.

## STRESS RELEASE POINTS

For the rapid, safe release of particular stresses, place small rose quartz stones on the slightly raised bumps to the sides of the forehead. You may need to tape the stones in place. Remembering the stressful event will begin the release process, which will be complete when you feel a change of emotion or a return of equilibrium. Placing a grounding stone by the feet and a balancing stone at the heart or solar plexus chakra may also help.

△ Rose quartz is useful to reduce any build-up of emotional stress and tension, and is also felt to encourage love and harmony.

▷ Keeping some rose quartz at your bedside can sometimes be effective as an aid to restful sleep.

illness. When the illness then causes pain and discomfort, the problem can be made worse by anger, irritation or disgust directed by the suffering person at their own affliction, as well as the draining emotions of fear, self-doubt and denial.

Local pain and inflammation can respond well to the placement of rose quartz as it calms and restores life-energy to the area. The addition of clear quartz points around the rose quartz, points directed away from the area, will also help remove imbalances.

# Rhodonite and rhodocrosite – clearing and balancing

Two minerals rich in manganese form crystals of a beautiful pink. Rhodonite and rhodocrosite are both valuable in helping to bring balance to the emotions.

## rhodonite

Named at the beginning of the 19th century after its colour – a rich rose pink – rhodonite $((Mn^{+2},Fe^{+2},Mg,Ca)SiO_3)$ is a hard, massive mineral, important in industry for its high manganese content. Rhodonite has become a popular semi-precious stone, especially the deep pink pieces patterned with dark brown or black oxides. It is cut as cabochons and carved into decorative ornaments.

Where the soft shades of translucent rose quartz may seem too gentle or soft, the balance of colours within rhodonite suggests a more robust and energetic character. The deep pink to magenta colours reflect the practical, down-to-earth vibration of caring

▽ **Rhodonite combines the pink of emotional balance with the red and brown of a practical approach to life.**

for oneself, having confidence and a sense of self-worth while remaining aware of the needs of others. The black or brown veins and patterns anchor rhodonite's energy into the solidity of the base chakra and through that to the earth itself. Because of its combination of colours, rhodonite works well at the base and sacral chakras. In emotional healing situations it complements and stabilizes the release initiated by rose quartz. Rhodonite will restore a sense of equilibrium without stifling the release processes that are underway. Always remember that grounding stones will quickly restore balance to a volatile emotional state.

Rhodonite can help to remove doubts about self-worth that prevent us from striving to achieve desired goals in life. A great deal of stress is created when personal ambitions are restrained or diverted. The entire structure of an individual's life energy can become distorted, leading to resentment, anger and aggression that may seem to have no apparent cause. Where

△ **Wearing a pendant of rhodocrosite can help to encourage a more positive view of oneself.**

these emotions are present rhodonite will help to divert the build-up of energy in positive and safe directions. Rhodonite used as a pendulum, wand or body sweep will identify the main areas of tension. Combined with blue stones, rhodonite will help us to find a way of achieving our ambitions.

## rhodocrosite

This stone can sometimes be mistaken for its close relation rhodonite. Both are manganese ores, but rhodocrosite ($MnCO_3$) often has additions of calcium, magnesium and iron. Whereas rhodonite is granular and opaque, rhodocrosite can be transparent or, more commonly, translucent. It usually forms in banded zones of pink, red, peach

▷ Rhodocrosite crystallizes in shaded bands of
pink, cream and peach. Large crystals form
translucent deep salmon-pink rhomboids.

and cream. Such a coloration lets rhodocrosite work on the base, sacral and solar plexus chakras, helping to blend their energies particularly where there is disruption due to emotional stress.

Poor self-worth and lack of self-confidence can manifest as problems in the digestive and reproductive systems. Anxiety creates tension in the stomach and pelvic areas, which can interfere with normal functioning. Particularly where there are emotional issues revolving around sexuality and fertility, rhodocrosite can help to ease negative perceptions.

In situations where there may be fear for one's safety, whether it is real or imagined, wearing a deep pink stone will help to reduce any anxiety and tension that themselves may create inappropriate reactions to those around you. Breathing through the stone, visualizing pink light around you, and allowing tensions to drain through the soles of the feet all help to achieve equanimity.

▽ Rhodonite or Rhodocrosite can help to identify
areas of emotional tension.

## STRESS RELEASE THROUGH BREATHING

Where obvious tension exists in the body, focusing the healing energy of pink light can help you to relax at a deep level. Use any kind of pink stone for this.

**1** Place the stone on or near the area. Take a moment to let the awareness centre on that part of the body.

**2** Now as you take a slow breath in, imagine that the air is focusing directly through the pink stone and right into the centre of the tension. Coloured by the pink stone, your breath will slowly begin to dissolve the pain and sorrow hidden there.

**3** Each time you breathe out, feel the tensions melt and relax. Continue this for a minute or two, then lie quietly.

# Other pink stones

If ever there is any doubt about which crystal will resolve an imbalance, consider using a pink stone of some kind. This will always allow deep healing to take place. Pink stones not only help to clear emotional stress, they can also be powerfully protective, expressing as they do the energy of unconditional or universal love, perhaps more accurately called compassion. This quality of non-judgmental, unequivocal understanding and acceptance is a result of deep experience of the underlying unity of life. When this unity is felt there can be no fear, and without fear, aggression melts away.

## kunzite

A pink variety of the mineral spodumene, (the green form of spodumene is hiddenite) kunzite $(LiAlSi_2O_6)$ is coloured by manganese. Kunzite can be identified by the parallel striations that run the length of the crystal and by the fact that the colour is more intense when viewed down the cross section of its main axis. Gem-quality kunzite can be transparent and clear, while low-grade stones when tumbled are opaque lavender-pink. Kunzite is an excellent protector of the heart chakra and of the integrity of the emotions. Emotional energy is such a powerful force that sensitive people

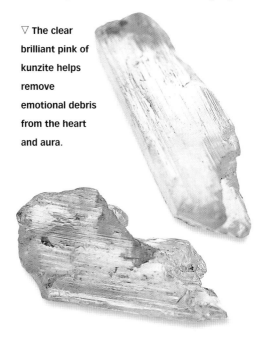

▽ **The clear brilliant pink of kunzite helps remove emotional debris from the heart and aura.**

## WAYS TO RELEASE NEGATIVITY

When you feel that you have acquired an uncomfortable or intrusive energy from outside yourself, or even if you are finding it difficult to let go of a certain emotional state, you can use kunzite to release negativity. In both these methods, the discordant energy becomes neutralized and harmless on passing through the crystalline structure of the 'exit' crystal. Make sure that all the stones you use are well cleansed before and after use to help them maintain their efficiency.

**1** Sit quietly and simply observe the energy patterns you wish to get rid of. Then take a kunzite crystal in both hands and imagine all the unwanted energy, thoughts or emotions are draining out of your body through the stone as if it were a stream of water.
**2** A variation of this can be to hold a kunzite or clear quartz in your left hand and another in your right hand. Visualize cleansing energy entering through the left and sweeping away unwanted energy through the right.

## CLEARING UNWANTED ENERGY

This layout can be used when there is a feeling of energies 'stuck' within the personal aura. Emotions or memories may be repeating in an obsessive loop, or there may be a 'bad taste' from an unpleasant experience that you want to dispel.
**1** Place a smoky quartz or a piece of kunzite between your feet pointing down and away from your body. Place a clear quartz or kunzite above the crown of the head pointing inwards. A third kunzite can be placed on the area where the negativity is most clearly felt.
**2** Alternatively place the kunzite at each chakra point for a minute or two, starting with the brow and moving down the body to the sacral chakra.

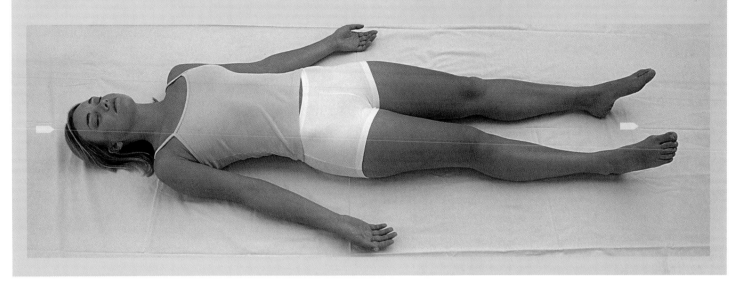

△ **Rubellite is red tourmaline and is one of the most attractive of pink crystals.**

▽ **Lepidolite, or lithium mica, is a sparkly pink stone often found with rubellite embedded within it. It can support self-confidence and the clearing of emotional debris such as guilt.**

can unwittingly pick up emotional debris from others. This can lead to unexpected mood swings and out-of-character behaviour. Placing or wearing a piece of kunzite by the heart for a while can help to sweep away this kind of negativity and any unwanted energy. Kunzite can be used as a release from any powerfully charged experience – such as a film, a song that gets stuck in the mind, or a hurtful remark.

If simply wearing a piece of kunzite is not sufficient, reinforce your intention with your imagination. This can be done in several ways, depending on what stones are available.

### rubellite

One of the most beautiful pink crystals is red tourmaline, also called rubellite. Its colour ranges from a delicate pink to a rhubarb red. Usually the crystals are translucent, but occasionally they can be very dense and almost opaque.

With all types of tourmaline the density of colour changes slightly depending on the angle of view. This is caused by light rays becoming polarized as they pass through the crystal lattice. Like kunzite, rubellite has parallel striations along its length, which help it to act as an energy conduit. It also

△ **The complex makeup of tourmaline means that it can contain many colours within a single crystal. 'Watermelon' combines red and green, a perfect heart chakra balancer.**

has great strengthening and protecting effects on the heart chakra. Rubellite provides an excellent way to balance the emotions when there is either too much aggression (caused by fear or nervous irritation from external or internal imbalances) or too much passivity (caused by a poor level of self-esteem). Rubellite is sometimes found embedded in lepidolite, a stone which shares its qualities.

Often tourmaline combines shades of both red and green. This complex variety is called 'watermelon' tourmaline, and it holds the best combination of colours to balance the heart chakra and the emotions.

# Carnelian and rutilated quartz – healing the wounds

Orange stones can often be effective repairers of the body, encouraging a rapid release of stress. Carnelian and rutilated quartz both encourage the body's own powers of regeneration.

## carnelian

A variety of chalcedony, carnelian ($SiO_2$) is a microcrystalline quartz formed from the dissolving of other minerals containing silicates. Chalcedony does not have the crystalline lattice usually found in quartz. Instead, it is made up of closely packed fibres arranged in concentric layers or parallel bands. This stone gets its warm colour from the presence of iron oxides. It is often translucent, showing colours ranging from pale orange to a deep orange-red. As iron is a very common metal in the earth's crust, carnelian is found around the world. The

▷ **Carnelian is a warming stone that links well to the creative energy of the sacral chakra.**

## ENERGY NET FOR HEALING THE ETHERIC BODY

Use this net regularly for five minutes at a time to help release trauma from deep in the body. It may sometimes bring old symptoms or pain to the surface before they can be completely removed. You will need six tumbled carnelians and an orange cloth to lie on.

**1** Place one carnelian at the top of the head and one at either side of the body at the level of sacral chakra.
**2** Place another stone between the legs at mid-calf level and another below it near the ankles. Place the sixth stone at the base of the throat.

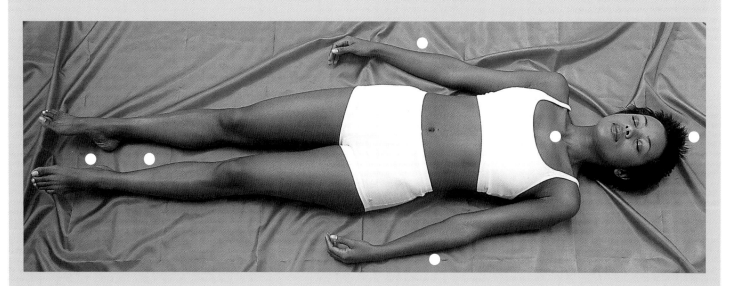

finest examples are used in jewellery – gem quality stones are traditionally known as 'sard'. Carnelian is one of the most useful stones for healing the etheric body when trauma and stress have accumulated to disturb physical functioning. Most will experience carnelian as a gentle soothing energy, though in some circumstances where it feels uncomfortable, the addition of some cooling green or blue stones may help.

## rutilated quartz

This is clear or smoky quartz that contains fine thread-like crystals of rutile, titanium dioxide ($TiO_2$). Rutile is a metallic, needle-shaped crystal that can have a remarkable deep red colour. In quartz it is usually straw coloured – a lustrous gold to golden brown. Titanium is a non-corroding, extremely strong and light metal so it is no surprise that rutilated quartz can help to knit together and strengthen tissues that have been strained or damaged. Like many long,

△ **Two pointed quartz crystals either side of the affected area, with the points facing each other, will diffuse a painful build-up of energy.**

▽ **Each crystal of rutilated quartz is different. Some have a few very long and fine threads of rutile running through them, which help repair nerve damage or connect energy pathways from different parts of the body. Other examples have tightly packed interwoven layers of rutile that might prove more effective in tissue repair.**

### TO EASE PAIN

Pain is a useful indicator of damaged tissue. Without that sensation we might not necessarily know that a problem exists. However, it is useful to be able to lower the levels of pain when they are very high. Pain is a concentration of energy, so by diffusing that energy the experience of pain can often be lessened. For repair of damaged physical tissue there must be a nourishing flow of energy to that area.

**1** To ease the emotional stress of the situation, and to help repair be more rapid and complete, use pink, orange or yellow stones at the sacral chakra or solar plexus, with perhaps an addition of violet stones at the brow or crown chakra to establish calm.

**2** To bring a cooling, quietening energy, place cool coloured stones, green, blue and violet, on or near a painful or inflamed area.

**3** To speed the repair of tissues, such as pulled muscles and broken bones, place rutilated quartz on or around the affected area. This will encourage the torn tissues to rejoin and heal.

thin crystals, rutile is an excellent energy shifter and will help remove energy blocks. Its golden colour suggests that rutilated quartz can reorganize and integrate scattered energy fields.

Very often symptoms of physical pain can be eased when the energy flow within the meridian system is repaired. Detailed knowledge of these energy channels is not necessary – simply placing rutilated quartz or clear quartz crystal points at either side of the painful area, points facing each other, will often bring relief.

Use your hand to scan over the area so that you can feel the flow of energy. The appropriate direction of flow will feel different from any other direction. If needed, the flow can be encouraged by sweeping over the area with a hand-held crystal.

# Other orange healers

Copper and topaz share the ability to create a healing flow of energy through the body. For an even more gentle, clear orange energy, orange calcite is perhaps the coolest and most soothing of the orange stones.

These stones are ideal for helping internal emotional pressures that largely arise from unresolved situations or subtle, unnoticed sources in the environment, such as subsonic vibration or conflict with people around you. Pressure can also be caused by the wrong food or drink, ionization in the air prior to a storm, planetary influences and so on. Like a pressure cooker, energy begins to build up and, with no means of release, turbulence increases until an explosion of some kind restores the equilibrium. To avoid explosions, which can be a sudden, unwarranted loss of temper or could even develop into a nervous breakdown, you need to safely ground and release the unwanted energy.

### RELEASING UNWANTED ENERGY

The following layout with orange stones can be used in acute cases of frustration or where there is a long term difficulty with a personal situation. The treatment helps to stimulate the creative flow of the sacral chakra and effectively grounds any excess energy through the feet.

Use any orange stones in this layout. Remain in position for 10-12 minutes.
**1** Place one stone below the left foot.
**2** Place another below the right foot.
**3** Place a third stone a couple of centimetres below the navel.
**4** Place a fourth stone a centimetre or so above the navel.

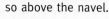

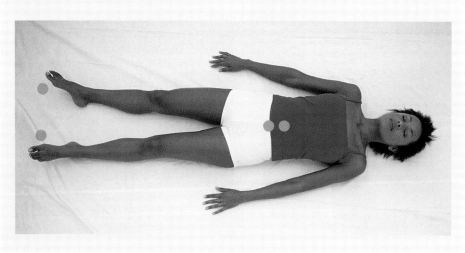

△ Golden topaz is associated with qualities of leadership and self-assuredness. It can, however, be rather susceptible to absorbing energy, so needs regular cleansing if worn.

## topaz

Found in many degrees of colours from completely clear to green or blue, topaz $(Al_2SiO_4(F,OH)_2)$ is best known in its rich golden-yellow and orange-pink varieties. The colour is caused by traces of iron or chromium and may change in sunlight, becoming stronger or more faded.

In any of its colours topaz is good to use when the physical body is tense and emotions are volatile. It encourages the relaxation of rigid areas. Topaz will charge up any area it is focused on and can also be used to draw off excess or negative energy.

For a more grounded and gentler effect, tiger's eye ($SiO_2$ variety) can be used instead. This stone will also help the individual to integrate and become comfortable in challenging social situations.

▷ Water is able to hold the energy patterns of crystals placed in it.

## copper

Metals can sometimes be found in a pure unmixed state in the earth, as nuggets or amalgamations known as native metals. All the precious and semi-precious metals have useful healing qualities, though sometimes they may be prohibitively expensive. Copper (Cu), a metallic red-orange that oxidizes to green, is a great conductor of energy. It is well known to be of benefit to rheumatic sufferers and its use can reduce inflammation of all sorts. Copper helps the flow of energy between all systems in the body and brings a stability and flexibility that protect against stress. When there is an energy build-up and an increasing sense of internal emotional or nervous pressure, copper can aid the flow of energy to safely release or ground it.

## gem waters and essences

Releasing stress and trauma can be a long-term process. Using techniques to maintain the momentum between crystal healing sessions can speed the healing considerably. Gem waters and gem essences offer easy and effective ways of doing this and are simple to make and use. The energy patterns held in the water will only be released as and when the body requires.

▽ Emotional turbulence, over-emotional states or irritability can be eased with copper.

### TO MAKE GEM WATER OR ESSENCE

When you are preparing to make a gem water or essence, choose a cleansed and washed sample of crystal. Members of the quartz family such as carnelian, and similar, harder minerals are ideal. Avoid very soft, water-soluble or potentially toxic minerals. Once you have made your gem water or essence, pour the water into a more permanent container such as an amber glass bottle and preserve it with alcohol or cider vinegar. Add a few drops to drinking water as required or rub on pulse points.

**1** To make a gem water, place the crystal in a clean, plain glass or bowl and cover with spring water. Leave overnight and drink in the morning or take sips throughout the day.

**2** To make a gem essence, place the stone in a clear glass bowl, cover it with spring water and put it in direct sunlight for at least two hours. This imprints the quality of the mineral on the water.

▽ Rub a drop of essence or gem water on pulse points for healing energy.

▽ Drink gem water within a day, while gem essences can be kept for much longer.

# Citrine – sun and the mind

One of the rarer varieties of quartz, citrine ($SiO_2$) forms from recrystallized quartz solution where nearby oxidized iron impurities become included in the atomic structure. These impurities create the characteristic golden-yellow coloration of citrine. The finest quality of citrine is transparent lemon or golden yellow. More commonly, crystals are golden brown to orange-brown with milky white areas. Most citrine these days is made by gently heating poor quality amethyst, turning it golden. This process can also occur naturally in metamorphic environments.

Whatever its origin, citrine quartz is invaluable as a healing stone. The range of colours allows it to work as a grounding stone (browns), as a balancer of the sacral

▷ **Citrine quartz is a translucent variety that shows a range of colours from brown to yellow.**

## CLARITY OF MIND LAYOUT

This energy net uses citrine to help clarity of mind, communication skills, adaptability and energy levels. It may quickly feel uncomfortable unless you really need the extra energy. Begin with short sessions of 5–6 minutes, and practise regularly, especially if you are studying. You will need three citrines, three clear quartz and a yellow cloth.

1 Place one citrine at the solar plexus, point down. Hold the other two citrines in the hands, points away from the body.
2 Place one clear quartz on the forehead with the point towards the top of the head. Tape the remaining clear quartz stones on the top of each foot, between the tendons of the second and third toes.

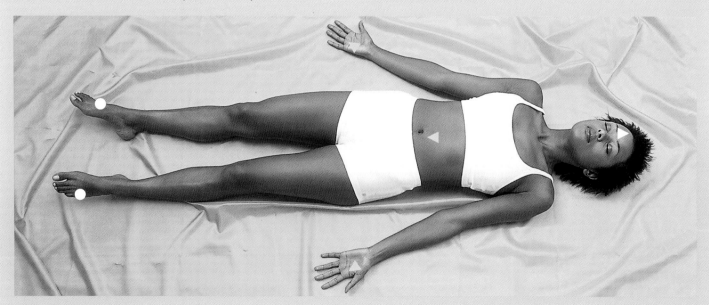

## A CHAKRA GOAL BALANCING

This exercise can be used to help a friend or partner. A chakra goal balance uses crystals that will bring each of the chakras into balance and release the stresses related to the issue being looked at. Repeat the process regularly.

**1** Encourage your friend or partner to share her problems and concerns with you, then together decide on a phrase or short sentence that sums up her intention.

**2** Help her to intuitively select a stone for each chakra that will both balance the energy and also support the process of achieving the desired goal. When all the stones have been chosen, settle your friend in a comfortable position.

**3** Place a stone on each chakra. Leave for 5 to ten minutes. Take away the stones, ground and centre her energies.

**4** After the healing session give your friend a piece of citrine to take with her; this will help to keep confidence high and reduce any emotional turbulence the release may cause. When you repeat the process, new stones should be selected.

chakra (oranges) and as a support for the energies of the solar plexus chakra (yellows). Citrine is gently warming, soothing and integrating. Working in harmony with the solar plexus chakra, it is effective at increasing self-confidence and the achievement of personal goals. This crystal smoothes away areas of irritation and friction, creating more optimism and relaxation through the body, emotions and mind. Thought processes especially are helped with citrine – the grounding qualities prevent the build-up of anxieties, the oranges encourage a flow of creativity

and the bright yellows calm the digestive system. Citrine has a calming effect on the nervous system, bringing clearer thought and improved memory.

The solar plexus chakra, with which yellow stones work so effectively, is the seat of our sense of personal power. From this centre arise our beliefs or doubts in ourselves. From here, confidence or anxieties, optimism or fear modify all our beliefs and our behaviour. Working with yellow stones like citrine can be an effective way to strengthen the positive aspects and release the fears within the body.

## goal balancing

Bad experiences, fear and anxiety often prevent us from achieving goals we would dearly love to reach. Removing the stresses that are linked to specific activities and personal behaviour patterns is one of the most rewarding techniques available to crystal healers.

There are many different ways of goal balancing. For example, with a pendulum it is possible to focus your intention on removing those stresses connected with the problem. The pendulum recognizes and releases only those related energy blocks.

# Other yellow stones

There is a crossover between crystals that work on the second and third chakras – the orange and yellow coloured stones. Citrine, topaz and tiger's eye, for example, will work well at either location depending on the exact shade of the stone.

The solar plexus chakra is especially important because it interfaces with many of the body's systems. The digestive system, the nervous system, the immune system, the brain and its memory function, all depend upon the solar plexus. The solar plexus is also the centre of emotional stability, the seat of personal power, hope and optimism.

Crystal healing is one of the best ways to release the tension that affects the solar plexus, causing stomach problems. Yellow stones help to support positivity and access reserves of personal initiative.

▷ Tiger's eye can be used at the base, sacral and solar plexus chakras, depending on the precise mix of colour in each stone.

▽ Nuggets of pure gold are rare. A very small piece of gold could be attached to a slab of clear quartz to enable its use in crystal healing sessions.

△ The beautiful, warm, glowing colour of amber echoes the gently activating effect it has on the body.

▽ The bright gold colour of iron pyrites from a distance resembles gold, hence its popular name, fool's gold. It is, however, an indicator that gold-bearing rocks could be nearby.

## amber

Not strictly a mineral or a crystal, amber $(C_{10}H_{16}O+H_2S)$ is fossilized tree resin more than four million years old. It can be brown, orange, yellow, green or red, perfectly clear or contain bits of debris from when it oozed from the bark of ancient pine trees. Amber containing whole preserved insects tends to be highly valued and is often imitated with plastic or resin. It can be worked very easily with abrasive papers and reheated to melt small fragments together into larger pieces, producing so-called Russian amber.

Amber is a soothing stone that is useful for correcting imbalances in the nervous system, or when there is a need for gentle activation and energizing. Amber can be helpful for detoxification and reduces confusion and anxiety.

## iron pyrites

With its high sulphur content, iron pyrites $(FeS_2)$ can have beneficial effects on the digestive system, helping with the elimination of toxins. More commonly known as fool's gold, pyrites forms brilliant

▷ Gold jewellery will have some beneficial effects on the energies of the body.

▽ Gold jewellery will have some beneficial effects on the energies of the body.

▽ Yellow coloured stones help to reduce tension in the solar plexus and encourage relaxation and positive attitudes.

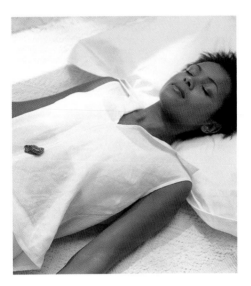

golden metallic crystals, often perfect cubes. As an iron ore, it is gently grounding, helping recovery from flights of anxiety and other emotionally charged imaginings that contribute to depression and frustration. If anxiety is a factor in digestive problems, pyrites can help reduce tension.

## other yellow stones

A commonly occurring native metal, though usually in quantities so small as to be uneconomical to retrieve, gold has been sought after and treasured since the Stone

▽ Sunstone is a variety of feldspar with a yellow-orange colour and a brilliant play of light. It is of the same family as moonstone.

Age. Forming from gold-bearing rocks or in hot water solution it is usually found near to granite rock masses and in quartz veins. As these erode the grains of gold are deposited in river gravels.

Gold rarely crystallizes but forms thin plates, wires and grains. Nuggets are very uncommon. Gold is not often used in crystal healing, simply because natural

examples large enough to be practical are rare. Small flakes of gold can be found in mineralogical shops boxed for display.

Like the other elemental metals, silver and copper, gold is a great conductor of energy, helping to harmonize many of the different levels within the body. Creating easy energy flow, gold is helpful in releasing stress from the nervous system, increasing the efficiency of the brain and the ability to repair damaged tissues. The immune system is strengthened by gold's positive effect on the heart chakra and thymus gland. In the absence of a piece of native gold, a clean piece of 24 carat jewellery can be used.

Stones such as fluorite, feldspar, beryl and tourmaline all have yellow varieties that can play a part in rebalancing the solar plexus chakra. Those stones with a warm orange-yellow work best with the digestive system and will be relaxing. The stones with a more lemon yellow colour will be effective in clearing the mind and nervous system, encouraging clarity and mental alertness.

# Balance and peace: green & blue stones

Crystals with the cooler colours of blue and green all tend to encourage a sense of balanced calm and a quality of peacefulness. These crystals work well with the energies of the heart and throat chakras.

# Green stones – balancing the heart

There are a great many minerals and crystals with a green coloration. All work very well to balance the heart chakra energies and introduce stabilizing and calming influences.

## green aventurine

A member of the quartz family, green aventurine ($SiO_2$) is one of the best overall balancing stones for the heart, because it acts without creating any turbulence or sudden release. Aventurine forms when quartz is subjected to heat and pressure, causing it to melt and resolidify, usually as large slabs, with inclusions of other minerals. It is these inclusions that give aventurine its colour. Green aventurine resembles green jasper but contains fuschite mica or sparkling fragments of haematite and pyrite, which catch the light and make it easy to distinguish from other similar stones. The inclusions have a slight grounding effect that increases the stabilizing qualities of the stone.

▽ **Aventurine is a massive form of quartz that can be found in a range of colours from emerald to very pale green.**

△ **Bloodstone of the finest quality is a dark green with bright red spots and splashes. It can also contain areas of grey, yellow and orange.**

## bloodstone

Another green member of the quartz family, bloodstone ($SiO_2$) is well known for its beneficial effects on the heart and circulation. In the past it was believed to be effective in staunching wounds and soldiers

△ **Verdelite can be distinguished from similar coloured stones because, like all tourmalines, the colour alters slightly with the angle of viewing.**

used to carry a piece with them into battle. Heliotrope, as bloodstone is also called, is a type of chalcedony with the same structure as jasper. The green colour is caused by small crystals of actinolite, while the prominent bright red spots and streaks derive from iron oxides that were present as the solution crystallized. With a combination of red and green, bloodstone can work with both the base and heart chakras, bringing either a sufficient energy or a sufficient calmness.

## verdelite

Green tourmaline ($Na(Mg,Fe,Li,Mn,Al)_3Al_6(BO_3)Si_6O_{18}(OH,F)_4$) is also known as verdelite. The green colour, which can vary from very light to almost black, is brought about by higher than usual amounts of sodium in the structure of the stone.

All tourmalines help to re-align the physical structures of the body and our connection to the energies of the planet. Its green colour attunes verdelite more to the heart chakra and to a relationship with the natural world. Like many green minerals, verdelite increases our receptivity allowing greater harmony with the surroundings.

## BALANCING THE HEART'S ENERGIES

The heart is the balance point for our entire energy system. Creating balance and stability in the heart makes it easier for other imbalances elsewhere to be corrected. Balancing the heart brings a life-supporting calm inside us, and an ability to relate positively to the world around us. The following layout of crystals helps to stabilize all the energies of the heart.

Beneath the heart chakra is another small energy centre that is particularly concerned with holding and bringing to fruition our most cherished wishes and desires. A Herkimer diamond placed just under the heart (pictured right) will help access this energy, bringing a sense of clarity and direction when there is confusion.

**1** For the layout shown below, first place a small rose quartz crystal at the centre of the chest.

**2** Then take four green tourmalines, and make a cross along the axis of the body around the rose quartz. Clear quartz can be used here if tourmalines are unavailable. It is important that, if the stones have natural points, these are all placed so that they are facing outwards.

**3** Between the four tourmalines make a second diagonal cross using smoky quartz crystals. Again, if these have natural points they should face outwards. This pattern will release stress from the heart while balancing and grounding its energies. The outward pointing stones ensure that a relaxing calm is established. Stay in this heart layout for five to ten minutes. Use grounding stones if necessary afterwards.

**4** For a variation of this layout, if you want to bring full potential closer within your reach, then you can add a Herkimer diamond underneath the layout.

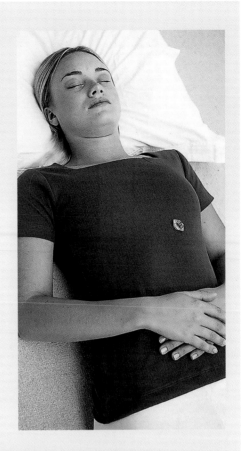

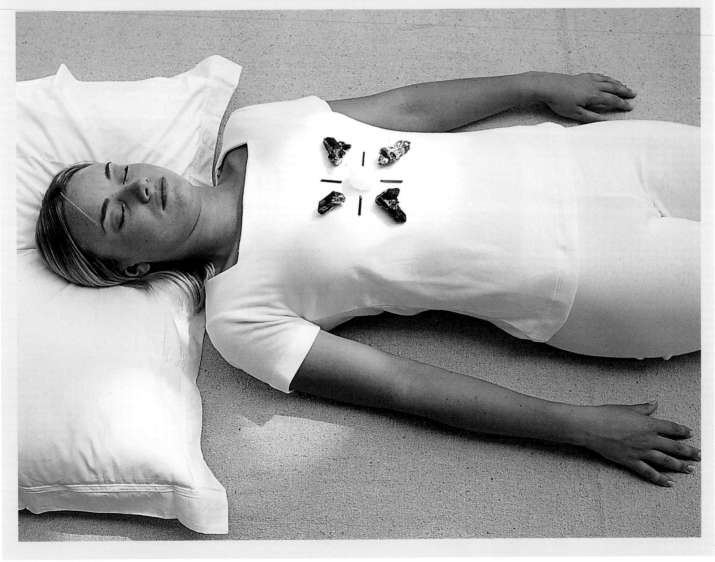

# Green crystals and the space of nature

Green is the colour of nature, the energy of expansion and space. The heart chakra establishes our own inner space and our relationship to everything in the world around us. Green stones and crystals can help to create the fine balance that we need in order to live harmoniously with the world without suppressing our own desires. Green crystals can also help to break down some of the barriers that keep us feeling trapped within our circumstances and the limits of our abilities.

## moss agate

Common symptoms of feeling trapped are tightness in the chest and breathing difficulties. Moss agate, a form of chalcedony, with coloured inclusions resembling trees, ferns or moss, can help to relieve the tensions that underlie these problems. Within the translucent or transparent quartz, which usually has a blue or yellow tinge, crystal growths of manganese oxides, hornblende or iron in various shades of green and brown suggest the ability to grow and expand. The inclusions often look like the fine structures within the lungs, suggesting freedom to breathe. Moss agate encourages a sense of increased confidence and optimism, allowing a much greater relationship with the world of nature.

▽ **Moss agate can be a useful calming stone for feelings of confinement and confusion.**

## jade

By connecting us to our physical instincts and earth energies, jade ($NaAlSi_2O_6$) increases the sense of belonging. Thus jade is an antidote to over-intellectual spiritualism – it calms the arrogance that sees the physical world as inferior to the flights of fancy the mind can conjure up.

## emerald

This stone is a gem-quality green variety of the mineral beryl ($Be_3Al_2Si_6O_{18}$). It balances the heart, speeds up detoxification and brings calm by removing hidden fears. Like many green stones, emerald can be a helpful aid to meditation.

## healing the garden

Green stones have a natural affinity with growing plants and they can be used to heal the energies of a garden. Simply place stones where you feel extra help is needed. Walk round your garden, allowing yourself to be receptive to energy changes. You will almost certainly be drawn to spots that feel dull or heavy in some way. This process is similar to scanning a body and is corrected in the same way by the placement of appropriate stones. Minerals with a significant copper content, such as turquoise, malachite and chrysocolla can all encourage plant growth.

▽ **Jade has been widely used for rituals and is linked to ancestor spirits and the gods.**

△ **Green stones make a space calm and restful for contemplation and meditation.**

## making space

Healing the heart can never truly be accomplished if whenever we reduce stress, we return immediately to a hectic and stressful life. For anything to grow, space is needed. If we wish to get more from life, sometimes it is necessary to do less instead of trying to cram more things in.

▽ **Emerald of gem-quality is rare and expensive but impure pieces work in healing just as well.**

## A SMALL CALM SPACE

Finding a few minutes once a day to be silent in your own company will help you to see opportunities and new solutions that would improve the quality of your life. Crystals can help to bring balance into our energy systems but it is up to us to maintain and build upon that state of balance.

Use some green stones to bring some of the qualities of nature into your home. Set a small space aside in a corner or on a table. Keep it clear of everyday clutter, and arrange some of your favourite green stones there, together with a beautiful plant and a candle, or other items that help you feel calm and relaxed.

**1** Take two minutes a day to sit and look at the stones. Sit comfortably in front of them, light the candle or burn some incense.

**2** Take up one or two of the stones and hold them in your hands, close your eyes and relax. You are making space in your mind, your emotions and your life for new things to enter.

**3** Open your eyes to look again at the stones and then close them again and think of the space you are creating in your mind. Repeat if you wish.

**4** When you have finished, return the stones to their place.

▽ ▷ **The energy of any room in the home can be enlivened by having a small quiet space somewhere within it.**

# Personal space – individual growth

Green stones strengthen the main quality of the heart chakra, which is to grow and expand in a harmonious manner in such a way as to fulfil the individual's core needs. Personal space and freedom to be oneself are essential for wellbeing and health. We can use crystals to help us achieve our goals in life, both by giving us quiet in order to see things more clearly and by encouraging the growth of qualities we need.

Before goals can be reached, it is necessary to clarify as much as possible what those goals are. A reminder of your aim keeps your attention focused in the right direction without becoming obsessive. Set aside a space that can be dedicated to your wishes. Have a representation of your goal; a picture, photograph or phrase. For example, if the goal is to pass your driving test, a picture of a car can be the centrepiece. Then choose crystals to encourage qualities that are needed for you to succeed. Encourage optimism and clarity with yellow crystals, calm with green stones, ability to learn with blue, co-ordination with violet. A clear quartz crystal can reinforce your intention if it is programmed.

▽ **This space is dedicated to a wish for personal control and confidence. The yellow crystals will help to encourage optimism and reduce anxiety.**

### GREEN BREATHING
This exercise easily creates a meditative state. Using a green crystal as a focus of attention naturally calms the mind and acts as a support to the entire process. Sit in a comfortable position and take a minute to settle yourself. Have a green stone in front of you – the type is not important.
**1** Look at the stone, letting your eyes rest on it gently. Keep looking at the stone and let your mind be aware of your breathing.
**2** After a few minutes, close your eyes and imagine you are breathing in the colour green. If you get distracted, open your eyes and gaze at the stone for a while longer, then close your eyes and breathe in the colour again.
**3** When you are ready, put the stone aside and relax for a minute before returning to normal activity.

▷ Exposing a clear quartz crystal to a range of coloured lights is an effective way of programming it, or modifying its energy.

## programming a crystal

To direct a crystal's energy towards a specific, clearly defined goal you need to programme it. This will always be most effective when your intention matches the natural quality of the crystal. Programming a blue crystal to radiate red energy is possible, for example, but will go against the flow of energy that crystal possesses. Always get to know a crystal well before you consider modifying its function with programming. Remember that a crystal that has always been used for its healing energy will always be better suited to healing rather than being used as a meditation stone. A meditation crystal will come to enhance and amplify the energies of the meditator each time it is used, and so will be less useful as a healing stone.

There are two ways to programme a crystal. The first way is by exposure to a type of energy, such as a light source. A clear quartz that is exposed for a prolonged amount of time to red light, for example, will after a while begin to resonate to that red frequency.

The second programming technique is to redirect the stone's energy through strong intention and affirmation. Hold the stone in your hands, or to your heart or brow, and project your intention into the centre of the crystal. Repeat this process several times until you intuitively feel that the crystal can now hold and broadcast the thought or intention. For sucessful programming, it is important that the intention you project is as clear and precise as possible. Vague or muddled desires bring vague results.

Once it is programmed, place the crystal carefully in a space where it can be seen, to remind you of your goals.

To remove the programming repeat the process with the intention that the stone reverts to its normal state. Cleanse the crystal and thank it for its help.

### GREEN HEART

This exercise will calm the heart.

1 Put a green stone at your heart. Hold a clear quartz crystal in your left hand, point inwards. Hold another clear quartz in your right hand, point outwards, away from the body.

2 Visualize a flow of energy from your left hand to your heart and from your heart to your right hand and out of your body. Feel calm energy filling you and tension draining away.

3 Change the quartz points around so the flow moves in the other direction. Repeat the process.

4 After five minutes put down the quartz points and experience the calm green energy at the heart chakra. If there is somewhere else that is in pain or in need of extra calming energy, put the green stone there, instead of at the heart.

# Expansion into the beyond – stones from space

Tons of dust land on the planet from space every year but it is rare to find larger fragments, even though meteorites have crashed into the earth since its creation. Metallic meteorites consisting mainly of iron and nickel are more common than rocky meteorites that have a composition similar to igneous rock. Many meteorites are thought to be the remnants of a planet that once orbited between Mars and Jupiter, a space now occupied by the asteroid belt.

## tektites

Even more mysterious than meteorites are tektites, a group of minerals found scattered around the globe whose exact origins are unknown. Tektites may be glassy meteorites but it is more likely that they formed millions of years ago when large meteorites struck the earth, melting rock in huge explosions of energy. The strange shapes of tektites are evocative of such cataclysmic events. Very often they have pitted, rippled or cratered surfaces and form pebble, teardrop or elongated extruded fragments. They are usually black-brown. In one area in the Czech Republic tektites are a brilliant green, and there they are called moldavites.

## moldavites

These are much sought-after, even though they are rarely found in large pieces. Moldavite is an excellent amplifying stone,

▷ **Meteorites remind us of the vastness of the universe and the possibilities of the unknown.**

**MOLDAVITE NET**

If you are lucky enough to have nine moldavite pieces you can try the following crystal net. This energy net will help expand awareness beyond its normal physical limitations. It will help connect you to the energy of the earth, and through its core energy out into the wider universe. This layout will help relax tensions in the chest, easing feelings of constriction and confusion. It will also help clarify your goals and directions in life. Moldavite can give a powerful and sometimes disorientating experience. Make sure you spend no longer than ten minutes in this net and ground yourself thoroughly when finished.

**1** On either side of the body between the head and solar plexus put three moldavites, evenly spaced.

**2** Position another moldavite midway between and below your feet.

**3** Place one above the top of your head.

**4** The last moldavite goes on the brow chakra in the centre of the forehead.

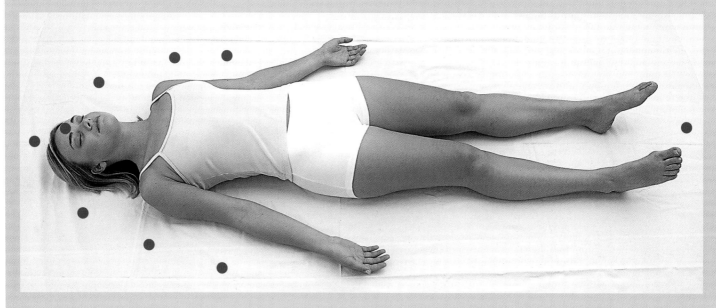

## EXPLORING MOLDAVITE

The energy of moldavite definitely seems to be unearthly at times, as befits a stone created from the meeting of earth and outer space. Comfortable exploration of moldavite's potential can be helped with this layout.

**1** Use eight pieces of amethyst or eight pieces of clear quartz. If they have terminations, place these so they are facing inwards towards the body.

**2** Once these are in place, place the moldavite on your heart, throat or brow chakra. Experiment with the moldavite on different chakras to see how your experiences alter.

**3** After a maximum of ten minutes remove the moldavite and replace it with a grounding stone, such as haematite or black tourmaline. Another grounding stone can be added near the feet if necessary.

**4** When you are ready, remove all the stones and relax for at least five minutes before resuming normal activities.

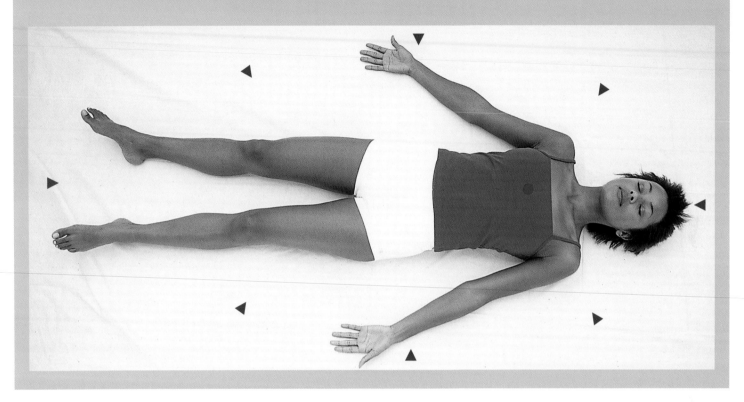

enhancing the properties of other stones placed with it. It usually feels expansive and enlivening and it may cause sensations of movement or sudden changes of energy and awareness, such as heat or flashes of imagery across the mind. It is well worth sitting for a time with a piece of moldavite and just allowing these tides of energy to come and go. If you wish to explore more deeply, place a piece of moldavite at your heart, throat or brow chakra and surround your body with clear quartz or amethyst. Keep a good grounding stone nearby for when you have finished. Do not place too much meaning on your experiences. Simply accept.

When exploring the qualities of crystals in this way remember to make notes of your experiences afterwards. Over time certain themes and types of imagery will emerge and these may suggest how the crystal is interacting with your own energy systems.

With stone such as moldavite there can be a powerful amplifying effect. This makes them useful in the exploration of other sorts of crystal. Green stones in general, and moldavite in particular, seem to enhance our natural sensitivity and psychic skills, particularly if we have learned the value of entering a quiet, receptive, calm state on a regular basis.

◁ **Moldavite has a characteristic bottle-green colour and a rippled or pitted surface pattern.**

▷ **Although attractive in its natural shapes, moldavite is also used in jewellery.**

# Turquoise and aquamarine – joy and the immune system

balance and peace

Activating and strengthening the body's own defences naturally improves quality of life, bringing an increased sense of optimism and happiness. Both turquoise and aquamarine can be used for this purpose. Happiness is one of the greatest antibiotics available to us. It rapidly creates balance in the blood chemistry and hormones, releasing stress and flushing out damaging toxins.

## turquoise

A hydrated basic phosphate of aluminium and copper, turquoise $(CuAl_6(PO_4)_4(OH)_8.4H_2O)$ is of medium hardness, and the colour – which varies – can alter when exposed to light or chemicals. Despite its lack of stability it has been used throughout the world as an important gemstone.

In North American Indian traditions, in China and Tibet, as well as in Europe, turquoise has a reputation for protection. There is a belief that the stone will become paler when its owner is in danger. Certainly it will react to chemicals secreted from the skin as well as to oils or perfumes being worn. Because of its susceptibility, the colour of turquoise is often stabilized with wax or resin. In the southwestern United States, turquoise was often powdered and presented

△ Turquoise is one of the most universal and oldest of gemstone amulets worn for protection.

▽ Turquoise is a soft mineral. Often in jewellery making it is crushed to a powder and mixed with resin, to make a more robust-coloured stone.

## INCREASING LIFE ENERGY

The thymus gland is located between the heart and throat chakras. It is an important organ of the immune system and at energetic levels regulates the amount of life-energy, or *prana*, within the body. All turquoise-coloured stones placed around this area will help to regulate and balance the thymus.

◁ **Aquamarine is so-named from its colour resembling the sea. It was once prized as a protection from shipwreck.**

as an offering to the spirits. In Central and South America it was used to decorate offerings to the gods. The delicate sky-blue tones suggest its affinity to the heavens – sky that has fallen to earth.

The colour of turquoise has a strengthening and supporting effect on the thymus gland, which is located just below the throat where the collarbones meet. This gland is one of the main organs of the immune system. In complementary medicine, it is of vital importance to the levels of life-energy available in the body.

Turquoise encourages the functions of this gland and so increases available energy, protecting the body from negativity.

## aquamarine

Blue-green in colour, aquamarine ($Be_3Al_2Si_6O_{18}$) is a variety of the mineral beryl, which can form very large crystals up to several metres long. Many of the finest crystals are found in Brazil, and it is a good source of the light metal beryllium, which is used in alloys. Aquamarine is excellent for energizing the immune system and is useful

in the recovery from debilitating illnesses, where it provides an energy boost, helping the body to get rid of the underlying causes of disease. Whereas turquoise is an absorbing stone with gentle actions, aquamarine can be stimulating and purifying. Occasionally it may appear to exacerbate symptoms as they are lifted from the subtle bodies. If this occurs, use it with a stone that will ease the process such as kyanite or selenite.

An important quality of the thymus, located midway between the heart and throat, is the expression of uniqueness. Repressing our natural qualities suppresses life-energy, leading to stress and susceptibility to illness. If you are in a situation where you cannot be yourself, use aquamarine to find a positive way to express your individuality. Aquamarine can help clear localized areas of imbalance and dulled energy. Placing it on or near an infected or inflamed area will help to release the difficulties that hamper the body's defence systems.

## TURQUOISE LAYOUT

Use this layout when healing energies are required or there is a lack of self-confidence. Turquoise stimulates the natural protective energies of the body, citrine reduces fear and balances the body's functions.

1 Place a turquoise just below the collarbones.
2 Place a bright yellow citrine at the solar plexus.
3 Place a rose quartz at the navel to calm and stabilize the emotions.

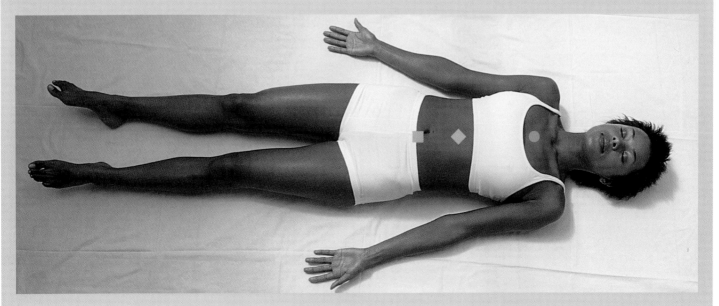

# Amazonite and chrysocolla – self-expression and creativity

Turquoise stones help to combine and harmonize the energies of the heart and throat chakras, easing the flow of personal expression and individuality. Amazonite and chrysocolla improve communication on many different levels.

## amazonite

A variety of the common mineral feldspar, amazonite ($KAlSi_3O_8$) has been used for centuries in jewellery and ornamentation because of its fine blue-green colour. Characteristic to amazonite is a streaky parallel patterning of different shadings, caused by the presence of lead, the impurity of which creates the intense colour.

Like turquoise, amazonite can sometimes be more blue and sometimes more green in colour, and this makes it useful both at the heart chakra and the throat chakra – but of special value for the thymus gland midway between them both.

Amazonite is particularly effective at activating the qualities of self-expression,

confidence, leadership and communication. Like many green and turquoise stones, amazonite may also help to enhance psychic skills, in particular the ability to receive images from the past. This ability is known as 'far memory'. The images received often relate to, or are symbolic of, current preoccupations and parallel or reflect the current goals of the viewer. Whether these

△ **Amazonite often shows streaks of different greens along its central axis. It forms clearly defined block-like crystals.**

far memories are actually past life information, or come from another subconscious source, their impressions can be useful in encouraging us to locate, order and pursue our unique path in life.

---

### AMAZONITE NET

An energy net of six pieces of amazonite can be used to release skills hidden deep within our genetic memory. It can also help the recall of distant personal memories, throwing light on repeating patterns of behaviour. This helps to clarify what prevents us from achieving our goals time and again, so that steps can be taken to remove hidden blocks. Place six amazonites evenly around the body: one above the head, one below the feet and two at either side. Allow five to ten minutes for a session.

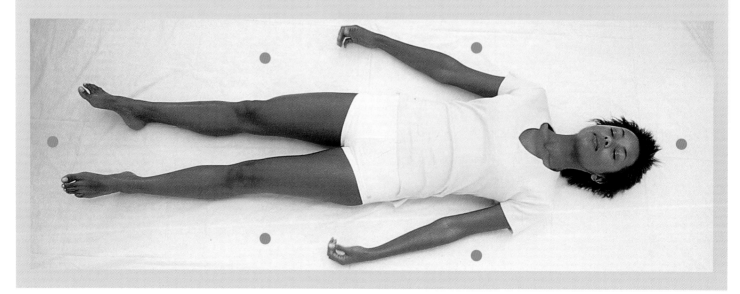

▷ Those who work creatively may benefit from chrysocolla, as it releases tension in the upper body and helps the flow of creative expression.

▽ Its effects on the thoracic cavity and throat make chrysocolla of benefit to singers.

# chrysocolla

A delicate and very beautiful mineral, chrysocolla $((Cu,Al_2)H_2Si_2O_5(OH)_4.nH_2O)$ is formed from solutions of copper, silica and water. Because it occurs near copper deposits it can be found intermixed with other copper-rich minerals such as turquoise, azurite, malachite and cuprite. Chrysocolla often intergrows with quartz, which makes it slightly more durable,

though still soft. In this form it is called gem silica. A variety of chrysocolla mixed equally with turquoise and azurite-malachite has a deeper, even blue-green colour and is known as Eilat stone. This variety is named for the region on the Sinai Peninsula where it was mined in the time of King Solomon.

Chrysocolla helps to balance the whole region of the chest, lungs, throat and neck. It cools and calms inflamed areas, stimulating

the immune system and quietening the mind. The mix of greens and blues acts on the heart and throat chakras, reaching up to the deeper blue of the brow chakra and the related minor chakra at the base of the skull, the medulla oblongata. This small energy point is important for regulating and directing psychic information and energy from other levels of existence. It clears away blockages in the emotions and belief systems, which cause confusion and failure.

Placing a piece of chrysocolla at the heart or throat, at the base of the skull or in the centre of the forehead can create a rearrangement of energies that results in a clearer view of issues. For particular problems, begin with a clear intention or a situation you wish to understand better. Focus clearly for a moment on that thought and then relax. The chrysocolla will help to bring resolutions to your conscious mind.

At a physical level, chrysocolla encourages relaxation and balance, allowing the green energies of the heart, with all its strength of feeling, to be manifested and expressed through the blue energies of the throat chakra and the voice.

◁ Chrysocolla can have strong areas of green next to rich, deep turquoise and blue. Its irregular and flaky appearance in natural form helps to identify it from other similarly coloured minerals.

# Blue lace agate and celestite – touching the clouds

Light blue stones, such as blue lace agate and celestite, are used to introduce a calming influence in situations where cool, peaceful energy is required.

## blue lace agate

This is one of the most striking varieties of quartz. The rich blue bands in blue lace agate ($SiO_2$) are created by larger quartz crystals intergrowing through chalcedony, which originally seeped as solution into cavities within volcanic rock. This natural blue agate is not commonly found, so it tends to be rather more expensive than other agates. Because of its microscopic structure, all agate is very porous and will take up dyes easily. Dyed agate is relatively easy to identify as all its bands are shades of one colour, whereas natural samples have some variation created by the different impurities in the surrounding rocks where they crystallize.

Few crystals have the soft, gentle energy of lace agate. It can be used anywhere that needs calming and cooling. Blue stones encourage the flow of energy and have a natural affinity with the throat chakra, our

▽ When polished, blue lace agate reveals undulating bands of blues and milky greys.

means of communication and expression. When the flow of communication is stifled, internal pressure builds up. Unexpressed, this energy can become resentment, anger and aggression; unable to flow, the blue vibration becomes red energy that will eventually explode. Blue stones can help to ease the pressure and release the energy.

△ All agates are a microcrystalline quartz in massive form only, though sometimes small crystals can be seen within the layers.

▽ A feeling of pressure is often felt at the throat when emotional stress is being released. A piece of blue lace agate placed at the base of the throat will quickly ease and release the energy.

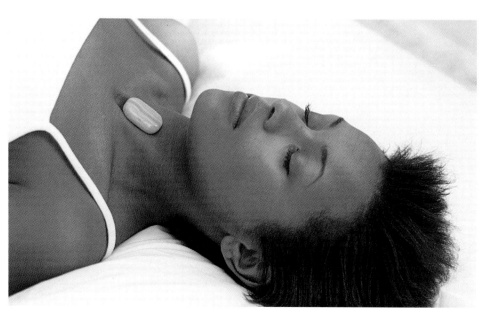

## celestite

Also known as celestine, celestite ($SrSO_4$) is a soft blue or grey mineral that has been used for centuries as an ingredient in fireworks and rescue flares. The strontium content burns with a bright crimson flame.

The finest celestite crystals come from Madagascar and are a beautiful sky-blue colour, hence the mineral name. Celestite has an uplifting, calming and expansive quality, making it good for contemplation and meditation. It is effective at lifting heavy moods and sadness as well as balancing the throat chakra. The ethereal quality of celestite crystals often helps the mind to travel beyond its normal perspective, promoting inspiration and intuitive leaps.

▷ **Celestite is easily damaged as it is very soft, so keep it away from harder stones in a collection**.

### ETHER NET

Using an energy net with seven small clusters of celestite and a white cloth will help you tune into spiritual states as well as encouraging communication skills and artistic creativity. Ether is the fifth element, the element of space. Within its fine substance are all the possibilities of creation. Lying in this energy net can provide a deep rest from the cares of the world, and an effective way to lighten heavy emotional burdens. It can also help dissolve negative patterns that have become attached to the auric field.

Lay out the seven clusters on the white cloth, one above the head, one at either side of the feet and the others evenly spaced between. Lie in the net for five to ten minutes.

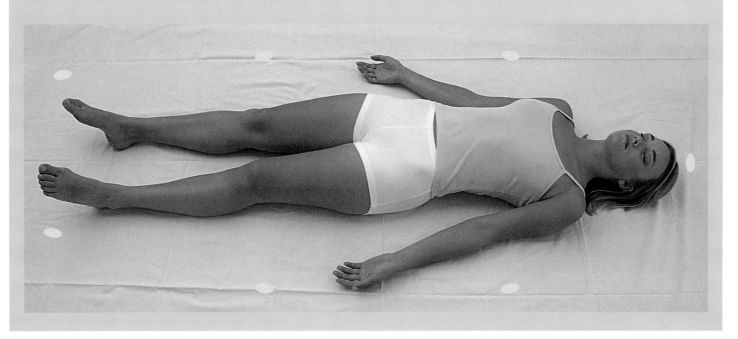

# Healing and beyond:
## *indigo & violet stones*

With deeper blue and violet crystals
the potential for change and growth
of awareness greatly increases as our
inherent abilities and buried talents
emerge to enrich our lives. These stones
attune to the brow and crown chakras.

# Indigo stones – lapis lazuli and sodalite

There are many deep blue minerals available, all of which can help us to regain a state of quiet peaceful awareness, in which we become more receptive to all sorts of information and communication.

## lapis lazuli

A rare gemstone that has always been highly prized, lapis lazuli $(Na,Ca)_8(Al.Si)_{12}O_{24}$ $(S,SO_4)$ forms only where limestone comes into contact with calcite and pyrites. Metamorphic conditions produce a new mineral, lazurite, which has an intense blue coloration. Lapis lazuli is a rock comprising several minerals: lazurite embedded in calcite and pyrites. Afghanistan has always been the best source.

▽ **The rich blues of lapis lazuli were once ground to a fine powder and used as pigment.**

Lapis lazuli works well with the whole area of the upper chest, throat and head. It can be very quietening initially, but this is often the prelude to deep cleansing at many different levels. Lapis can help those who are shy or introverted to communicate and express themselves. It can also benefit those who project their voices, such as teachers, singers and sales personnel.

Like other deep blue and indigo stones, lapis lazuli attunes to the throat and brow chakras and enlivens communication, the processes of thought and memory. The energy of lapis lazuli is not comfortable for everyone, provoking detachment and floating into uncharted depths. This apparent emptiness, when patiently absorbed, reveals a wealth of information and solutions to problems. It can also reveal past errors and bring up unresolved fears.

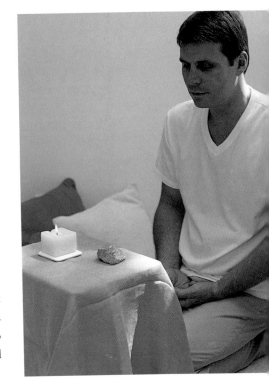

△ **The peaceful, calm presence of lapis lazuli brings a lively silence to a meditation room and aids thought processes.**

## sodalite

This mineral can be easily confused in appearance with lapis lazuli. Indeed, sodalite $(Na_4Al_3Si_3O_{12}Cl)$ can often be found as one of the minerals making up lapis. The main differences are a slight variation of blue – lapis is more brilliant, sodalite darker. Lapis contains specks of golden iron pyrites and has a speckling of different colours, while sodalite has thin veins of white running through it. Sodalite is named from its high sodium content. It is a useful stone for the brow chakra. It can be less penetrating in its energy than lapis lazuli, but can help nevertheless to access fine levels of intuitive knowledge and promote understanding of ideas and concepts. It is therefore a useful stone for the student and the philosopher.

Physically sodalite will, like all dark blue stones, have a sedating and quietening effect on overactive systems, particularly the nervous system and the lymphatic system,

◁ A flow of fine levels of information is suggested by the web-like structure and veins of colours within sodalite.

▽Sodalite promotes understanding and is helpful placed close by when studying.

which is suggested by the web of fine white veins throughout the stone. This visual characteristic also reflects the ability of sodalite to strengthen communication, particularly in groups.

Indigo stones should be used sparingly with those suffering from depressive states as the colour can exaggerate the condition. Choose activating, warm coloured stones to encourage optimism and dynamism.

## LAYOUT FOR INCREASING EASE

Sometimes there is a feeling of unease, of things being not quite right without any apparent symptoms of illness or upset in your life. Because of its potent cleansing energy lapis lazuli can be used to alleviate this in a simple procedure that can be remarkably powerful.

**1** Place a clear quartz, point upwards, above the crown of the head. Place a smoky quartz, point down, between the feet.
**2** At the centre of the brow place a piece of lapis lazuli. Remain in the layout for five to ten minutes and repeat for a few days if necessary.

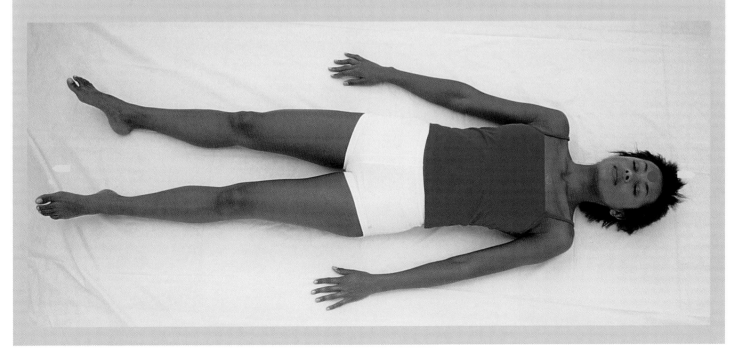

# Other blue stones – intuition

Becoming a good crystal healer requires a degree of knowledge about tools and techniques, but most of all it is necessary to have confidence in your own intuitive abilities. Crystals can be described only in general terms – each person will react slightly differently to a given stone. The ideal stone for one person may not have any effect on another. Intuition lets the crystal worker choose the most appropriate stone for each case.

## guided by instinct

Intuition is the sum of information that is received by the mind at levels of awareness that we do not usually access. Though an important factor in our everyday lives, intuitive choices usually go unnoticed. Often they are things we 'just do' without any conscious justification.

Paying attention to where our awareness moves – where the eyes may be resting, what the hands are doing, the sorts of thoughts in our mind, how the body is feeling – is important. It's also useful to take note of the actions we perform 'by mistake', like picking up a stone other than the one intended, or having a stone fall out of place time after time – all these are clues to intuitive knowledge. Intuition rarely operates at the level of spoken thoughts – it is necessary to have a quiet mind so that these subtle impressions are not drowned out by our usual mental chatter. This is why developing a regular meditation practice and removing our own stress is important. Taking time to experience calmness and clarity increases the likelihood of noticing what is really happening around us.

Regardless of how large or small your collection of stones, intuition will guide you to choose the most appropriate crystals for the work you are doing. When you go to select stones for a healing, notice those that first catch your eye. See if, when you pick up the stones, there is an instant of hesitation before you select a particular crystal.

### USING INTUITION IN CRYSTAL HEALING

Noticing your instinctive actions, thoughts and feelings greatly increases the effectiveness of a crystal healing session. Be aware of hesitation before or after placing a stone – you may need to adjust the position. Notice if there is a feeling of rightness or completion when all the stones have been placed. If there is not, maybe another stone needs adding or some other change should be made.

Working with crystals teaches you to become aware of slight changes in your mental and physical state. When working with others, scan quickly across the patient's body to discover how they feel. Then note which crystal or group of stones comes immediately to mind. Practise your sensitivity all the time, not only with hand scans but also with visual scans. Remember that the individual energy field is greater than the physical body. When you quickly scan someone – does the energy feel balanced? Is there a sense of being top or base-heavy? Do you sense grey areas or energy hollows?

◁ **Intuition develops at its own pace. Regular work with crystals will ensure accuracy.**

▽ **Focus on maintaining a relaxed awareness rather than on any desired outcome.**

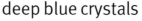

△ Regardless of how large or small your collection, intuition will guide you to choose the most appropriate crystals.

▽ Kyanite forms fan-like clusters or blades of thin crystal ideal for restoring energy balance.

## deep blue crystals

Crystals of a deep blue colour will stimulate the latent abilities of subtle perception and intuitive skills. Stones with striations will speed the flow of information, as well as initiating levels of peacefulness through

▽ Indicolite is the blue-green variety of tourmaline ideal for working on the upper chakras and wherever a peaceful flow of energy is needed.

△ Sapphire can balance the higher faculties of the mind as well as reducing levels of stress.

which information can be recognized. Blue tourmaline, also known as indicolite, will energize and balance throat, brow and crown chakras in this way.

Kyanite ($Al_2SiO_5$) is a blue variety of the mineral disthene, which forms thin blade-like crystals. Kyanite is a very effective energy conduit that can balance most systems in the subtle anatomy. It can quickly create great stillness and tranquillity, which makes it ideal for meditation.

Corundum ($Al_2O_3$) can often be found in the same rock as kyanite. The presence of iron and titanium colours corundum blue, creating the stone we call sapphire. Forming hard, barrel-shaped or hexagonal crystals, sapphire will enhance the functions of the higher levels of consciousness, reduce tension and bring calm, especially to the crown and solar plexus chakras.

# Amethyst and other violet stones

Violet stones have a natural affinity to the crown chakra just above the top of the head. This chakra relates to functions of the brain and mind, but most of all it is the master control centre for the whole chakra system. Violet stones combine the vibrations of practical, down-to-earth red energy with the energy of blue – the expansive, spacious, undefined flow of peace. Combining the two extremes allows violet stones to bring a state of balance wherever it is required, while having a special focus on the workings of the mind.

## amethyst

A violet form of quartz, amethyst ($SiO_2$ + Fe) has always been prized as a beautiful gemstone and master healer. Coloured by

▷ **Clusters and geodes of amethyst are ideal for placing in rooms as a focus for healing and peace.**

### AMETHYST HEALING NET

The amethyst net is an excellent method to explore the qualities of other crystals. It also aids any deep healing work and is especially useful for creating calm.

**1** To enhance the effect of this net, lie on a yellow or violet cloth. Place eight amethyst crystals evenly spaced around the body, with one below the feet and one above the head. If you have amethyst points, place them so they face inwards. Have the stones you want to investigate close at hand.

**2** When you are settled in the amethyst net, experiment by placing a stone at your brow chakra (or any other chakra point you want to try). Finish off all exploratory sessions holding a piece of black tourmaline to ground and centre.

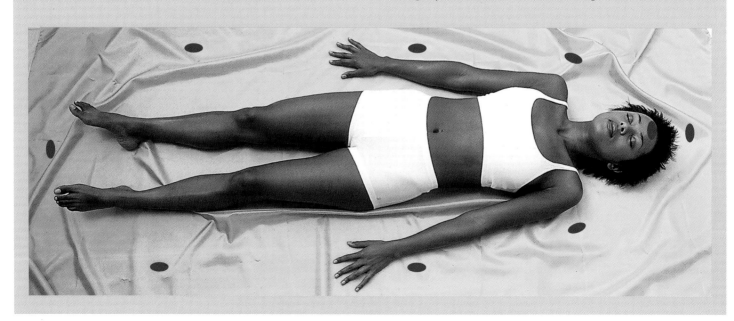

△ Fluorite is characterized by internal bands of colour and clearly visible planes of cleavage.

▽ First found in Japan, then South Africa, sugilite has become a popular stone for quality jewellery.

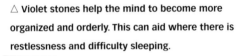

△ Violet stones help the mind to become more organized and orderly. This can aid where there is restlessness and difficulty sleeping.

▽ Dynamic rest and effortless action are the characteristic qualities that violet stones can bring to our lives.

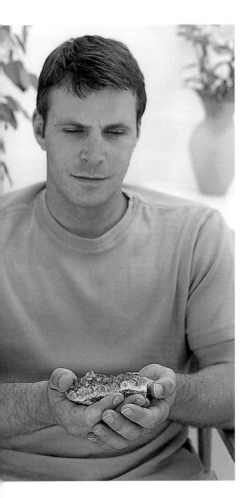

iron, amethyst tends to form geodes of densely packed short crystals all pointing inwards towards the centre of the hollow. Colour varies from very dark, almost black, through purple to a delicate violet. Amethyst is calming and stabilizing to all areas, particularly the mind. It can be a useful stone to reduce restlessness, irritation and worry. Amethyst balances brow and crown chakras but can be used anywhere. Held or placed upon the forehead or above the crown, it is helpful for meditation. The combination of the grounding effects of red together with the expansive quality of blue allows amethyst to be an effective guide in the exploration of different states of being.

## fluorite

A common mineral found in metamorphic rock, fluorite ($CaF_2$) has many uses in industry and is the main source of fluorine gas. Fluorite often has bands of different colours running through it, making it a popular decorative stone despite its softness and fragility. Common colours are blues and violets, green, yellow and clear. Fluorite is particularly useful as a balancer of brow and crown chakras – though it will help to integrate spiritual energies in a balanced way to any level of the body. It will encourage orderliness and structure and is especially helpful at improving levels of physical co-ordination and mental agility.

## sugilite

A stone that was only discovered in the first half of the 20th century, sugilite ($KNa_2(Fe^{2+},Mn^{2+},Al)_2Li_3Si_{12}O_{30}$) is another purple mineral that helps the co-ordination of the left and right hemispheres of the brain. The nervous system is balanced by this stone and it helps sensitive individuals who feel unable to keep up with the changes within society and technology. This inability can create confusion and alienation or can manifest as allergy problems. Sugilite helps integration with the everyday world, and can help prevent a withdrawal from it.

# Multi-coloured stones – unlimited possibilities

healing and beyond

Crystals displaying more than one colour can be especially useful for healing as they will introduce a mixture of colour energies simultaneously. A combination of red and green, for example, will be energizing but in a very organized way. Red-and-green stones, such as bloodstone or ruby in zoisite, can energize the heart chakra and calm the base chakra. A combination of complementary colours (red-green; blue-orange; violet-yellow; black-white) very effectively harmonizes and integrates related chakra energies and can help energy flow better throughout the whole system.

Azurite-malachite and chrysocolla display different shades of blue and green and therefore broadly balance the area of the throat and chest. Where one colour predominates, that will be the main energy involved, and other colours present will modify that primary focus. So a bloodstone will work mainly at a green level, lapis lazuli at a blue level and so on.

Some crystals display a whole rainbow spectrum of colours. These stones naturally attune to the very rarefied levels of energy above the crown chakra. They can also be used in the same way as white or clear stones, bringing in the whole potential of the spectrum of light. The colour in many of these multi-coloured stones is created by light refracting off their internal structures – microcrystals, fractures, inclusions and so on. Their appearance changes depending on how the light catches them, giving them an extra liveliness. Organic gems such as mother of pearl and abalone exemplify this very well.

## opal

A member of the quartz family, opal ($SiO_2.nH_2O$) crystallizes in a slightly different form and has a high water content. Its watery quality and great range of colours aligns the stone naturally with the emotions and emotional balance. The opal will work with emotions in the area of its dominant colour.

Brown, black or dark blue opals will work well with the lower chakras and are particularly effective at releasing tensions in the reproductive system, being useful for painful periods and PMT. Fire opal, a bright orange colour, will energize and help recovery after emotional upset. Water opal, which is colourless with a sheen of rainbow colours, can help to stabilize mood swings and energize the subtle systems of the body.

◁ **The high water content and microscopic structure of opal gives it a unique variety of rainbow colours and patterns.**

△ **Stones that combine red and green, such as ruby in zoisite, shown here, or bloodstone, help to enliven with their polarity of energy, both the heart and base chakras.**

## labradorite

A variety of feldspar, labradorite ($(Na,Ca)Al_{1-2}Si_{3-2}O_8$) looks dull grey until light hits the inclusions of magnetite crystals. The iridescence created is a vivid mix of peacock blues, yellows, oranges and greens. Like all stones with a vivid play of rainbow light, labradorite can inspire many different levels of energy and awareness. It brings energy into the body and works well with any of the chakras.

One of labradorite's most important characteristics is the ability to protect the auric field and prevent energy being drained by other people. This sort of energy drain is usually an unconscious process between people who are in a close relationship of some kind – family members or co-workers – where one person habitually absorbs the energy they need from the other. This leaves

▽ Ametrine can be useful for easing worries, increasing creative imagination, restoring balance to the digestion and improving memory.

## ametrine, azurite-malachite

Amethyst, when subjected to heat, turns golden yellow. Where the heating is uneven or localized there may be areas of yellow next to the original violet colour. This variation is known as ametrine. A combination of violet and yellow is ideal for balancing anxiety, fear and nervousness as it affects the solar plexus and brow chakras. Azurite is a deep blue copper mineral that gradually breaks down to form green malachite. Both are therefore often found together.

△ The play of colour in labradorite helps to disperse enervating external energies to maintain personal energy integrity. A white variety is known as spectrolite or rainbow moonstone.

▽ Azurite-malachite is a good stone to calm the heart and emotions, restoring a sense of peace.

the second person feeling tired and drained, put-upon or overwhelmed. Wearing or carrying a piece of labradorite effectively prevents this excessive loss of energy. There may have to be some changes in the relationship as it comes to terms with a new balance of energies.

▽ Abalone shell is formed from layers of crystallized calcium carbonate, a substance known as nacre.

# Crystal reference guide

These lists are best used as a reminder of the general areas of function rather than a rigid framework that must be adhered to at all times. The names of the crystals in the book are common throughout the English-speaking world. However variations do occur, due to the older names used in jewellery or mining that can sometimes be misleading. The chemical formula of a mineral remains a constant identification regardless of common names around the world and lists the constituent elements of a mineral and the relationship each atom has to the others. The formula for quartz, for example, is $SiO_2$, which indicates that every atom of silicon (Si) is bonded with two atoms of oxygen (O).

The colours listed here for each crystal are those most commonly found. Although colour is one of the best identifiers of a stone, most minerals can occur in most colours, and beginners can become confused, so other

| Crystal | Chemical Formula | Colour |
| --- | --- | --- |
| Amazonite | $KAlSi_3O_8$ | Green, blue striated |
| Amber | $C_{10}H_{16}O+H_2S$ | fossil resin Yellow, brown, green, red |
| Amethyst Quartz | $SiO_2+Fe$ | Violet-purple |
| Apophyllite | $KCa_4Si_8O_{20}(F,OH).8H_2O$ | Clear, green, grey, pink |
| Aquamarine | $Be_3Al_2Si_6O_{18}$ | Blue |
| Azurite-malachite | $Cu_3(CO_3)2(OH)_2 + Cu_2CO_3(OH)_2$ | Dark blue and green |
| Black Tourmaline (Schorl) | $Na(Mg,Fe,Li,Mn,Al)_3Al_6(BO_3)_3Si_6O_{18}(OH,F)_4$ | Black |
| Bloodstone | $SiO_2$ | Green with red spots |
| Blue Lace Agate | $SiO_2$ | Blue, banded |
| Botswana Agate | $SiO_2$ | White, grey banded |
| Calcite | $CaCO_3$ | Colourless, all colours |
| Carnelian | $SiO_2$ | Red-orange |
| Celestite | $SrSO_4$ | Grey-blue, clear |
| Chrysocolla | $(Cu,Al)_2H_2Si_2O_5(OH)_4.nH_2O$ | Green to blue |
| Citrine Quartz | $SiO_2$ | Yellow-brown |
| Clear Quartz | $SiO_2$ | Colourless |
| Corundum | $Al_2O_3$ | All colours, white streak |
| Danburite | $CaB_2Si_2O_8$ | Colourless |
| Diamond | $C_4$ | Colourless, all colours |
| Emerald | $Be_3Al_2Si_6O_{18}$ | Bright green |
| Fire Opal | $SiO_2.nH_2O$ | Red, orange |
| Fluorite | $CaF_2$ | All colours |
| Garnet | $SiO_4$ plus various metals | Red, brown, green |
| Gold | $Au$ | Yellow, orange |
| Green Aventurine | $SiO_2$ | with inclusions Green, blue |
| Haematite | $Fe_2O_3$ | Metallic grey/black |

identifying qualities such as crystal shape (crystal system) and hardness can be useful to know. Crystal system is not always easy to recognize because of the many variations within each system. However, certain characteristics of each system can really help identification. Mohs' Scale of Hardness is a scale of relative hardness. Minerals of 1 or 2 are extremely soft and easily scratched. A hardness of 3 to 5 can be dulled or scratched easily and so are rarely used in jewellery. Most gemstones range from a hardness of 6 (like moonstone) to 8 (like emerald). Stones harder than 8 are rare: corundum (ruby and sapphire) has a hardness of 9 and only diamond has a hardness of 10.

The influence each stone has with an individual's energy systems will depend on the state of health. However, the general qualities of each stone will suggest that they will work well in certain broad areas.

| Crystal System | Hardness | Chakra | Subtle Body |
| --- | --- | --- | --- |
| Triclinic | 6–6.5 | Heart, throat | Mental, etheric |
| Amorphous | 2 | Solar plexus | Mental |
| Trigonal | 7 | Brow, crown | Emotional, mental, spiritual |
| Tetragonal | 4.5–5 | Heart, crown | |
| Hexagonal | 7.5–8 | Throat | Etheric, mental |
| Monoclinic | 3.5–4 | Throat, heart | Etheric, mental, astral |
| Trigonal | 7–7.5 | Base | Etheric, astral |
| Microcrystalline trigonal | 7 | Heart, base | Etheric |
| Trigonal | 7 | Throat | Emotional, mental |
| Trigonal | 7 | All | |
| Hexagonal | 3 | All | |
| Trigonal | 7 | Sacral | Etheric |
| Orthorhombic | 3–3.5 | Throat, crown | Soul |
| Monoclinic or orthorhombic | 2–4 | Heart, throat | Emotional, mental |
| Trigonal | 7 | Solar plexus | Causal |
| Trigonal | 7 | All | Etheric, emotional |
| Trigonal | 9 | Crown, solar plexus | |
| Orthorhombic | 7 | Crown | Spiritual |
| Cubic | 10 | Crown | Mental |
| Hexagonal | 7.5–8 | Heart | Astral, etheric, emotional |
| Amorphous | 6 | Base, solar plexus | |
| Cubic | 4 | Brow | Etheric |
| Cubic | 6.5–7.5 | Base | Etheric, astral |
| Cubic | 2.5–3 | Heart | Emotional, mental, spiritual |
| Trigonal | 7 | Heart | Etheric, mental, emotional |
| Trigonal | 5-6 | Sacral, solar plexus | Etheric |

| Indicolite | $Na(Mg,Fe,Li,Mn,Al)_3Al_6(BO_3)_3Si_6O_{18}(OH,F)_4$ | Blue, blue-green |
| Iron Pyrites | $FeS_2$ | Metallic yellow |
| Jade – Jadeite | $NaAlSi_2O_6$ | Clear, rich green |
| Jade – Nephrite | $Ca_2(Mg,Fe)_5Si_8O_{22}(OH)_2$ | Green |
| Jet | Organic carbon | Black, dark brown |
| Kunzite | $LiAlSi_2O_6$ | Lilac, clear, green |
| Kyanite | $Al_2SiO_5$ | Blue |
| Labradorite | $(Na,Ca)Al_{1-2}Si_{3-2}O_8$ | Grey, green iridescent |
| Lapis Lazuli | $(Na,Ca)_8(Al.Si)_{12}O_{24}(S,SO_4)$ | Deep blue with white and gold |
| Magnetite/Lodestone | $Fe_3O_4$ | Black |
| Malachite | $Cu_2CO_3(OH)_2$ | Greens with black |
| Milky Quartz | $SiO_2$ | White |
| Moldavite | Rock silicates | Green |
| Moonstone | $KaSi_3O_8$ | Pearly/cream |
| Moss Agate | $SiO_2$ | Clear with green/brown inclusions |
| Obsidian | Igneous rock with inclusions | Black, grey, red-brown |
| Opal | $SiO_2.nH_2O$ | Various |
| Red Coral | $CaCO_3$ | Red, orange, pink |
| Red Jasper | $SiO_2$ | Red |
| Rhodocrosite | $MnCO_3$ | Pink, orange, cream |
| Rhodonite | $(Mn^{+2},Fe^{+2},Mg,Ca)SiO_3$ | Pink with brown or black |
| Rose Quartz | $SiO_2$ | Pink |
| Rubellite | $Na(Mg,Fe,Li,Mn,Al)_3Al_6(BO_3)Si_6O_{18}(OH,F)_4$ | Pink, red |
| Ruby | $Al_2O_3$ | Red |
| Rutilated Quartz | $TiO_2$ (in $SiO_2$) | Yellow-brown |
| Sapphire | $Al_2O_3$ | Blue, violet-blue |
| Selenite | $CaSO_4.2H_2O$ | Pearly |
| Smoky Quartz | $SiO_2$ | Brown, black |
| Sodalite | $Na_4Al_3Si_3O_{12}Cl$ | Blue with white veins |
| Spinel | $MgAl_2O_4$ | Scarlet, pink |
| Sugilite | $KNa_2(Fe^{2+},Mn^{2+},Al)_2Li_3Si_{12}O_{30}$ | Lilac, purple |
| Tektite | Rock, silicates | Brown, black |
| Topaz | $Al_2SiO_4(F,OH)_2$ | All colours, clear |
| Turquoise | $CuAl_6(PO_4)_4(OH)_8.4H_2O$ | Light blue–turquoise–green |
| Verdelite | $Na(Mg,Fe,Li,Mn,Al)_3Al_6(BO_3)_3Si_6O_{18}(OH,F)_4$ | Green |
| Zircon | $ZrSiO_4$ | Brown to clear |

| | | | |
|---|---|---|---|
| Trigonal | 7.5 | Throat, brow | All |
| Cubic | 6.5 | Solar plexus | Astral |
| Monoclinic | 7 | Heart | Astral, etheric, emotional |
| Monoclinic | 6–6.5 | Heart | Astral, etheric, emotional |
| Amorphous | 2.5 | Base | Etheric, emotional |
| Monoclinic | 6.5–7.5 | Heart, throat | Etheric |
| Triclinic | 4–7 | Throat | All |
| Triclinic | 6–6.5 | All | All |
| Cubic | 5.5 | Throat, brow | Etheric, mental |
| Cubic | 5.5–6.5 | All | All |
| Monoclinic | 3.5–4 | Heart | Etheric, emotional |
| Trigonal | 7 | All | Emotional |
| Amorphous | 5 | Heart, throat, brow, crown | All |
| Monoclinic | 6–6.5 | Sacral, solar plexus | Emotional |
| Trigonal | 7 | Heart | Emotional, mental |
| Amorphous | 6 | Base, sacral, crown | Mental |
| Amorphous | 6 | Sacral, solar plexus, crown | Emotional |
| Hexagonal or trigonal | 3 | Heart | Etheric |
| Trigonal | 7 | Base | Etheric |
| Trigonal | 3.5–4.5 | Base to heart | Emotional, mental, astral |
| Triclinic | 5.5–6.5 | Heart | Emotional |
| Trigonal | 7 | Heart, throat | Emotional, mental, astral |
| Trigonal | 7–7.5 | Sacral, heart | Emotional, astral |
| Trigonal | 9 | Heart | Mental, spiritual |
| Tetragonal | 6–6.5 | All | All |
| Trigonal | 9 | Solar plexus, heart, throat, crown | Emotional, mental |
| Monoclinic | 2 | Sacral, throat, crown | Emotional, soul |
| Trigonal | 7 | Base, sacral | Solar plexus |
| Cubic | 5.5–6 | Throat, brow | Emotional, mental |
| Cubic | 8 | Base | |
| Hexagonal | 5.5–6.5 | Crown | Astral, causal |
| Amorphous | 5–5.5 | Base, brow | Etheric, astral |
| Orthorhombic | 8 | Solar plexus | Etheric |
| Triclinic | 5–6 | Throat, all | All |
| Trigonal | 7–7.5 | Heart | All |
| Tetragonal | 7.5 | Base | |

# Colour
# fundamentals

Colour is a universal language. Everything under the sun is affected by colour. Plants, animals, bacteria, chemical reactions, all exhibit changes of behaviour when exposed to different colours. It is also a subconscious language that we use instinctively in every area of our lives.

# Natural environments

The human characteristic of adaptability allows us to successfully inhabit all sorts of environments. Whether living in a forest or a desert, people adapt to the unique qualities of their surroundings. We get used to the colours and shapes around us, which is why a change of scene, such as a holiday, makes us sharply, refreshingly aware of many different details of colour, light and shape. Colour plays a big part in creating the ambience and mood of a place because its vibrational energy charges our emotions and energy levels.

## the calm of nature

When escaping from the crowded and grey environment of towns and cities, most people experience a noticeable relaxation and lifting of mood as the green of nature fills their vision. Walking through woodland where the light is predominantly filtered through green leaves creates a sense of calm in the emotions and an expansive, increased sense of connection with our surroundings.

△ **Inside a wood or forest the trees alter the quality of light to something completely different from the one that exists outside it.**

The feeling of relaxation and the renewed sense of mental perspective during and after a country walk is so common that few will stop to think about it when the walk is over, but they will subconsciously feel profound benefits from the experience.

## holiday happiness

Many people enjoy relaxing by the seaside in summer. The predominant colours are the blues of the sea and sky, which introduce a feeling of expansiveness and peace. Turquoise tempers the deeper blues with an extra sense of calm and comfort. The golden yellow of sand and sunlight energize the body's systems, helping to restore balanced functioning by reducing anxiety and stress levels, and creating happiness and clarity in the mind. It is no wonder with today's hectic lifestyle that two weeks doing

▽ **When we dream of holidays, the first image that often comes to mind is a beach. The yellows and blues of the seaside revitalize our energies.**

△ **Deserts provide endless variations of a few colours and their calm stillness has inspired visionaries and mystics for centuries.**

## special places

Colour in the landscape separates and defines special places. The white cliffs of Dover symbolize more than simply the end of the land of England. Their very starkness suggests both a barrier of otherworldliness, a mystical separation from the mainland of Europe – and, when seen from afar – an invitation to explore new possibilities.

In Australia, Uluru (Ayer's Rock) is sacred to the Aborigine peoples, not just because of its shape and size, but because of the amazing red coloration the rock has, especially at sunset. The colour of blood, the energy of life and heat, it rises dramatically out of the vast landscape and is regarded by the Aboriginals as the birthplace of the gods. In the south-west states of America, the canyons, especially the Painted Canyon, were held in the same awe by the people living in the region because the powerful colour symbolism was so suggestive of the generative forces of life. In the same way certain mountains – Mt Shasta in California, Mt Fuji in Japan and Mt Kailash in the Tibetan Himalayas – are held in awe as focuses of power and transcendence because their white peaks dominate the landscape and evoke the purity of the heavenly realms.

▽ **Uluru, formerly known as Ayer's Rock, in Australia is a perfect example of how the natural colour of rock can take on magical and sacred significance for the people who live near it.**

△ **Archaeological evidence shows that our earliest ancestors felt exactly the same as we do about flowers, offering tokens made from them at important ceremonies and life-events.**

nothing and simply being on a beach in the sunshine is regarded by many as the perfect holiday, and one which they will repeat each year with unfailing regularity.

The same colour combination of blues and golds occurs in many desert or near-desert conditions and it is perhaps significant that in the past many people have sought the deserts of the world as places of mysticism, for contemplation, visions and religious inspiration. With such isolation, very few distractions and the stimulus of blues, golds and yellows directly affecting the function of the nervous system, such places encourage the deepest thought.

# Nature's use of colour

In the natural world colour is used in two main ways: to hide and to reveal. Considering that full colour vision is a very rare development in the animal world it is surprising how sophisticated nature's use of colour can be.

## the seeing world

In the simplest of eyes there is only the ability to distinguish between light and dark. In creatures that live in darkness, for example in the depths of the ocean, colour vision is not as important as other sensory mechanisms for identifying electromagnetic radiations such as electric currents. But where there is sunlight, colour vision does become important. Experiments have shown that though many insects are sensitive only to green, blue and violet light, they can see beyond the human range, well into ultraviolet. Birds, dogs and cats have different degrees of colour recognition depending on the importance of sight

▽ **The courtship and mating rituals of birds rely heavily on dramatic displays of colour in the male's plumage.**

△ **Bees' eyes see different frequencies of light from those that the human eye is able to recognize. Ultraviolet frequencies play a vital role in the bee's ability to locate flowers.**

compared with their other sensing mechanisms. Owls and hawks need acute visual sensitivity to movement, while dogs rely less on colour vision because their highly effective sense of smell is their dominant sense for gathering information. Full-spectrum colour is seen by the higher vertebrates, including humans, as well as a few unexpected animals, such as tortoises and the octopus.

The eye is not the only mechanism for recording light and colour, nor does the greatest use of colour belong to those creatures with the best colour vision. The eye is simply a specialist organ for recording colour and light. Light is an energy and its vibrations can create many changes in physical matter. It is thought that within the human skin there are specialist cells that have a great sensitivity to light, and that it is possible to notice subtle changes that take place when these are exposed to colours. It seems that this method of sensing increases when there is impairment of vision.

△ **The male peacock has evolved a fabulous display of tail feathers to attract a mate.**

Plants have no specialized organs for colour recognition as such, yet colour is employed magnificently as a communication device. Bees and other insects are drawn to flowers by their colour and this ensures the fertilization of seeds and the continuation of the species. As it ripens, fruit accumulates sugars, so changing colour to indicate that it has become edible to animals. The animals then eat the fruit and spread the seeds through their droppings.

▽ **Some animals use colour to imitate aggressive species as a form of protection. Some butterflies, for example, have large eye-like markings.**

colour prevailing in a habitat. So, for example, the ragged vertical stripes of the zebra help it to blend into the tall grasses of the African plains, by disguising its size and shape. Some creatures have the ability to change colour very quickly, to achieve an almost perfect match with their background. The slow-moving chameleon has an amazing range of colour changes as does the bottom-feeding flatfish, the plaice. Both of these creatures are virtually impossible to see until they move. Perhaps the most unusual and striking use of colour is the protective warning or camouflage device of the squid, which has evolved a complex and beautiful language of expression and mood by sending constantly changing waves of rippling colours across its body.

▽ No colouring is accidental or superficial, it is a survival strategy, an evolutionary advantage that all creatures, such as this jellyfish, utilize.

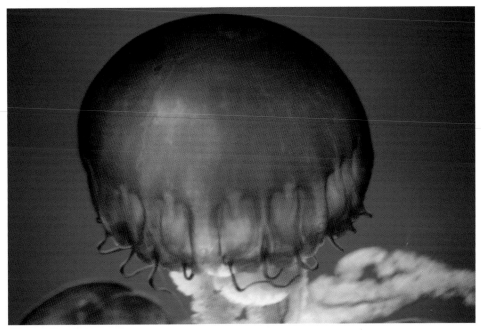

## warning signals

In some creatures bright and striking colour displays are used to attract a mate or to act as a warning of aggressive superiority. The male peacock displays its fan of wonderful tail feathers when trying to attract the attentions of a female and to demonstrate superiority to a potential rival. In insects and snakes, bold, distinctive markings, such as the yellow and black stripes of the wasp, are recognized as danger signals by other species. This colour strategy can be so effective that even some completely non-toxic and harmless animals mimic the coloration of a poisonous or dangerous species to avoid unwanted attention from predators. The eye and face patterns on the wings of some butterflies and moths mimic the aggressive displays of much larger animals to much the same effect.

## camouflage

Using colour to blend with the surroundings is a common strategy. Camouflage often mimics the light and

▷ The chameleon has developed special pigment cells that rapidly blend with its surroundings to disguise it from predators who rely on sight.

# Climate, culture and colour

Although the physical effects of colour are biologically constant, people living in different climates understand and interpret colour in ways that can differ, and even oppose each other. Colour becomes a language of tribe and culture, and to members of the tribe the messages of colour are easy to read on a subconscious level. However, these colour messages mean little or nothing to people from a different culture. The energy of colour remains constant but the significance of that energy changes.

## black and white

For people of the northern hemisphere, the north is a region of ice and snow where the sun never travels. The north therefore is associated with the white of snow or the black of winter and night. In the southern hemisphere, however, winter weather comes from Antarctica, from the south, and therefore white and black are linked to the south rather than the north. This affects other colours and elements accordingly.

In Europe, for example, death has traditionally been associated with the colour black. Funeral cortèges use black cars, and coffin bearers and mourners dress in black. In China, however, mourners wear white, because white is the colour of winter when all things return to the earth in a dormant state. In fact, traditionally minded Chinese will avoid wearing white, because it reminds them of the death shroud, whereas in the West, white is associated with innocence.

## red and white

There are some colour combinations that seem to have the same resonance in most parts of the world. Two of the colours most frequently found together are red and white, symbolizing the polarities of male and female. In Tibetan symbolism and in some pagan traditions, red is the colour of the female Sun, white the male Moon. The two together are the power of creation, the union of opposites, the joining of Heaven

and Earth. Right across the northern hemisphere, in the Arctic and temperate zones, these colours appear each autumn after the fertilizing rains, in the form of the fly agaric mushroom, characterized by its red top and white spots. The fly agaric is a favourite food of the reindeer of Lapland, and the native Sami peoples of that region observed the apparent intoxication that the animals showed after eating the fungi. The Sami, along with every Siberian tribe, woodland American Indians and others, learned to dry and eat small portions of the mushroom in order to enter exalted altered states of reality, the realms of the spirits and gods. Ceremonial costumes of red, decorated with white polka dots, were worn by the shamans and healers of these peoples and still are today.

It is interesting that the Western image of Father Christmas retains all the symbolism of the Arctic shaman: dressed in red and white, he is drawn in his sleigh by reindeer, and he travels across the sky-worlds to bring the magic of gifts to his people in their time of hardship – the depths of winter.

◁ **White has become traditional for Western weddings where it is regarded as a symbol of purity and new beginnings.**

## green

In Western Europe forests dominated the landscape for thousands of years. The colour green was always associated with the wildness of nature, the power of growth and of freedom. The woodland world was believed to be inhabited by spirits, elves and fairies, who were often dressed in green. The dominant energy, the intelligence of nature, was represented by the Green Man – a fusion of human and plant life. In the Arabic world, green is the sacred colour of Islam. In a landscape that is dominated by desert and arid wilderness, green is the colour of oases, providers of life, food, water and shelter. To the Arabic mind, green represents the refuge of heavenly paradise. In the West, green is the force and wildness of nature.

▽ **Each figure in this Tibetan mandala is identified by its colour, denoting the exact energy each manifestation displays to the meditator.**

△ In Peru traditional clothing tends to be as bright and colourful as possible.

## traditional uses of colour

Mankind's use of colour grew from the needs and limitations of the environment. The first colours were of the earth – the red, ochre and black of cave paintings created from ground-up iron-bearing rocks and clays, and soot. Red ochre is the earliest dye used worldwide, and sacred red is found in burial chambers in most parts of the world.

## development of dyes

Plant dyes provide a range of browns, yellows, blues and greens. The rarity of a colour or the difficulty of producing a dye quickened the birth of the fashion industry. Only the rich and powerful used the expensive colours, which became symbols of privilege and power. Blue was difficult to produce so the plant woad was precious and its use probably had spiritual significance to the ancient Britons and Picts who were famed for its use. In the long history of the Roman Empire, the most prestigious colour was purple, extracted from the shells of Mediterranean shellfish, by a secret process originally known only to the Phoenician traders of the eastern seaboard. Wearing purple robes was the exclusive right of the emperor. Lesser nobles were ranked by the precise widths of purple stripe that they were allowed to wear on their togas. Wearing too much purple was a serious offence.

## display and concealment

Colour is used in dress to display and to conceal, as it is in nature. Tartans show a mix of the practical and social uses of colour. Woven tartans have been found on mummies in the Taklamakan desert of Mongolia, though today this cloth is more often associated with Scotland and Ireland.

The choice and blend of colours as well as the pattern of warp and weave in Scottish tartans are unique to each clan or tribal grouping, and no clan would dream of wearing another's tartan. Every tartan has several variations of colour and pattern – for example, hunting tartans use a blend of tones to act as a camouflage in the Highland landscape. Dress tartans have bright reds and yellows, and are worn at social occasions.

## group identity

While hunters favour camouflage, warriors aim for maximum display. Colour can be a means of identification, and an aggressive statement, so red is a common military colour. The bright red uniform that the British Infantry wore for hundreds of years was worn to intimidate. Other groups, such as the Masai, also dress warriors in red.

Traditional clothing around the world tends to reflect tribal unity. To an outsider the group may be perceived as dressing alike, but to the insider there are subtle differences that clearly denote rank and status.

△ Bold colours and extravagant designs have characterized war dress for millennia. Colour is used to threaten the opposition and create a sense of unity among warriors on the same side.

▷ In this Byzantine mosaic each figure's rank and status is identified by the amount of purple worn. The central figure is the Emperor Justinian, dressed all in purple.

# Colour co-ordination

colour fundamentals

An instinct for harmonizing and co-ordinating colour is a gift that some people are born with, but the rest of us can manage if we follow a few guidelines. In practice, shades, tones and tints that work well together do so because of their natural visual relationship, and there are simple rules to mixing and matching colour.

When similar colours are placed next to each other, each loses some of its vibrant qualities. Complementary colours, those opposite to each other on the colour wheel, will augment each other's qualities. Colours that are next but one to each other on the

▽ **Colour in nature, designed for survival, often makes harmonious juxtapositions that are borrowed by fashion designers.**

## HOW COLOURS ARE DEFINED
• A hue is the quality of a colour that enables us to classify it as red, green, yellow etc.
• A tint is a hue with white added.
• A shade is a hue with black added.
• A tone is a hue with grey added.
Tints look good together, as do shades or tones, but mixing tints, shades and tones does not always work well.

True Colour Wheel, present pleasing combinations that are often employed as tints by interior designers to create a comfortable space.

## colour categories

Carol Jackson, the author of the book *Colour Me Beautiful*, formulated categories of colour into a practical and easy to use system, based upon the four elements (fire, earth, air and water) and the seasons (spring, summer, autumn and winter). She applied the colour groupings to décor, furnishings, clothes and make-up.

△ **Plants naturally grow together in swathes of the same species. Garden designers develop this theme of group planting to create stunning displays.**

Spring colours are those linked to the water element. They feature warm and light tints, and no dark colours. Spring colours include turquoise, lilac, peach, coral, scarlet, violet, emerald, sunshine yellow, cream and sand. All the colours in this category are clear and almost delicate. They create a joyful and nurturing ambience.

Summer colours, linked to the air element, are all tones (that is, they have a lot of grey in them). This range of colours is

▽ **Colours that appear with the season's changes become associated with the qualities of that time of year, and are reflected in our clothes.**

▷ **The colour wheel here is often described as the True Colour Wheel. This presentation of colour was put together by Sir Isaac Newton and has been used by many famous colour workers, such as Goethe and Steiner. It shows the complementary colour to red as turquoise. In the Artist's Colour Wheel, not shown here, the complementary colour to red is shown as green.**

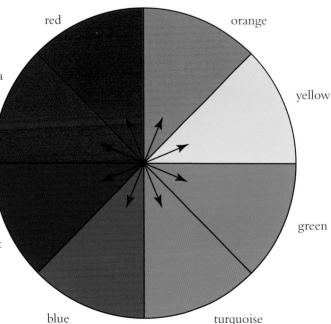

red

orange

yellow

magenta

green

violet

blue

turquoise

◁ When it comes to choices in fashion, no one system will suit everyone. Colouring and personality are factors to consider but the colours should also 'feel' right to wear.

△ Experiment with a wide range of colours in your clothing, and don't be afraid to mix strong shades together if that's what feels right.

▽ Try dressing in a colour range that complements your natural colouring and also dress in a contrasting style to compare. See how your behaviour is modified.

very subtle and includes maroon, rose, powder blue, sage green, pale yellow, lavender, plum, oyster and taupe. This is a 'middle-of-the-road' selection, that includes darker colours, but not heavy colours. Summer colours have an elegance that is also cool and contained.

Autumn colours are related to the fire element. These are warm colours. All are shades, which means they have black in them. They include mustard, olive green, flame, peacock, burnt orange, teal and burgundy. These colours are very rich and striking. They suggest maturity and depth.

Winter colours are connected with the earth element and feature a big contrast between hues, tints and shades. Winter colours include black, white, magenta, cyan, purple, lemon, silver, indigo, royal blue and jade. None of these colours are subtle, they are all bold and powerful.

These colour groupings can also reflect psychological personality types, not simply a person's natural colouring or skin type. For example, winter colours are often favoured by people with strong business sense, confidence and a practical nature. Spring colours, on the other hand, are popular with those of an artistic, sensitive and quiet disposition.

There can also be a strong second preference in colour groupings. Occasionally the second preference can be useful in choosing clothes that are designed to create a particular effect, for a presentation or interview for example. However, wearing colours to impress people may feel rather uncomfortable compared to wearing your natural, instinctive choice. Both men and women can use these colour categories for choosing clothes, and women often use it too when selecting make-up.

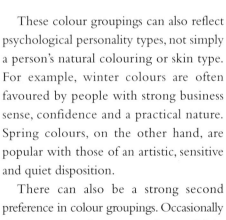

# Colour for commercial use

Colour affects everyone at an unconscious level, that is, below the awareness of normal everyday thought. So politicians, businesses and advertisers have learned to manipulate the desired response by using the language of colour. Careful use of colour can bypass the viewer's ability to discriminate or make instant critical judgements.

## advertising

The human eye can distinguish between hundreds of shades of colour, and each shade elicits a slightly different emotional and behavioural response. The advertising industry exploits this ability and constantly bombards us with subliminal messages through the use of colour. As those who work with hypnosis and auto-suggestion know well, subliminal messages, because they are not recognized by the conscious mind, can have a profound effect on our behaviour and attitudes. It is the advertisers' job to select the most appropriate colours for their product 'message' as well as an image that is uniquely identifiable. The right colour or combination of colours can make all the difference to product sales.

△ Retail outlets depend on being seen and recognized. Colours and logos that can be seen from a long way have a distinct advantage.

▽ An effective interior design will match the colour and shape of a room to its function, creating an ideal atmosphere. Muted colours and soft lighting will promote relaxation in this restaurant's customers.

## colour manipulation

Red is the key colour in products that suggest energy, vigour, excitement and speed. Fast food outlets very often combine a bright red with yellow or white in their logos and décor. Bright yellow stimulates the digestive system, so we feel hungry, while white combined with red suggests clean, efficient service. Using bright red and a creamy white as interior colours in eating places ensures that customers are focused on the business of eating rather than on socializing. Whites and greys also prevent people from relaxing and becoming too comfortable. On the other hand, in up-market restaurants, dark, rich reds are often combined with subdued lighting to create an atmosphere of comfort and security. This encourages people to talk quietly or intimately, while taking time over a meal. Orange or yellow walls in eating places make for a convivial and a lively atmosphere, with more bustle and noise. These colours are often used in bars, bistros and coffee houses to create an ideal atmosphere for chatter and socializing.

Blue suggests sobriety, control and responsibility, and is used in products where a sense of stability and authority is required.

◁ **This interior, though at first glance, abstract and random, draws the eye to a reception area by using warm, more welcoming colours.**

▽ **Warm colours in a bar setting often encourage relaxation and enjoyment.**

Light or mid-blue is rarely used in food advertising as we tend to associate it with decay in that context. Dark blue labelling combined with a rich yellow or gold is often effective in the promotion of specialist gourmet foods, suggesting a certain level of detachment and even superiority from the everyday. The qualities associated with blue make it a popular colour for the interiors of public service buildings such as banks, where it helps to keep a subdued, serious and unemotional ambience.

Green colours and tones are used to promote products that suggest freshness, and naturalness. Often green coloured packaging will form part of a claim made by the manufactuer that the product will bring health benefits. Dark greens and mid tones are used in preference to olive and yellow greens, as these lighter green colours may suggest and even at times create feelings of unease and nausea.

## colour at work

There is ample evidence, both anecdotal and researched, that colour is an important factor in every environment. The same pale greens that can suggest nausea in food environments, especially the sallower shades,

are often used in large public meeting spaces and corridors where people need to be encouraged to keep on the move rather than loiter and socialize. The wrong colour combinations in an office, greys and cool blues for example, or browns and tans, not

▽ **In this office colours have been kept cool to encourage quiet efficiency, but avoid the sedating effect of dark blues.**

only affect the mood of the staff but can also reduce profits, while creams and pale tones can create a rather uninvolved attitude from the workforce. Yellows, oranges and peachy pinks with turquoise and warm shades of green can transform a company's workforce and productivity from mediocre to efficient.

Colour should never be thoughtlessly applied. It is a vibrant, life-sustaining energy that should be used with care and skill.

# Colour inside the home

The home, whatever its shape and size, always becomes a reflection of the people who live in it. Our own space speaks volumes about our personal tastes and attitudes. Becoming more conscious of the effects of colour on behaviour, and learning what colours reflect our own energies, makes us better able to choose the right colours for our home.

Recommendations about using colour in the home, like all opinions of what is considered fashionable, are usually very culturally specific and change from one year to the next. Formulas can be helpful, but

△ Tints of orange, creams and browns create a spacious feel while bringing a quality of warmth.

they should never supersede personal choice. In general, colours with red in them will warm up a cool space, such as a north-facing room. Warm colours will also make a space feel smaller. Colours with blues in them will make a room feel cool and appear larger. Dark hues will reduce the apparent size of the space and light hues will make it seem larger than it is.

## entrance halls

Hallways are the first rooms entered in many homes. They are rarely large enough to be a living space and so can be treated as a transition between the outside world and the inner privacy of the rooms beyond. Hallways immediately reflect how we wish to be seen by the world. They can be extremely formal or simply act as a storage space. Colours here will suggest whether the hall is a barrier or a welcome sign. White or cream is often chosen as a neutral colour that acts as an emotional air-lock. Rich, deep colours, whether warm or cool, will create a strong impression of personality and a clear boundary to demarcate territory.

The colour used in an entrance hall will directly affect the visitor, so choose wisely. Strong reds are energizing while slightly

▽ Subdued earth tones are enlivened here with the use of complementary blues and yellows.

▽ The cool blues here create spaciousness and neatness. Stairs and banisters in red and yellow articulate depth and distance in a practical way.

△ A mix of yellow and green items in a kitchen that is decorated in neutral colours creates a bright and cheerful room.

muted reds (with a hint of brown) suggest solid, powerful and practical comfort. Pinks, depending on the tint, offer a warm, friendly, non-threatening atmosphere. Blues are calming and sedating, useful for city homes where the outside world is noisy and hectic. A deep blue will help to cool over-stressed and over-stimulated nervous systems, generating relaxation and a sense of peace and quiet. Greens and browns suggest the natural world, though here it is very important which shades and tones are used. A strong, bright green can look fine in nature where light levels are so complex that they create a huge variety of subtle shades. Follow nature's example and imitate the diffusion of light by using a range of tones and shades of greens, rather than one strong block of colour.

## kitchens and bathrooms

Utilitarian rooms like the kitchen and bathroom need colours that harmonize with their functions. For example, it is a good idea for bathrooms to be painted in warm tones – yellows, pinks and oranges. These give a comfortable, relaxing brightness and reflect the energies of cleansing and caring. Yellow in the kitchen, on the other hand, can be over-stimulating to the digestive system unless tempered by other colours, such as blues and greens. Red can heighten emotions and can cause recklessness and a lack of consideration, whereas warm shades of terracotta connect to the practical earthiness of cooking and baking.

Blues and white are cool and efficient. They are not the best main colours for a kitchen that is a social space as well as an area of food preparation, but their clean freshness together makes them ideal as a colour for plates and other crockery. Cool colours in both rooms could be enhanced by the addition of a strong third colour to offset them. A luxurious space can be created by adding gold or a rich green to a stark blue and white setting.

Modern design's trend for wide expanses of stainless steel in kitchens is practical in commercial premises but can give an empty, unemotional feel to a family room that should be warm and welcoming.

△ It is important to choose the appropriate shade of colour in decoration. A warm yellow in a kitchen is refreshing, a yellow that has more green in it may create the opposite effect.

◁ Bathrooms in bright, warm colours are enlivening and uplifting – though might encourage too much dawdling in a large family.

▽ Blue and white are classic colours to use in a bathroom, and in a room where there is plenty of natural light will bring a sense of clean tidiness without overwhelming coldness.

△ **Brown promotes calm but this corner would benefit from a splash of yellow to add life.**

△ **This choice of colours will allow feelings of comfort, restfulness and a certain dreaminess to develop – ideal for a quiet space.**

▽ **Warm tones on large areas keep a space comfortable while spots of brighter colour bring individuality and visual interest.**

## living rooms

The only golden colour rule in the home is that if you dislike a particular colour – you should change it. Living in an atmosphere that you find disturbing in any way does not support health and wellbeing.

The main living area in the house needs to be a reflection of the owner's personality and should also be flexible enough to remain comfortable and generate a positive influence throughout all sorts of activities

▽ **A collection of items with a range of complementary tones and hues creates a balance of energy, both visually and emotionally.**

highlights of these colours will add depth and equilibrium to the home, maintaining a healthy balance of vibration.

Acquiring small items, such as cushions, throws or ornaments, that can be changed or their placement in the space rearranged, can be far more practical and flexible than adjusting large areas of colour in a room to reflect the energies of the people using it. Careful use of single coloured items can enhance a particular space. These items can be of similar tones or can be complementary colours for a subtle approach. Choosing contrasting colours can add a much more dramatic effect that draws attention to a particular area of the room.

## INSTANT COLOUR

Keeping the main colour in the living area neutral means that it is a lot easier to change your surroundings from a cool, calm environment to a rich vibrant one, simply by swapping fabrics and soft furnishings. Add to this an adjustment in lighting, or even the addition of a few candles, and you have a cost-effective way of adjusting the overall ambience to suit your needs.

▽ Even though complementary colours from the artist's colour wheel are used here, the red by its very nature is more dominant, bringing energy into a neutral white area.

▽ Blues with a hint of pink or violet have the quality of a warm summer sky and are inviting rather than isolating. A vase of vibrant orange flowers adds to the warmth.

▽ A calm blue background can be quickly enlivened with temporary elements if you are in need of some stimulation and energy.

▽ Chair covers that can be changed allow you to alter the feel of a space to suit your preferences at different times.

△ Greens in nature display variation with the constant play of light. Indoors, greens are best in subtle, tempered shades.

and moods. A background colour chosen from a pale version of one's favourite colour will be generally supportive and in harmony with the individual's energy field. If more than one person lives in a space a neutral tone can be chosen, or a compromise needs to be found so that everyone feels equally comfortable. For example, if one person's favourite colour is green and their partner's is blue, a turquoise colour scheme might be a good choice. Or, a complementary colour could be chosen, in this case a peach, gold or a pink tone.

Many people's choice of colours follows a similar pattern to other preferences in life. We prefer certain types of music and food, for example, but few of us would be happy just eating one thing all the time or listening endlessly to one piece of music. The same is true with colour. You may prefer tones that are within the turquoise through light blue to violet range of the spectrum, sometimes tending towards turquoise, other times towards magenta. If so, it is less likely that a yellow or red would appear in your colour scheme, but nonetheless, a few

## bedrooms

Perhaps the most important room in the house for most people is the bedroom, as this is where we spend the longest periods of time. These rooms are also our most individual and personal spaces so we need to be as comfortable in them as possible. Even a favourite colour can become a depressing influence if there is not a balance with other colours.

▽ **Cool colours in a bedroom are perfect as they encourage the mind to quieten down and release the hectic activities of the day.**

△ **Blues and whites, especially with a hint of violet or purple are quietening, restful colours that help the body's natural sleep rhythms.**

Colour favourites can also change quite quickly, especially with a greater awareness of the energy of colour vibrations. Generally speaking, colours that are restful and calming are better in bedrooms. Remember that the colour on the walls and fabrics will be having some effect on your energies even when you have your eyes shut. Muted and mixed tones are probably preferable to strong, bold colours. Blues calm the mind and lower the body's levels of activity, naturally encouraging sleep. Yellows, on the other hand, may be overstimulating – fine for waking up in the morning but not so good for getting a good night's rest. Pale violets will encourage relaxing, dreamy states and pale pinks will give a feeling of security.

▽ **Pink and violet hues are light and calming and are good healing and recuperating colours.**

▷ Creative spaces are often made more effective when there is a range of colour energies – this encourages play but not necessarily mental focus.

▽ Restful expanses of colour can help mental focus for thinking and communicating.

## studies and workrooms

Work rooms such as studies and offices should reflect and complement the energy of the activity. Mental clarity and inspiration, for example, are promoted by bright yellow. and small amounts of yellow like a lampstand or letter rack, work just as well as yellow walls or curtains. Even a sheet of yellow card that can be placed in view can

be very effective when you are feeling particularly tired. Cool blues are useful for calming down thought processes so that intuition and new ideas can emerge. In a busy space, where there is high energy and a fast pace, the presence of some blue can help to keep a peaceful ambience.

For physical dexterity and practical work, reds and oranges provide energy and focus, balanced by complementary greens to encourage calmness of mind and emotions. These colours are ideal combinations for sewing, painting and other creative arts, as they provide a comfortable space where work can be carried out for long periods.

◁ Your own character will determine whether you work more effectively in an energizing or a sedating environment.

# The colour palette

Each colour has a set of clearly defined influences and meanings, which can be invaluable in understanding the world around us and our behaviour patterns. These qualities can also be used to create particular impressions on others. A desired image or a subtle message can be sent with colour much more effectively than with words.

# Red

Red is the colour with the longest wavelength. It is the nearest visible light to infrared in the electromagnetic spectrum. Although red occurs beyond the infrared, it maintains close connections with heat and warmth. Even rocks will become red when they are heated sufficiently. This is seen in volcanic eruptions when lava pours out on to the surface of the earth.

## living red

Instinctively, the occurrence of red makes us wary, as we connect it with heat and the potential danger of burning. Red lights are

△ Red is the colour of heat and burning. Infrared is invisible to the human eye but its heating effects are evident when hot objects appear red.

▽ The effect of red on the eye is quite unusual. For the colour to be seen, the eye itself makes internal adjustments. This alteration means that we see red objects as closer than they really are.

built into artificial fires to help simulate the cosiness of a real fire. Too much heat and red burns, but at the right level it supports our lives and gives us comfort.

Being the colour of blood, red has symbolic links with living and life. Spilling or losing blood brings illness and death. Wearing red, eating red foods and surrounding yourself with red increases the body's ability to absorb iron, the metal that is responsible for the colour of haemoglobin in the blood. The presence of haemoglobin allows the blood to absorb oxygen in the lungs and to transport that life-giving oxygen to the cells of the body.

Physical activity and the energy that supports it also has a red vibration. If speed, danger, daring or courage are involved, the red quality of the activity increases. Mountaineers, racing car drivers and stuntmen all have 'red' careers.

## feeling red

Phrases like 'red light district' and 'scarlet woman' aptly describe the sexual nature of red. Some aspects of red behaviour are not socially acceptable. Red together with black is associated with evil, for example in the archetypal 'red devil' of medieval artists.

△ The cliché of what the red sports car is thought to represent sums up the dynamic, direct, self-absorbed quality of red energy.

**PUT RED IN YOUR LIFE WHEN THERE IS ...**
- a lack of enthusiasm and interest in life
- a lack of energy and a feeling of over-tiredness
- an inability to make your dreams a practical reality
- a feeling of insecurity, unwarranted fear, or anxiety

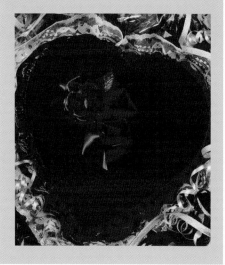

◁ When a woman wears the colour red, it has an immediacy and boldness. It says 'I am here, notice me' and is closely associated with sex appeal, and also with illicit passion.

who abuse it. These people often display some of the negative qualities that are associated with red – selfishness and an interest only in personal, rather than global, survival and short-term security.

To be healthy in a long-term sense, we need the colour red to reconnect ourselves to the planet and support it as it supports us. For our personal development, the role involves taking responsibility for our own wellbeing and survival as part of humanity as a whole, not being separate from it. Although often seen as a 'green' issue, global and local conservation is also about survival, which is a red issue. Red and green issues are intrinsically linked, as they are complementary colours.

Blatant expression of emotion is not always easy to handle, whether it is sexuality, passion, anger or aggression. When expressing red emotions, the heart beats faster, the capillaries dilate and the skin becomes flushed and feels warm.

Red is thought of as an immediate colour. This affects the thinking processes, causing restlessness and impatience. Red can result in very selfish behaviour, a focus on personal needs and survival above everything else. Sometimes the drive to survive is what fuels

◁ Red can easily lead to excess as its own nature is impulsive and reckless. Drunken behaviour exemplifies many qualities of too much red energy.

impulsive actions and rash comments. When these traits are managed well they create capable business people who are innovators and entrepreneurs, preferring to move from one project to another, getting an operation on its feet then moving on. They are gifted with being able to manifest new ideas. Often people with red traits are also renowned for their daring exploits, and they can be somewhat extrovert and boastful about their skills.

Red brings focus to the physicality of life, to the process of living. The colour is symbolic of what we need to survive. Life should be grabbed and lived with a sense of immediacy. Without red we become listless and out of touch with reality and we fail to live our dreams in this world. Without the foundation that red gives us we just daydream of escaping into fantasy worlds.

Red keeps us rooted in the red energy of our planet. People who become detached or divorced from the planet tend to be those

### USING RED

If you want to come across as a bold and dynamic person, wear a red scarf or a tie. This is especially effective if you have an event coming up at which your confidence needs a boost, such as an interview or a presentation. You might also find this useful for a social occasion when you feel nervous about some new people.

# Orange

While red is associated with fiery heat, orange is more closely linked to the benign warmth of the sun and of fire. Like fire, orange energy displays some sense of direction and purpose – it moves along those pathways which fuel its own existence. Orange is certainly dynamic, but more thoughtful and controlled than explosive red. As a mixture of red and yellow, orange blends the properties of both primary colours. (The secondary colours – orange, green and violet – are also able to balance contrasting energies.) Curiosity is one of the driving characteristics of the orange vibration and this brings exploration and creativity, particularly on a practical level.

## PUT ORANGE IN YOUR LIFE WHEN THERE IS ...

• a feeling of bleakness and boredom, particularly where there is a sense that time is really dragging

• a lack of interest in what is going on around you, even to the degree of disdaining to become involved in any way

• a resentment of changes in familiar routines and an obsessive need to have things in their 'proper' place

• over-seriousness – taking oneself too seriously, being unable to see humour and playfulness in life

• a fear of experiencing pleasure through the senses and of enjoying sensuality

• an inability to let go of the past. This can be especially apparent after an accident or shock where the mind continually revolves around the issues involved – the 'what if ...' and 'if only I had done this instead of that ...'

• a problem with blocked experiences in life, such as a decrease in personal creativity

△ Orange warms without burning. The light of sunrise and sunset encourages a sensitivity to creative ideas and contemplative thought.

▷ A fox cub illustrates how orange promotes exploration, play and creativity.

▽ Orange combines the new energy of red with the organizing qualities of yellow.

## playing at life

While red is a focusing or self-centred energy, orange reaches out to see what it feels like to be somewhere else – it is the toddler trying to grasp and wanting to taste everything. Orange is learning to experience the world with a sense of play and enjoyment.

Strangely, surveys have often found orange to be the least popular of colours (the favourites being green and blue). Exploring and reaching out can sometimes be painful. We learn that stroking a cat's fur is enjoyable and fun, but pulling a cat's whiskers can lead to the pain of a swift retaliation. Learning by exploring is somewhat risky, full of unknowns – this is the element of excitment, but it can also bring shock and stress. Yet because the orange energy is purposeful and has an instinct for moving on, it can creatively remove blocks to restriction and stagnation.

Orange represents instinctive rather than intellectual or thought-out problem solving. Orange energy often manifests itself

△ **Orange peel – washed first, or from organic sources – makes a soothing tea that aids digestion and helps to relax the body and release any feelings of stress.**

when someone is working on the design of their garden. It can also emerge through a potter working clay, or an artist roughing out a sketch, or a poet scribbling ideas. Even doodling on a pad while listening to someone on the telephone is exhibiting the natural urge to explore through creativity – to allow a flow of energy to balance the sense of identity characterised by red.

A balance of orange energy brings a willingness to get involved, to 'get one's hands dirty' with practical exploration. It gives the ability to fill time creatively and to be aware of the needs of the body. Without orange energy, attention tends to get drawn to the head, filling our lives with ideas, thoughts and theories. Orange enables us to put these thought processes into practice in the world in a creative way, and to enjoy the experience of doing so.

**USING ORANGE**
In times of stress, or after a shock or a surprise, wearing shades of orange can help the body to return to a state of balance.

# Yellow

Yellow is a bright, sunny colour. Most people will recognize the sensation of warmth and vitality when looking at a strong, pure yellow. Like the energy of a bright, sunny morning yellow brings clarity and awareness. As with all colours, different yellows will create markedly different responses. An orange-yellow or golden colour imparts a sense of establishment, of solidity and assuredness, a rich, round sensation of inner warmth. A clean, light yellow seems to clear the mind while keeping it alert and active

**PUT YELLOW IN YOUR LIFE WHEN THERE IS ...**

- confusion and indecision
- fear and anxiety caused by unknown factors leading to nervous and digestive disorders
- a weak and confused immune system – frequent minor illnesses, intolerances and allergies to foods and other substances
- nervous exhaustion, nervous breakdown, 'burn out', panic attacks, hot flushes
- poor memory, inability to concentrate or study
- tendency to Seasonal Affective Disorder (SAD) or lethargy and depression in dull weather
- digestive difficulties, malabsorption of food

△ The light of the morning sun is stimulating and enlivening to plants and daytime creatures.

▽ Yellow enriches, lightens and activates many of the systems of the body. It tends to encourage orderliness and clarity.

in a state of readiness. An acid yellow can be stimulating and enlivening, a shade of yellow that has just a touch of green, however, will create a degree of discomfort, disorientation and even nausea.

## decisive yellow

The functions of the yellow vibration have to do with decision-making, with what to do in any given situation. Decisions rely on information, but more importantly on the ability to select bits of information that are relevant. Discrimination, knowing what is what, is a 'yellow' skill upon which we constantly rely for our wellbeing, physically as well as mentally.

The digestive system, the immune system and the nervous system all reflect yellow frequencies. The functions of the digestive system are to break down, identify and absorb those substances that the body requires for maintenance and growth, and to eliminate from the system those substances that are harmful or unnecessary. The

▷ The colour yellow is naturally associated with the sun itself, and so with its life-giving and sustaining energies. Lemons and yellow flowers are instant reminders of these qualities and an easy way to access them.

▽ Honey, the concentrated energy of sunlight turned into nectar sugars by plants and processed by bees, has many yellow qualities: it helps the digestive system, is gently energizing and is a powerful immune system booster.

immune system works in a similar way. Its various organs and defences are able to identify and destroy cells that are in the wrong place or have come into the body from outside, such as bacteria and viruses.

The digestive system and the immune system rely on correct decisions about what is useful and what is dangerous. Both need qualities of intelligence, memory and discrimination. If for some reason, such as stress, the systems fail to work as well as they should, mistakes are made: the digestion may not absorb nutrients that are needed and the immune system may identify harmless substances as dangerous, creating intolerance or allergic reactions.

The nervous system relays information to the brain, which then categorizes, interprets and acts upon the signals. Correct identification of priorities leads to an easy relationship with the world. When this yellow function is lacking, confusion and indecision creep in. Fear and worry are the consequence of an imbalance of yellow energy, when wrong information and a lack of clear and logical thought result in an inability to act positively.

Society in the West is currently very focused on the yellow qualities of acquisition of knowledge, organization, structure and information exchange. The senses are continually bombarded with information, and large amounts of yellow energy are used up. However, people in this work environment spend the day in artificial light and are badly lacking in the yellow energy of sunlight. As a result, they need additional yellow from food, furnishings and sunlight to help keep the balance in their busy lives.

**USING YELLOW**
When working at a computer use a yellow mouse mat to improve your concentration and stay alert.

◁ Eating outside in natural sunlight improves digestion and gives a feeling of wellbeing.

# Green

Green is the colour of nature, the colour of the plant kingdoms. The human eye has its greatest sensitivity in the range of frequencies we perceive as green. Perhaps this skill evolved during mankind's early development as a forest dweller. The qualities of green are characterized by balance, and indeed green itself is found midway in the spectrum. Whereas the reds and yellows are warm colours, and the blues and violets are cool, green can be seen as either, depending on the shade.

△ Personal space and a sense of freedom helps to relax emotional and physical tensions. We respond to such views by taking a deep breath.

▽ The human eye recognizes more variation of colour in green than in any other colour. Individual choice can therefore be very particular.

## green growth

The power of nature is green power. Green stands for growth and the desire to expand and increase. Yet growth requires change, and change means that what has been must disappear to be replaced by what is to come. The process of life is the process of transformation from one state to another, the death of one form giving birth to another. Balance and a sense of order must be present for growth. Growth is an expansion of

△ The need to expand, grow and increase is a core quality of green energy expressed in nature.

orderliness that must be sustainable, with each stage acting as a foundation for the next period of expansion.

## green relationships

The colour green is the vibration of relationships, because in growing and expanding we meet others in the world around us.

## PUT GREEN IN YOUR LIFE WHEN THERE IS …

- a feeling of restriction caused by circumstances such as being housebound or confined
- a need to let change happen, but also a fear of the unknown
- a feeling of being trapped by other people's rules and regulations and a need to break rigid patterns
- a need for new ideas
- a need for a new state of balance
- a problem with personal relationships, especially with over-dominance or subservience
- a negative green tendency – feelings and emotions like envy, jealousy and greed

Learning how to relate to others is a skill of balancing our needs with the needs of the other person. If it is possible to develop a mutually agreeable relationship of caring and sharing, both lives are enriched and expanded – our interaction with the world is broadened. When a relationship is formed that is negative, manipulative or unpleasant in some way – very often because one per-son is trying to gain power and control over the other (a negative green tendency) – then

△ **For people who work and live away from a natural environment, gardens and urban parks help to restore balance and perspective. Even a simple window box can have this effect.**

our own potential for understanding the world is curtailed and restricted.

Green energy inevitably has to do with the pushing out of boundaries, of growing beyond what is known. Because it is expan-sive it must develop relationships with those things around it, but it must also have a degree of power and control.

The power of green can be expressed in a harmonious way, as in an ecological bal-ance where all elements are accommodated and mutually supportive, or it can be destructive to everything around it, simply absorbing or taking over, enforcing new order on others. The energy that green cre-ates is the energy of finding direction and new paths. Green enables us to find the means to the desired end; it provides the power to accomplish rather than power to dominate. In this way green shows how to balance difficult extremes to enable progress to be made.

### USING GREEN
When there is a sense of thwarted ambition, restriction or being trapped by external circumstances, surrounding yourself with greens, or taking a walk in green gardens will restore equilibrium.

# Blue

 △ **The blues that are found in the sea and sky help to free the mind from its normal activity.**

Blue is the colour of distance. When artists of the early Renaissance began to consider how to represent perspective, they employed the simple observation that in nature the further away an object was in space, the more blue it appeared. When we think of blue in this way it is associated with looking beyond what is in the immediate environment – and the colour itself also has the effect of stretching the perceptions outwards to the unknown.

▽ **The peaceful, restful energy of blue has almost universal popularity, and imbues the qualities of steadiness and reliability.**

## communicative blue

There are two aspects of blue. On the one hand there is the experience of going beyond what is known – the active search for information or detail – and on the other hand the experience of rest and peacefulness, simply being happy to be alive without any particular focus of thought.

In some respects these seem to be contradictory qualities but in fact the uniting factor is the desire for equilibrium. For example, the teacher is better informed than the student. Communication allows the student to learn what the teacher knows. The teaching will stop when the teacher and student know the same information. This is a new state of equilibrium and peace that will continue until a new source of information is found and interaction begins again. All kinds of communication, like talking, listening, learning and the exchange

**USING BLUE**

Blue will help the easy flow of communication whether it is with other people or listening to your own thoughts and feelings. To help remember a speech, write your notes on blue paper.

▷ Using the colour blue in a situation of relaxation and repose will encourage quiet communication and feelings of peace.

of information and viewpoints are blue activities. So too, are the expressive arts – not just the performing arts such as acting, singing and music, but any art form that seeks to communicate with other people. Any of the five senses can be used to tell the story or carry the message.

Although blue is the colour of communication and the flow of energy it is a cool vibration. We can understand this property when we consider that redness or heat is often caused by a concentration or build-up of energy that cannot flow freely. Thus inflammation – a red, energetic state – in the body can be reduced by cooling the area down by using a blue vibration. This will counteract the red quality, or will help to remove the block and to create a flow of energy, thus enabling the area to return to normal functioning.

▽ Blue encourages an effective flow of peace and understanding. Many compassionate deities are associated with blue. The robes of the Virgin Mary are predominately blue indicating her ability to hear and respond to humanity.

## distant emotions

The sense of distance gives blue a quality of detachment and devotion. Gazing into the sky naturally brings a sense of peace. The colour blue somehow seems to free the mind from its normal activity, removing us slightly from involvement with thought, emotion or physical action. A 'cool' personality avoids getting caught up in emotional turmoil or any particular belief. That impersonal quality is like the blue of the distant mountains, not overwhelmed by detail or closeness, but offering the possibility of greater perspectives. Blue is also linked to devotion. This is the quality of the vibration that can be understood as a constant stream of energy or communication towards the source of devotion, which is usually a powerful, universal focus of great depth such as the Virgin Mary, Krishna or Shiva – all of whom are associated with the colour blue.

Without some injection of blue in our lives helping the flow of information and energy, we will inevitably experience frustration, disappointment and lack of progress in whatever we do.

**PUT BLUE IN YOUR LIFE WHEN THERE IS …**
- a need to calm agitated, excitable, or chaotic states
- a need to communicate clearly
- a need for help with new information or in seeing information in context
- a need for peace, detachment, solitude and rest

# Indigo

the colour palette

There is a different quality to the experience of looking at a cloudless blue sky and a midnight blue sky. The indigo of the midnight sky amplifies the characteristics of blue in a profound, resonant way. At a physical level, while blue is a quietening and cooling colour, indigo is sedating. In a depressed state indigo is to be avoided as it can easily deepen the mood.

## how indigo works

In a way, indigo turns blue energy inwards: while blue promotes some form of communication between people, indigo creates an internal communication in an individual that might manifest as profound thought processes, new insights, philosophy and

△ The midnight sky has an infinite depth that reflects the timeless quality of indigo light.

intuition. The flow of blue can be fast, but the flow of indigo can be almost instantaneous, often leading to the sensation of inspiration 'coming out of the blue', with no previous development or build-up of thoughts and ideas. Intuition and sudden clarity of awareness, startling realizations and innovative concepts occur in the 'super-cooled' state of indigo.

The depths of indigo may seem unfathomable and mysterious, but they can yield useful perceptions. Indigo is related to clairvoyance, clairsentience and clairaudience (clear seeing, feeling and hearing) and other psychic skills.

▽ Indigo pigment was derived from azurite and lapis lazuli and was an expensive commodity. Woad is one of the few vegetable dyes to produce the same deep blue colour.

### PUT INDIGO IN YOUR LIFE WHEN THERE IS ...

- a need to focus on personal issues, beliefs and ideas
- a need to develop sensitivity to the inner senses and intuition
- a need to cool and quieten normal mental processes
- a need to relieve physical, mental and emotional pain

- inability or difficulty in assimilating and understanding new concepts or philosophies
- a need for temporary relief and removal from everyday problems and difficult experiences in life
- a need for space and a desire for a period of solitude

△ The wonderful stained glass windows of Chartres cathedral in France are a masterpiece of medieval design, bathing the interior with a deep blue light that heightens the sensitivities and elevates awareness from the mundane world.

▽ Blueberries and sloes are some of the indigo foods that can be found growing wild.

△ In an indigo state of awareness, the stillness of the mind is unperturbed by thoughts that come and go – like fish moving through deep water.

## profound indigo

The deep, directionless depths of indigo can sedate the conscious mind to a degree where more subtle, delicate perceptions can be registered. Blue energy is the skill of language and eloquence personified in the talker. Indigo energy definitely belongs to the listener. Blue energy can be frivolous and superficial, but indigo energy never fails to be profound and significant.

The internal quality of indigo and the enhanced sense of removal from normal, everyday communication can mean that those using a lot of indigo energy are able to step away from how the world is usually seen and come up with new and startling ways of thinking. The inventor has these qualities, going beyond the consensus view of what is possible while often appearing to be socially out of step or isolated. The internalizing qualities of indigo make it an ideal colour to use in contemplative and spiritual contexts, particularly in solitary meditations, and in visualization, where the inner senses are given a higher importance than the physical senses. Without the qualities provided by indigo we would need to find other resources to help provide deep quiet in our lives.

### USING INDIGO
To find peace for reflection, look up at the clear night sky. Contemplation and deep meditation come easier in the indigo depths of night. Night-time is often when inspirations and solutions to problems naturally arise.

# Violet

Violet is the colour at the opposite end of the rainbow spectrum to red. A combination of blue and red, it can be seen both as a completion and as the beginning of another cycle of vibratory energy, the rest of which ascends beyond the visible spectrum. Violet is the door to the unseen, both in terms of the electromagnetic spectrum and in human experience.

## how violet works

The key to understanding the energy of violet is to see how its component colours work together.

Red is a focusing, concentrating, dynamic and activating energy, while blue is a cooling, quietening and expansive energy. Violet brings a new dynamism to the unfocused expansion of blue and a stabilizing energy to the frenetic activity of red. The rather undirected spaciousness of blue is made practical by the addition of

◁ Aubergines (eggplant) are part of the *solanacea* family which also includes deadly nightshade and tobacco, and contain toxic alkaloids, which can distort our perception of reality, a very violet characteristic.

△ Healing is represented by the colour violet – the blue giving detachment and the ability to be devoted to the flow of energy, and the red supplying motivation to be of use to others.

the red. Concepts and ideas are thus better able to find some real application in the world. The energy that red brings allows more creative qualities to emerge from the blue, so violet is associated with the imagination and with inspiration.

## violet and fantasy

The difficulty with the world of violet energy is that it can become very self-contained. The red and blue make such a balanced whole that it is easy not to look

△ The silhouette of an industrial landscape, beautifully etched on a violet sky, illustrates this colour's ability to combine and balance the practical with the ideal, dreams with reality.

◁ Violet energy ranges from blue with a hint of red, to purple, where the red and blue are more equally mixed.

▷ Quiet, meditative spaces can benefit from a touch of violet colour.

△ **Violet encourages the flow of the imagination and the integration of ideas, or it can degenerate into daydreams and fantasy.**

## PUT VIOLET IN YOUR LIFE WHEN THERE IS ...

- a need to rebalance life
- a need to speed up the natural healing energy of the body
- a need to use the imagination in practical ways
- a need to integrate new skills into everyday life
- a need to remove all sorts of obstacles in life
- a need to calm hyperactivity, or energize lethargy or depression

beyond it. Where this happens, imagination transforms into fantasy, and inspiration becomes fanaticism. Violet energy, because it seems to extend beyond our current knowledge into the unknown, can trap the spiritual dreamer in a fantastic world of miraculous happenings and unrealistic wishful thinking. Here the practical world and all its tangible solidity is rejected in favour of a make-believe, usually very selfish, sense of personal evolution or spiritual progress.

▷ **Violet and purple suggest luxury, even today, a lasting memory of the time when these colours were exclusive to the rich.**

If the lure of the glamorous unknown can be avoided, violet energy can become one of the most effective colours to bring balance and healing in any situation. It helps to integrate energies at every level and as healing requires the building up of new systems (red energy), according to accurate information (blue energy), violet can speed both physical and emotional recovery.

Violet is an important energy to those who use the blue and indigo skills of psychic perception, because it helps to supply the grounding energy for the work. Without the anchoring abilities of red, the use of subtle perceptions can seriously imbalance and exhaust the life-energy of the practitioner.

The skill of integration is aided by violet. As the colour combines opposite energies, it can help people who need to work with an array of disparate things. Violet is often associated with the richness and diversity of ceremony, perhaps originating from its ability to psychologically balance the minds

and actions of the participants. Violet is often thought to be the most spiritual of all colours. In bygone days, violet dye was expensive and reserved for the priesthood and the rich. In practice, though, no colour is more spiritual than any other.

### USING VIOLET

Lavender is a traditional remedy for insomnia or restlessness at night. It is also one of the most versatile essential oils for scratches, burns, headaches and worry. Dried lavender flowers beside the bed, or a drop of oil on the pillow, will encourage peaceful sleep.

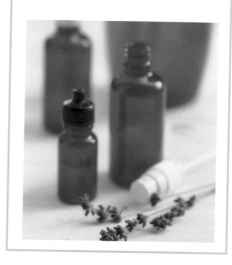

# White and black

When people speak of opposites it is usually in terms of black and white. Strictly speaking neither are colours – simply characteristics of the presence or absence of light. As in all polarities, black and white cannot be defined without each other. Like day and night, white and black are part of an unceasing definition of existence.

## white absolutes

The presence of white is what humans perceive as the entire visible light spectrum seen

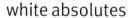

▷ **Coal and soot consist of black carbon – one of the earliest used pigments.**

together – the complete energy of light. In this sense it stands for wholeness and completion – nothing has been taken out, everything is present. In many cultures white is associated with purity and cleanliness, openness and truth – everything is shown in bright light, nothing is hidden. This is why white is often used to denote holiness. White is also the colour of bone and the snow of winter, so for some, the energy of white relates to the starkness of death and endings. Both of these interpretations – purity and death – are connected by the act of setting things

**USING BLACK**
If you want to become inconspicuous, consider dressing in black. Black can be inconspicuous, or it can make a bold statement of mystery and self-control. Black clothes often say; 'notice my presence but don't intrude into my space'.

△ **Light and shade, black and white, the zebra takes advantage of random contrasting patterns to disappear into its surroundings.**

◁ **Black and white are associated with viewpoints where no mutual ground can be found yet neither can exist without the other.**

apart from normal life, creating a sense of specialness. Entering or leaving the world, white signifies beginnings and the end of one cycle that enables another to start.

White is uncompromising. Everything is clear, open and explicitly manifest. It has a cold quality. White can be of use when clarity is needed in life. But it can also take on a hint of the other colours around it and so acts like a mirror to the energies that are in proximity. This can make it a rather uncomfortable colour for those who do not wish to have their hidden feelings reflected back to them. As a vibration of purification,

△ **Where there is light and three-dimensional form there is shadow, each defines the other.**

white can help to clarify all aspects of life, giving the energy to sweep away blocks in physical, emotional and mental patterns. There are no degrees of white, and its action can be as uncompromising and rapid as a flash of blinding light. White gives the potential to move towards every other colour, as it allows development in any direction. It is a good choice for new beginnings.

## black contrasts

White reflects all aspects of light, but black absorbs all aspects of light. So while white reveals, black conceals. In the simplicity of symbolism white is translated as whole, holy and good, so black inevitably becomes linked to the hidden, fearful and bad experiences. Black is the fear of a starless, moonless night where everything is unseen and unknown and anything might be hiding out there to wish us harm. Where white is the colour of emergence, of birth and change, black is the colour of continuity, of withdrawal from definition, of the hidden. White continually makes its presence felt: it shouts 'I am here, look at

me!' Black withdraws, refusing to take a stand or be noticed. White is the energy of completion, an expanse outwards. Black is the energy of gestation and of preparation. Black has often been associated with the energies of the earth and the fertile soil. The rich earth from which all life and sustenance springs is the same earth where the dead are placed.

In a way, both white and black reflect the particular beliefs of the individual. White can be seen negatively as blankness, and positively as a clean slate, offering a new beginning. In times of fear and uncertainty, black is a threatening unknown, a silence in which our own terrors and nightmares can be amplified. But at other times, black may simply be experienced as a restful emptiness that allows many different possibilities to emerge and disappear again.

▽ **Black can be seen as a threatening colour, representing a cloak over what lies beneath or within. At other times it is mysterious, allowing a sense of potential or possibility. It is the energy of gestation and preparation.**

**USING WHITE**
White has the ability to clear away all clutter, all extraneous noise. Fresh starts and new beginnings all benefit from its energy. Looking at a picture of snow-clad mountains brings clarity and freshness to a mind that feels crowded.

# Turquoise and pink

Turquoise is a blend of green and blue. It is so named because the Turks were fond of the colour and decorated many of their buildings with turquoise ceramic glazed tiles. Turquoise has the calming, expansive nature of green and the cool, quiet flow of blue. It can bring to mind a particular quality in the sky before or after sunset, a calm, warm sea, a beautiful lagoon, a pure mountain stream or distant hills in the mellow light of late summer.

## functions of turquoise

The energy of turquoise allows the expression of our wishes. The green quality of growth is added to the blue quality of communication. Turquoise is the colour of the desire for freedom to be a unique individual. The blue ingredient ensures that, whatever the need may be in the heart of the individual, it will communicate itself and be recognized for what it is. Turquoise

△ **Turquoise and pink are both blends of colours that can be warm and cool. Both balance and strengthen life-energy at many levels.**

▽ **The Turks were skilled tilemakers and with access to the mines of Persia they were able to use turquoise pigments to great effect.**

▽ **Turquoise is a copper ore with varying degrees of blue and green. Each mine produces a slight variation of colour.**

also represents the exploration of information through feelings and emotions. This creates the possibility for new interpretations of established ways for doing things, of new uses for old ideas.

Space and freedom are essential for every living creature. Restriction of natural behav-

**USING TURQUOISE**
Throughout the world turquoise stones have been used as protective amulets for promoting health and guarding against harm. A large proportion of everyone's energy comes from the turquoise motivation to experience life to the full. Wear turquoise jewellery to give yourself confidence and strength. Turquoise has a strengthening influence on all systems of the body bringing a sense of inner confidence.

iour patterns and the inability to find a p[ ] in the community cause a rapid build[ ] of stress and toxins in the body. This le[ ] to a decrease in energy and greater susc[ ] tibility to disease. Turquoise can help w[ ] there is low energy, a lack of interest in l[ ] a failure to fit in with the surroundings[ ] a lack of courage to strike out on your o[ ]

◁ Dark pink, bubble-gum pink and magenta are much more stimulating than pale tints. They provide the energy to make changes to improve one's life and are dynamic and assertive.

light rapidly defuses aggressive attitudes and behaviour. These deeper shades of pink can also help to improve self-confidence and assertiveness, while pink's paler shades are more protective, promoting peace and being supportive of self-acceptance and feelings of self-worth.

Pink is sometimes seen only as a soft, feminine colour, a colour representing the qualities of caring and tenderness. It will also help to take the heat out of any turbulent or aggressive situation. The dynamic mix of red and white is a useful balance of male and female energies that can also be valuable as a healing colour, reducing the effects of disease as well as the fear and anguish disease can cause. Pink can help where other colours may have drawbacks, as it fundamentally supports the integrity of an individual.

## functions of pink

Pink is red and white combined in varying degrees. The quality of the energy will depend on how much red vibration is present. White is the potential for fullness, and red is the motivation to achieve that potential, so pink is a colour that promotes both these energies together.

Pink gives an underlying confidence to existence, it provides a level of support that means that it has the ability to neutralize any negative or destructive tendencies. Aggressive behaviour patterns arise where there is fear at an emotional level, or friction at a physical or mental level. Pink

provides sufficient energy to move out of that negative state and enough clarity to recognize and clear away misconceptions.

Deep shades of pink that veer towards magenta have proved to be extremely effective in situations of disorder and violence, such as in prisons and police cells. In places such as these, a limited exposure to pink

▽ Pink promotes relaxation and acceptance of where one is in life without false views or feelings of complacency.

**USING PINK**

In any aggressive or threatening situation, or where there are simple misunderstandings leading to anger, visualizing pink around everyone can help to calm the mood and reduce tension.

# Brown and grey

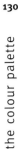

Brown clothes were worn by the large majority of manual workers until the introduction of blue denim. As a mix of the primary colours, brown can blend into many surroundings. It is a disguise that shows no preference, no specific direction or attitude. It can be used very effectively to hide the true nature of the individual. Grey clothes are the favoured uniform of managers, businessmen and politicians. Grey reflects the desire to project coolness of mind, emotional stability and the ability to look down on the rest of the world with a detached neutrality. It epitomizes the myth of efficiency.

## practical brown

Brown is a mixture of red, yellow and blue. Like every colour, brown has a wide range of shades and tones, each having a different effect. It is primarily a colour of the earth and the natural world. Brown acts as a solid background colour, a base upon which other, more striking colours can arise. As a combination, brown is neutral and non-threatening. Its warm tones are comfortable and familiar.

The red content makes brown a colour of practical energy and this mixed with the mental qualities of yellow and blue can encourage study and focus of the mind. However, in too great a quantity brown can also have a dulling effect, as it lacks the overall clarity to break out of established patterns

▽ **Brown is a varying mixture of red, yellow and blue. It can range from a burnt orange tone to a chocolate brown with hints of red and purple.**

of behaviour. Brown gives a state of solidity and reality from which one can grow. It suggests reliability and the desire to remain in the background, unnoticed.

In the traditional surroundings of an oak-panelled library or study, brown aids the transformation of inspiration and thoughts into practical, everyday reality. Discoveries and inventions need time devoted to painstaking detail, and involve going over the same set of ideas repeatedly until a solution emerges. Brown acts as a supporting colour in this process.

◁ **Brown is a warm, comfortable colour, reflecting wholesomeness, naturalness and dependability.**

▽ **Deer, like other forest or woodland animals, use their brown hides or coats to blend into the background and become virtually invisible.**

### USING BROWN

Brown in the home can be overbearing. Adding a few richer colours to brown wooden furniture and neutral coloured floor coverings will create a warm, stable atmosphere where it is easy to feel comfortable for long periods.

## neutral grey

Grey is the true neutral colour. It is usually thought of as a combination of white and black, but a mixture of any complementary colours will produce grey. Grey is the colour of void, of emptiness, lack of movement, lack of emotion, lack of warmth, lack of any identifying characteristics in fact. Because of this, grey can be restful. If it contains a high proportion of white it will tend to take on the qualities of surrounding colours. If it has a greater amount of black, it can feel very heavy and depressing. Grey lacks information and this has a numbing effect on the mind, though not in a particularly peaceful way, as with blue or indigo. Indeed the inability to see into the colour can be reminiscent of the experience of fear or terror where decision-making processes seem frozen and even time stands still. With its emptiness, boredom and lack of direction, grey has an enervating and draining effect: its neutrality prevents us from moving towards an energetic state.

Unlike brown, grey has no connection to the solid earth or the life of nature.

▽ Grey pigments appear to be that colour because they scatter all light that hits them in a random way.

◁ **Where grey skies are common they can have an oppressing influence on people as it reduces the intensity and effect of all other colours.**

Immovable stone and cloudy skies reflect the impersonal, implacable nature of grey. Grey has a detached, isolated and unemotional feel. While brown suggests a down-to-earth practicality, grey has a cool, calculating mental neutrality, an unwillingness to get one's hands dirty.

Grey clothes can suggest that the wearer wishes to remain unsullied or uninvolved, but they can also suggest sophistication – being cool. When placed next to other colours, grey does have a cooling effect. It is moderating and stabilizing, making neighbouring colours stand out while muting their vibrational energy.

▽ **Grey clothes suggest efficiency and are often used in the business world. Grey can also suggest a lack of imagination, however.**

### USING GREY

Grey clothing will emphasise neutrality. However, too much grey, or a wrong shade, will suggest lack of character, lack of initiative and extreme detachment. A hint of another colour that reflects individual preference will make all the difference: efficient, wellbehaved but with personality. If you want to emphasize your willingness to comply, wear grey.

# Self-healing with colour

An understanding of how the body uses the language of colour helps an individual to discover their personal colour needs. Selecting from a range of coloured, everyday items can provide unique guidance to enhance wellbeing, and provide guidance and clarity in life.

# Human responses to colour

The only real difference between coloured light and any other radiation of the electromagnetic spectrum is that we can see it. Under the light of the sun, which reaches the earth with greatest strength in the visible spectrum, humankind has evolved to respond and make use of colour. The fact that the warm colours of reds and oranges activate and stimulate us while the cool colours of blues and violets calm us, probably derives from the biological triggers of daylight and nightfall.

## eyes and light

Our eyes serve not only as a sense organ but also directly stimulate vitally important, fundamental and very primitive parts of the nervous system located deep in the brain. The hypothalamus, pituitary and pineal glands are all extremely light sensitive. Light reaching these areas of the brain has an immediate effect on the involuntary autonomic nervous system, changing our physical, mental and emotional states. The human eye is a complex and sophisticated

△ It is thought that our sensitivity to colour has evolved over time, in order to respond to the changing conditions of sunlight in our world.

sensing device. Light passes through the transparent lens and stimulates the retina at the back of the eyeball, which consists of specialized light-sensitive cells called rods and cones. The rods are sensitive to blue and green and work in dim light. The cones work best in daylight and are sensitive to different colours depending on the pigments

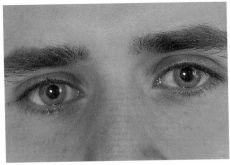

△ The human eye is one of the most complex structures in the whole animal kingdom, the product of millions of years of evolution.

◁ The warm colours in fire combine with the physical sense of heat, and promote feelings of warmth and comfort.

tors and healers can therefore find ways of using colour to manipulate our responses – for better or worse. Colour, as well as the amount of full-spectrum sunlight, has been shown to initiate profound changes in the nervous system. We are all moved by colour whether we are aware of the process or not, but increasing our knowledge of how colour influences us can help us to be aware of any attempts to manipulate us.

they contain. These photoelectric cells, when stimulated, send electrical impulses via the optic nerve into the brain where they are interpreted. The process of vision is primarily a function of the brain, for the eyes 'see' only a small area of the world at any one time. The eyeballs move very rapidly, 50 to 70 times a second, scanning the field of vision. It is the visual cortex in the brain that makes sense of this information and tells us what we are seeing.

△ **Colour is the food of our emotions. It reflects our thoughts and moods consciously and unconsciously. Combinations of bright, festive colours, for example, are powerfully attractive, particularly to young children.**

▽ **Although we think of colour as a decorative, superficial thing, our choices and reactions are dictated by the energy each wavelength exerts on important areas of the unconscious brain.**

## NATURAL LIGHT

It has been recommended that people spend at least 20 minutes outside in direct sunlight every day. If you wear glasses or contact lenses it is also a good idea to remove them for five or ten minutes every few hours, in order to get the benefit of natural light.

## the energy of light

Light impulses do not go just to the visual cortex in the brain. Some nerves go from the retina directly to the hypothalamus, a small organ that regulates most of the life-sustaining functions of the body, such as control of the autonomic nervous system, energy levels, internal temperature, cycles of rest and activity, growth, circulation, breathing, reproduction and the emotions. The hypothalamus directly affects the pituitary gland, which is the major controlling organ for the endocrine system and all its hormonal secretions. Light from the eyes also directly affects the pineal gland, which modifies our behaviour patterns according to the amount of light it receives. The pineal gland regulates our energy so that we can remain in balance with our environment. The correspondences between the endocrine glands and the subtle energy systems of the body, indicate that colour affects all levels of our being.

The eyes are thus not simply a source of information about the world around us, they also allow light energy to be carried to the centre of the brain where it can create profound changes at the level of cellular function, physical activity, emotional and mental states. Advertisers, interior decora-

# Light as healer

The sun is the motor that drives this world. A change to the energy we receive on the surface of the earth is like a change in gear that speeds up or slows down all life processes. It is not a matter of choice – life has evolved to take advantage of the energy of the sun and so is automatically connected to its cycles.

## cycles of light

At sunrise, the sun low on the horizon is red. As it climbs into the sky, the widening angle with our point on the earth's surface allows more orange and then yellow light to reach the ground. Experimentation has clearly shown that red light increases blood pressure, pulse rate and breathing rate, and that these functions are further increased in orange light, reaching their peak in yellow light. The human physiological response to light has evolved so that the rising sun stimulates us into activity and alertness.

▽ Only the comparatively recent introduction of artificial lighting has changed our patterns of rest and activity, triggered by sunrise and sunset.

△ Sun, moon and stars are the earliest deities in many religions. Light is a universal metaphor for enlightenment and spiritual fulfilment.

Other experiments have shown a decrease in blood pressure, pulse rate and breathing rate when people are exposed to green light. Relaxation increases with blue light and is at its fullest in complete darkness. White light has been found to have similar quietening effects to blue light. As daylight fades the subduing green light changes to the blue of evening, then the

△ Energy levels, hormone activity and mood are all automatically regulated according to the quality of light.

darkness of night, with perhaps only the moon for illumination. Night is the natural time of rest and reflection. Emotionally and physiologically we respond to colours as they fit the times of the day, just as our distant forebears did before artificial light sources were available.

## light reaction in cells

Studies with plants grown under different colours and ranges of light have demonstrated that the wrong kind of light can seriously damage their growth and health. Full-spectrum natural sunlight with normal levels of ultraviolet light (which is filtered out by most types of glass) is essential to maintain the normal, healthy functioning of plant cells. The same has been found with animal cells. Filtering light or exposure to a single colour for long periods causes cells to function abnormally and even eventually die. These studies seem to suggest that humans, as well as plants, need a balanced environment of light and colour. Until 1879 when the electric light bulb was invented, most people lived and worked outdoors in natural light. Now more and more people spend a large proportion of their lives in enclosed environments exposed to artificial light and completely cut off from the sun.

△ All life has evolved to take advantage of the different qualities of sunlight through the year.

When full-spectrum, balanced fluorescent lighting was tested in schools against normal white tubes, there appeared to be a significant decrease in irritability, hyperactivity and fatigue in students after just one month. Interestingly, there also seemed to be a correlation between poor quality lighting and the amount of tooth decay!

The reduction of sunlight on a cloudy day or, more profoundly, in the long months of winter, significantly changes the mood of most people, but for some, the lack of sunlight can be seriously debilitating. Seasonal Affective Disorder (or SAD) causes mood swings, low energy levels and depression that begins as the days grow shorter and only gradually improves with the onset of spring. Effective treatment is by exposure each day to several hours of bright full-spec-

trum light that resembles sunlight and which resets the chemical balance within the pineal gland, the organ that is disrupted. Without sufficient exposure to the full spectrum of light from the sun, the finely balanced chemical reactions in our bodies tend to falter, leaving us prone to ill health.

△ An indoor lifestyle may be a factor in our lack of health and sense of wellbeing, spending time outside will counteract this.

▽ During the long winter months the grey rainy weather in some countries can contribute to feelings of seasonal depression.

# Single colour guidance

Our instinctive emotional response to colour can tell us a lot about ourselves. It reflects back to us how we are functioning. It can show life-long tendencies, immediate situations or a potential direction in personal development. Sometimes certain colours stay with us as favourites for many years. This is reflected in the colours we choose to paint our home, inside and out, and the predominant colours in our wardrobe. It is possible to interpret these colour preferences through their known correspondences to our physical, emotional, mental and even spiritual state.

## colour choice

Given a range of colours to choose from, the process of self-reflection and self-revelation can begin. The simplest approach is to make spontaneous choices:

★ Which colour do you like the most?
★ Which colour do you like the least?

The colour you like the most will, as likely as not, be present in your home or in

▽ **Sometimes our instinctive choice of food reflects our energy needs of the moment.**

△ **Coloured candies can be used as a way of identifying colour energies that are lacking.**

▷ **Flowers, with their vibrant colour and variety of shape, are an excellent way to introduce a balancing colour into the surroundings.**

your clothes. It may also be a colour that you need to help you in a current situation. By looking at the full range of correspondences for that colour, as discussed earlier in this book, you may get insight into a new direction in life. However, if the colour you have chosen is an absolute favourite and you have no desire to reflect on other choices, you may have become stuck in particular habit patterns. Again, look at the correspondences for that colour to see what these habits might be.

The colour you like least will suggest areas of your life that may require attention and healing. Each colour has positive as well as negative attributes, so it is a good idea to bring the positive energy of a colour you dislike into your life to create balance. Do this through new activities, the choice of food, by wearing that colour in clothing or adding it to your surroundings.

The process of self-analysis through colour can be developed a step further by deciding, before you make your choices, what each choice will represent. For exam-

ple, a series of three choices could be selected to show:

**1** What your physical needs are now (e.g. activities, food, clothes)
**2** What your emotional needs are now (e.g. peace, space, fun, company)
**3** What your mental needs are now (e.g. time to study, standing up for yourself)

## how to do it

**1** Collect together a selection of different coloured items, for example ribbon lengths, pieces of card or buttons so that you have at least one of each colour of the rainbow plus a selection of other colours.
**2** Lay the items out at random on a plain background.
**3** Close your eyes and have in your mind your first question.
**4** Relax, open your eyes and pick up the colour that you are immediately, and instinctively drawn to.
**5** Repeat these steps for each of your questions in turn.

## what does it mean?

The colour that you have instinctively selected will give you the answer in the language of colour. You can then introduce the colour energy into your life by whichever means seem appropriate. The colour choices may highlight some aspects of your life that have not been clear to you. This process can bring issues to the surface so they can be looked at and healed.

## taking it further

You can invent any number of permutations for a series of questions or choices. For example:

1  Where am I now?
2  What are my main difficulties?
3  What is at the root of those difficulties?
4  What are my priority needs?
5  What is the next possible step and the way forward?

The colour choices can be interpreted through colour correspondences and then introduced into your life using the information in this book.

▽ **Use collections of differently coloured items, such as ribbons or pieces of fabric, for single colour guidance exercises.**

**CHOOSING COLOURS**

Try not to think about the choice you make. Just pay attention to where your eyes settle as soon as they are open. For a moment or two you may find your eyes just scan over the colours, but soon they will focus on one in particular.

△ **Lay out all your colours so that your eyes can easily scan all of them at the same time.**

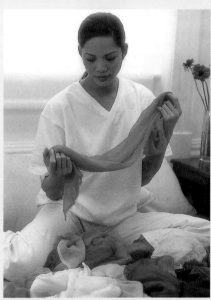

△ **Close your eyes, take a moment to relax, and think of the area you wish to investigate.**

△ **When you feel ready, open your eyes and pick the colour that first draws your attention.**

# single colour assessment

A simple way to determine your day-to-day colour needs is to carry out a single colour assessment. This process can be done as often as you like. Sit quietly with these pages open in front of you and go through the steps below one by one.

## how to assess yourself

1. Cover the chart showing the keys to colours with a sheet of paper. This helps to stop the logical and judgmental part of the mind from interfering with the instinctive choice of colour.

2. Note down on a piece of paper the number of choices you will make and what each will represent. For example, a one-colour choice could represent what you most need today; a two-colour choice could reveal firstly a problem you are encountering, and secondly, a possible solution.

3. With the framework decided, close your eyes. For each choice, open your eyes and record the colour that your eyes are immediately drawn to.

▽ **Relax before starting a single colour assessment and remember that you are being guided towards a colour by your intuition.**

4. Repeat the process for each choice, then look up the correspondences on the chart.

5. Consider the questions and phrases linked to each of your colour choices, and where appropriate, decide to bring that colour more into your life.

▷ **Any coloured items can be used for colour assessment. The important thing is to decide on an appropriate framework of questions.**

### KEYS TO COLOURS

| Colour | Key phrases and questions that may help you to focus ideas |
| --- | --- |
| Dark red | Need to keep your feet on the ground<br>What is taking your attention away from where it needs to be? |
| Red | Need to take action, now<br>What is stopping you doing what is necessary? |
| Orange | Need to let go of old, worn out ideas, things, emotions<br>What is blocking you? What are you allowing to block your way? |
| Gold | Need to relax, enjoy life<br>What is making you doubt yourself? |
| Yellow | Need to start thinking clearly<br>What are you afraid of? |
| Olive green | Need to reassess where you are going<br>What hidden factors are stopping your growth? |
| Green | Need for space to gain fresh perspective<br>What is restricting you? |
| Turquoise | Need to put into words exactly what you feel<br>What are your strengths? |
| Light blue | Need to talk to people around you<br>What do you need to express to others? |
| Dark blue | Need for peace and time on your own<br>What are you so close to that you cannot see clearly what is happening? |
| Violet | Need to heal yourself<br>What are you sacrificing to appear as a 'good' or 'helpful' person? |
| Black | Need to be quiet and listen<br>What are you wanting to hide from? |
| White | Need to make some changes<br>What is painful to look at in the real world? |
| Pink | Need to look after yourself more<br>What thoughts do you have about yourself that are too critical? |
| Magenta | Need to take time out to repair all levels of yourself<br>What have you been overdoing at the expense of your own health? |
| Brown | Need to focus on the practicalities of life<br>In what areas of your life have you been too dreamy? |
| Grey | Need to disappear into the background<br>What do you want to hide and why? |

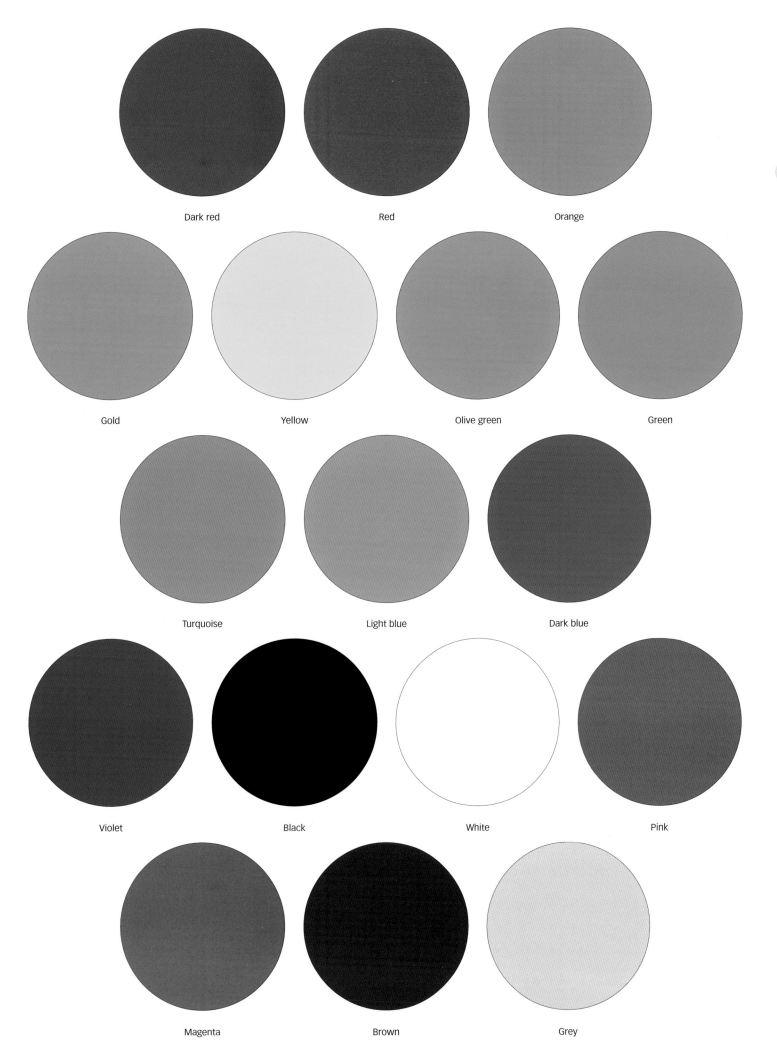

Dark red

Red

Orange

Gold

Yellow

Olive green

Green

Turquoise

Light blue

Dark blue

Violet

Black

White

Pink

Magenta

Brown

Grey

# Specific colour placement

In certain situations it is helpful to introduce specific colours into the environment for immediate short-term effect. This can often be more effective than redecorating whole rooms, or enthusiastically pursuing certain foods or activities. Once the situation changes, the colour can be removed until it is needed again in the future.

## everyday uses of colour

When you use visualization techniques for relaxation and stress removal, it can sometimes be difficult to return to everyday activities or focus on practical tasks, especially if your experience has been deep. The same problem sometimes occurs in people who meditate regularly, as returning to the realities of the world can be disruptive. A rich red object such as a cushion or a piece of fabric can help. After relaxation or meditation, try gazing at the colour red for about a minute. This will integrate the benefits of meditation into your body and prepare you to return to the normal world.

Students studying for examinations will find the process less tiring and generally more effective if they introduce a shade of yellow into their study-space. An acid yellow will keep the mind alert, while sunshine yellow combines alertness with relaxation.

▽ **Small areas of bright colour, like cushion covers, are excellent ways to temporarily bring colour energy into a room.**

## colour and reading difficulties

American psychologist Helen Irlen introduced the idea of reading through coloured overlays in 1988. Her attention was drawn to a type of dyslexia called SSS or Scotopic Sensitivity Syndrome. People with this difficulty are very light-sensitive. They have trouble dealing with high contrasts, such as black and white, find that letters and numbers 'move' on the page and have difficulty with groups of letters or numbers. They also

△ **Having a red object in a meditation space helps to ground spiritual energies at a practical level. Tibetan monks often wear red shawls or robes for this purpose.**

have a poor attention span. Irlen has devised a series of tests for people with reading difficulties which enables her to help them by recommending reading through different coloured overlays or tinted spectacle lenses. These measures can alleviate, or even sometimes remove the problem entirely. Irlen's

## THE WORK OF BARBARA MEISTER VITALE

Barbara Meister Vitale, a well-known educator and lecturer in the USA, has used colour in her work since 1970. During her research with children and the way they learn, she has concluded that:

• Lots of different coloured pieces of material in the classroom help to reduce hyperactivity and increase children's attention span.

• Children behave differently when dressed in different coloured clothes.

• Using several different coloured pens and coloured paper increases children's learning skills and aids their ability to recall.

• Using a blue light helps both adults and children in their reading and studying.

• People with reading difficulties respond well when a transparent colour overlay is placed on their reading material.

• The effect of colour is unique to each individual. It might be their favourite colour, or its complementary colour, that is most helpful to them.

△ **Bringing colour into a space is more than a design or fashion whim. Colour has an impact on every activity around it.**

work has centred on people with SSS, who make up approximately one-fifth of those with dyslexia or other identified learning difficulties. Irlen believes, however, that her findings could benefit a much wider section of people, and that about one-fifth of the general population could benefit from reading through colour. There is medical evidence to suggest that wearing coloured lenses can also reduce the incidence of migraine by up to 80%.

The benefits of using colour in health and in education are only now being investigated scientifically. Perhaps in the future these inexpensive and simple tools could help in many situations, and may well transform many peoples lives.

▽ **Study can be helped by having objects of lemon yellow around that help the memory functions of the brain. If exam-stress is a problem, a bright golden yellow encourages relaxation and reduces nervousness.**

# Rainbow diet

Each of us has colours that we prefer and some that we dislike. Any reaction of an emotional nature to colour, either positive or negative, can indicate how colour can be used to promote healing and wellbeing.

A balance of attractive colours in the food we eat plays a large part in a healthy diet. But few people recognize their instinctive reaction to the colour of food, or notice that they get drawn towards that colour in a foodstore or marketplace. Manufacturers of convenience foods play on this reaction, which is why many packaged foods contain dyes and colourings to tempt our palate.

The effect of a food is not always gauged by the colour we see; its colour-related action or quality is also important. One of the qualities of orange is to eliminate toxins. Brown rice and oats are good detoxifiers, so can be described as having an

△ **Fresh fruit and vegetables provide a banquet of colours to feast the eyes and tempt the poorest of appetites.**

orange action. Often the body tries to direct us to the foods we need to rebalance our health. It is worth observing the types of food that appeal to someone after an illness or shock. Allowed a free choice we will always tend to be drawn to the foods we need by colour as much as by smell or taste but we rarely recognise or allow ourselves to follow through and eat the foods.

## CHOOSING FOOD BY COLOUR

• Foods that display our favourite colours will always be needed because they give us the particular energy that supports our body's function.

• Foods belonging to the least-favourite, or even hated, colours will provide the nutrition and colour energy that we are lacking.

• Food colours that we are attracted to temporarily reflect the immediate nutritional needs of the body.

• If you have problems that correspond to certain colours, you may wish to introduce foods of that colour into your diet to help your body with its healing.

▽ **Unprocessed natural sugars could be thought of as better for us than the white, processed varieties. We do, however, get enough sugar for our daily needs from eating fruits and vegetables without having to add it to other foods.**

# RED FOODS AND FOODS THAT WORK IN A RED WAY

Red foods are generally rich in minerals and provide good sources of protein. They are good for increasing levels of vitality. Red deficiencies are shown through low energy levels, anaemia, light–headedness and lack of stamina.

Foods have different kinds of colour energy, one is its obvious outwards appearance, the colour it actually is, another is the inherent energy it supplies. Chocolate is a good example of this, although not red in colour it is an important red energy food because of the instant energy it supplies. In appearance watercress and parsley are both green foods, but their high levels of minerals give them a red quality. Red wine is red in colour and provides iron, but its high alcohol level means that it also provides violet energy, so it can be classed in either colour category.

△ Redcurrants are widely used to accompany rich, red foods, such as meat and game.

△ Chocolate is an important red energy food as it gives instant energy.

| Red fruits | Strawberries, raspberries, cherries |
| --- | --- |
| Red vegetables | Red cabbage, beetroot, radishes, peppers, onions, tomatoes, chillies, watercress, parsley |
| Other red foods | Meat, pulses, nuts, fish |
| red Vitamins | B12 (vital for the absorption of iron) |
| red Minerals | Iron (helps the blood to carry oxygen), magnesium (good for nerve responses, cell energy, hormones, healthy bones), zinc (good for fertility; healthy hair, skin and nails) |
| Other red nutrients | Fatty acids (improve function of cells and promote healthy blood, skin, hair and nails) |
| Red non-foods (foods with little or no nutritional value) | Red wine (stimulates and relaxes in moderation), coffee (stimulates the adrenals, diuretic), chocolate (gives instant energy), sugar, the ultimate non-food (very addictive but gives instant short-lived energy, followed by a big energy 'low') |

◁ Red foods can be very attractive when energies are low or following periods of illness.

▽ Soft red fruit is many people's favourite way of absorbing red energy and natural sugars.

# ORANGE FOODS AND FOODS THAT WORK IN AN ORANGE WAY

Orange foods help with the release of toxins and stress from the body, they support the reproductive system and encourage creativity at all levels. Orange deficiencies are shown in constipation, artist's block, difficulties with fertility and stiffness of the joints. Orange foods help with the release

| Orange fruits | Oranges, peaches, apricots |
|---|---|
| Orange vegetables | Pumpkin, peppers, carrots |
| Other orange foods | Brown rice, sesame seeds, oats (provides roughage which is mucilaginous and gentle), shellfish |
| orange vitamins | Vitamin A (for healthy eyes, skin, stable energy levels), vitamin C (strengthens cells and blood vessels, helps absorption of iron) |
| orange minerals | Calcium (for muscle relaxation and healthy bones), copper (helps absorption of iron, improves flexibility of arteries), selenium (free-radical scavenger, helps reduce the effects of ageing), zinc (for healthy reproductive organs). |

◁ **Seafood is rich in many trace minerals and Omega 3 fatty acids that support the reproductive system.**

▷ **Oranges contain the key nutrient Vitamin C and carotenoids that support the body in healing the effects of disease and ageing.**

foods into a system that is tired or toxic is easier for the body to handle than the strong, direct energy of red foods that could appear on first glance to be the solution.

▽ **The vitamin C and zinc in carrots provide an excellent combination to help the body detoxify metals and other pollutants.**

of toxins and stress from the body by encouraging the system to become more efficient in the natural elimination and excretory processes. This, in turn, aids relaxation and the release of stress as the body lets go of unwanted and waste products.

Orange foods contain key nutrients that support and maintain the reproductive systems. These foods can also aid the flow of creativity on other levels too.

Lack of orange and orange-energy foods can be evident in physical constipation, but also in stagnation in other areas, such as artist's block and stiffness in muscles and joints. Introducing orange or orange-energy

◁ **We are often attracted to orange foods when our bodies need to release significant amounts of stress or toxicity.**

# YELLOW FOODS AND FOODS THAT WORK IN A YELLOW WAY

The sun gives us our main source of yellow during daylight hours, but as modern life uses up the yellow vibration in dealing with pollution, chemicals, living indoors and high stress levels, yellow foods are needed in large amounts by much of the industrialized world's population.

Lack of yellow leads to irritability, tension, poor memory, restlessness, inefficient absorption of nutrients, digestive problems,

▷ Bananas are rich in potassium that helps to maintain healthy muscles. Grapefruit and lemons help to fight infections.

▽ Yellow foods are a useful addition to the diet for those who are studying, or coping with worries that they can do little about.

a drop in immunity, a tendency towards hot flushes, feelings of depression, and inability to make decisions.

Problems with learning, concentration and memory can indicate a lack of yellow energy in the body. Sometimes this lack is made worse by the modern lifestyle, lighting and high levels of stress. However, recent research into learning and attention difficulties has concluded that fish oils (Omega 3 fatty acids) have a crucial role in the internal body chemistry. The systems of people experiencing these problems seem to be unable to assimilate these vital nutrients correctly. This indicates that what were once thought of as behavioural problems are actually difficulties with nutrition. Giving children experiencing these problems daily supplements of fatty acids – a yellow food – resulted in significant improvement in over 40% of cases, confirming the research.

▽ Grains that are made into flours form the staple diets of most cultures.

| | |
|---|---|
| Yellow fruits | Lemon, bananas, grapefruit |
| Yellow vegetables | Grains (rice, corn, wheat, rye etc.), peppers, pumpkins |
| Other foods | Eggs, fish, oils, food rich in fatty acids |
| Vitamins | Vitamin A (for healthy tissues, blood, eyes and immune system), vitamin B complex (helps the body to convert food into energy, support nerves and muscles), vitamin D (for absorption of calcium, promotes healthy muscles, nerves and parathyroid), vitamin E (antioxidant, good for healthy tissues and wound repair) |
| Minerals | Sodium and potassium (for healthy blood pressure, cell function, smooth muscle function), selenium (for smooth skin, protects blood cells), phosphorus (for healthy bones, teeth, kidneys, nerves and energy levels), iodine (for balanced function of thyroid, healthy arteries), chromium (helps metabolism of sugars and the function of the pancreas), molybdenum (facilitates use of iron and fats), manganese (stabilizes hormones, improves nerve function) |
| Non-foods | Food additives (interfere with natural digestive processes), alcohol (depletes the liver of nutrients, overworks the pancreas), sugar (overworks the pancreas) |

▷ One serving a day of green leafy, raw vegetables is thought to be the minimum for a healthy body.

## GREEN FOODS AND FOODS THAT WORK IN A GREEN WAY

Food that is green, or that works in a green way, tends to be rich in vitamins and minerals, though these can be lost in cooking or storage. Some parts of the world do not support the growing of fresh green foods, so people living in these places have to find

△ Dark, leafy greens are some of the best sources of vitamins and anti-oxidants, that help us to deal with old or dysfunctional cells throughout the body.

▽ Green foods calm our emotions, by providing the nutrients that the body uses to balance all of our energies.

other sources of green nutrients. The Inuit people of northern Canada, for example, live on a diet almost entirely based on fish and fish products, which supply the green energy they need. All minerals act in a green way and all therapeutic herbs, as well as culinary ones, also come under this heading.

Lack of a green vibration creates depression, a feeling of being trapped, breathing difficulties and a lack of self-value. Being in a large space, in the open air, and among natural surroundings is a quick way to bring a green vibration into your life if you feel your green food intake is insufficient.

Eating foods in their natural season, or where possible, foods grown locally, allow the body to settle into the rhythms and patterns of our immediate surroundings.

Many leafy green foods are categorised as bitters by nutritionalists as they stimulate the liver and help to keep the whole of the digestive system in balance.

| Green fruits | Apples, pears, avocados, green grapes, limes, kiwifruit |
| --- | --- |
| Green vegetables | Cabbage, calabrese, broccoli, kale, sprouts, green beans, peas, leeks, spinach |
| Other foods | Most culinary herbs – marjoram, basil, oregano |
| Vitamins/minerals | All vitamins and minerals |

| Blue and violet fruits | Plums, blueberries, black grapes |
|---|---|
| Blue energy vegetables | Kelp and all seaweed products, asparagus |
| Violet vegetables | Purple sprouting broccoli, aubergines |
| Violet energy herbs | St John's wort (acts on the pineal gland) |
| Blue and violet energy vitamins | Vitamin E (stabilizes oxygen in the body, improves pituitary gland function) |
| Blue energy minerals | Iodine (enhances the function of the thyroid gland) |
| Violet energy minerals | Potassium (stabilizes electrolytes in the body, keeps oxygen supplied to the brain) |

# BLUE AND VIOLET FOODS AND FOODS THAT WORK IN A BLUE AND VIOLET WAY

There are very few foods that are blue or violet coloured. However, some foods work in a blue or violet way. Blue foods are useful when the voice, glands and organs of the neck, and communication skills need help. Violet vibration foods have a remarkable effect on the workings of the mind.

## negative violet effects

Food additives and colourings serve to create illusion (a violet function) and relate to the shelf-life or appearance of foods. Some

△ **Good crops of asparagus need special fertilizers, usually seaweed or from a seaweed source, to ensure an adequate supply of iodine.**

▽ **Dark-coloured grapes produce varying shades of red wine. The violet qualities of otherworldliness are encountered when drinking too much.**

▷ **Purple and violet foods bring unusual colouring to dishes or culinary displays.**

additives also have an addictive quality, a trait that also belongs to a violet vibration. Both alcohol and sugar belong in this violet category when they are used in excess to escape from the reality of the world. Alcohol in particular is often the socially acceptable face of addiction and escapism.

Genetically modified foods also reflect a violet vibration because of the false idealism associated with their production. They are being upheld as the solution to world hunger, when in reality, there is already more than enough food to go around, but it is not being shared and distributed appropriately.

## healers and intoxicants

Plants that have a violet resonance have long been used in healing all over the world. When used carefully under experienced supervision they can open the consciousness to other realms of experience. The use of intoxicants is a topic where cultures clash and legal entanglements abound, creating confusion and subversion which are strong violet traits.

In Meso-American traditions, a small cactus plant called peyote (*Lophophora williamsii*) is ritually harvested

and widely used for its mind-expanding effects in religious and healing ceremonies.

Throughout the region of the Amazon basin a vine grows called ayahuasca (*Banesteriopsis caapi*) that is collected from the forest, cut into small sections and boiled for many hours with combinations of other plants. Ayahuasca too, is an intoxicant used in healing and religious ceremonies, though it requires a special preliminary diet to give maximum benefit. Both ayahuasca and peyote are valued as purifiers of the body and are used to remove the causes of infection and illness.

Basil, the common pot-herb, used in Mediterranean cooking, has specific and therapeutic effects when taken in small amounts. Drunk as a tea, it can help relax the body while keeping the mind alert.

▽ **Purple basil belongs to the same family as holy basil, which is used in the Indian subcontinent as a sacred herb of meditation.**

# Colour therapies

Colour has been used as a therapeutic tool for thousands of years. Today many of the traditional uses of colour for healing have changed little. The original practices have created a firm foundation for new ideas and applications of colour in the quest for health and wellbeing.

# Theories of colour healing

Colour has always been associated with certain types of energy that are useful to both the healer and the magician. In the Middle Ages, colour was one of the correspondences used in magic along with planets, elements, spirits and angelic beings, metals, herbs, shapes and numbers. Tibetan and Chinese traditional medicine requires knowledge of the relationship between the colours of the elements and the compass directions to balance health. Yet it was only in the 19th century that science began to verify the healing possibilities of colour.

The German natural philosopher J.W. von Goethe (1749–1832) greatly influenced 19th-century ideas about light and colour. His book *Die Farben Lehre* (*The Theory of Colour*), published in 1810, combined scientific observation with metaphysical concepts, describing colour as an interplay

△ As an artist and scientist, Goethe was an important influence on colour theory.

of the polarities of light and dark. Goethe saw colour as an expression of spirituality and a way of expressing the inner nature of humanity. His thinking influenced artists such as Turner and teachers like Rudolph Steiner, who became influential in forming the colour theories of the 20th century.

During the 19th century there was an increasing interest in the healing properties of light. In 1851 Jacob Lorber wrote *The Healing Power of Sunlight*, which advocated exposing diseased parts of the body to the sun's rays as well as taking sun-charged mineral water and even sun-energized salt and other substances for speedier healing. In 1877 the American physician Dr Seth

▽ As in the 19th century, sunlight is still seen as part of the healing process today, and is often used as a therapeutic tool.

◁ Blue light has been found to significantly reduce the pain of a form of arthritis – the longer the exposure the better the results.

▽ Gradual and consistent exposure to yellow light decreases blood pressure and heart rate and increases energy and endurance.

Pancoast published *Blue and Red Lights*, in which he discussed using coloured filters to alter the body's function. He found that red filtered light would energize the nervous system while blue would sedate it. A year later, in *The Principles of Light and Colour*, another American physician, Dr Edwin Babitt, focused on the healing properties of the three primary colours. He began by creating small cabinets through which he shone filtered sunlight on to his patients. He later developed ways of projecting electric light through filters on to the patient. Babitt also recommended his patients should drink solarized water charged with coloured and filtered light. Many thought him a miracle worker, as he would frequently treat the most stubborn ailments with success.

Dinshah Ghadiali, a scientist who was born in India in 1873, devised a complete system of healing involving colour. He proposed that sound, coloured light, magnetism and heat were all different frequencies of one single energy. He correlated colour and other vibrations directly to specific areas of the body and its functions. In 1939 he published his theories in *The Spectro-Chrome Metry Encyclopedia*. He proposed that just as every chemical substance showed a unique

spectral analysis, which means that each substance absorbs and reflects different frequencies of light energy, so the body would absorb and reflect colours depending on its state of health. Ghadiali also devised a machine that projected colour.

At the beginning of the 20th century in the USA, optometrist Dr Harry R. Spitter developed a colour healing system he called syntonics. He founded the College of Syntonic Optometry in 1933, where he

▽ Transparent coloured filters are an important tool in colour therapy that can be used to carry specific energies.

taught that light shone through precise combinations of 31 colour filters directly into the eyes could have profound healing effects on many aspects of the glandular and nervous systems, as well as significantly improving vision. Spitter's work was continued and developed after his death by Jacob Liberman, who uses a system of 20 coloured filters in holistic healing.

The use of colour and light as healing tools faded into the background as the use of new drugs became more widespread. Pharmaceutical drugs became available to treat conditions where sunlight and fresh air had been recommended. As more drugs arrived, the knowledge of utilizing light, colour and other natural resources to heal was no longer used. Recently, the popularity of colour and light as healing tools has increased, particularly as the limits of pharmacology and the complex difficulties of certain diseases are being recognized.

# Colour essences

Many of the pioneers of colour healing found that their patients benefited from drinking water charged with natural sunlight or specific wavelengths of colour. Some theorized that the atomic structure of the water was somehow altered and given particular life-enhancing properties. These theories hold renewed interest for scientists today. Medical researchers are currently investigating techniques to target specific light frequencies on diseased tissue to restore normal functioning to the cells.

Colour essences are regaining popularity as vibrational healers. They contain nothing other than water that has been subtly energized and altered by the action of natural sunlight through a coloured filter.

△ The purity of single coloured light that is shown in a rainbow is what makes colour essences such a powerful healing tool.

▽ Medieval doctors would often use the early morning dew gathered from flowers, knowing that it possessed unique balancing properties.

They are easy to make and, like all vibrational remedies, have the advantage of being self-regulating. This means that the body will only make use of the energy within the essence if it is appropriate. Vibrational healing seems to work by reminding the body of its natural state of balance, which it needs to return to after some stress or shock.

Although simple to make, colour essences can be effective tools for healing. Rapid release of stress can sometimes feel uncomfortable. If this is experienced, simply reduce or stop using the essence for a day or two. Taking essences last thing at night and immediately on waking is a good way to bring a person back to a state of balance.

▷ Water can be charged with a colour using sunlight. Take a glass of water and surround it with a coloured gel and cut a disc from another piece to cover the top. Make sure the glass is surrounded then leave it in direct sunlight for two hours.

## TO MAKE A VIBRATIONAL ESSENCE

You will need:
* Clean drinking water, spring water or mineral water is best
* A plain glass container
* Colour gels from theatrical lighting suppliers or other coloured filters
* Brown glass storage bottles
* Labels
* A preservative, such as alcohol, cider vinegar or vegetable glycerine

### method

**1** Pour the water into the glass vessel. Stand it on a colour filter of your choice and cover it with another filter in the same colour. (Colour gels can be made into cones or laid across the top of the vessel.) Leave the vessel in bright natural sunlight for at least two hours.

**2** If you are going to keep the essence for future use it will need to be bottled – preferably in brown (neutral amber) glass to reduce exposure to light.

**3** It is a good idea to add a preservative to your essence to keep it stable unless you are going to use it immediately. A 50/50 mix of energized water and alcohol such as brandy or vodka will

keep for many months. Cider vinegar, honey or vegetable glycerine can also be used as preservatives if you can't use alcohol.

### uses

* A little can be drunk each day in water. If kept in a dropper bottle, the essence can be taken as and when you need it, either directly dropped into the mouth or mixed with a little water.
* Drops can be placed straight on to pulse points at the wrists, side of the neck or on the forehead.
* Add colour essence to a diffuser sprayer filled with water. Spray around the room or around the body for immediate effect.
* Rub a drop or two on to the area needing help, or the related chakra point.
* A drop or two can be added to bath water or massage oil.
* A few drops can be added to water in an oil burner, with or without the additions of essential oils.

△ Taking a few drops of a colour essence three or four times a day can quickly restore balanced energy.

▽ Rubbing a drop of essence into an area of imbalance can speed up the healing process.

▽ Using a diffuser spray with water and a couple of drops of essence can quickly bring a colour vibration to a whole space.

# Plants and colour

All over the world plants have been used to help keep the body healthy and to fight disease. Today, herbalism is still the most practical source of healthcare for a majority of the planet's population. Many of the herbs that are in common use indicate by their colour, shape, habit and popular associations how they can be used in healing. The name given to this information is the Doctrine of Signatures, and it has been used as a guide to healers for centuries.

## HEALING FLOWERS

Two types of yellow flowers are particularly powerful healing plants. Yellow helps release tension, boosting optimism and relaxation.

St John's wort (*Hypericum perforatum*) is a roadside plant that in midsummer produces a head of bright yellow flowers. This suggests that it acts on the upper abdomen and, through its complementary colour violet, on the brain. In recent years St John's wort has been used as a treatment for depression and for lightening heavy moods. When extracted, the essential oil of the plant is a rich deep red, which can be helpful in boosting energy and the immune system.

The familiar dandelion (*Taraxacum officinale*) is another yellow flower with a wealth of healing properties. Its leaves and root are two of the best known liver tonics and diuretics. Leaves can be eaten in salads and the roasted root makes a coffee substitute. Dandelion flower essence and oil are wonderfully effective muscle relaxants that also help release rigid mental belief systems. The way the seed heads disperse at the slightest breeze is seen as a signature for the quality of letting go.

△ The sunflower is sacred to the sun in its native Mexico, and its seeds have been used to treat cold, damp illnesses such as coughs and colds.

▷ Flower essences are a simple way to use plants' energetic and vibrational properties.

## flower essences

Paracelsus, the 16th-century Swiss physician and occultist, is believed to have used the dew of flowers for his healing practice and there is some evidence that flower waters were also an integral part of Tibetan medical practices.

Early in the 20th century the gifted homeopath Dr Edward Bach made his own important discoveries about the healing properties of flower essences. He energized

▷ Essential oils are made from the concentrated extracts of plants. They can often be linked to colour energies and used alongside other colour healing techniques.

water with sunlight and flowers or other plant parts to create a set of 38 remedies. They were designed to rebalance the emotional disharmony that Bach saw as underlying all diseases. Dr Bach was often drawn to choose his remedies by the colour as well as other qualities of the plant. Flower essences are now made all around the world to help people bring balance into their lives, and colour plays an important part in explaining how they work.

## energizing flowers

Red flowers often boost energy levels, for example, scarlet pimpernel (*Anagallis arvensis*) is a bright red, ground hugging plant whose flowers open only in sunshine. It used to be a popular remedy for heavy moods and depression, but today the flower essence of scarlet pimpernel is more often employed to energize and clear deep-seated blocks. The elm tree has tiny deep red and purple flowers, and their flower essence helps to clear the body and mind when

▽ Red coloured plants and flowers often have rich, heady perfumes that can be sensual, energizing and grounding.

fatigue and confusion have set in. Here the red stimulates the energy reserves and the purple balances the mind.

## calming flowers

Blue flowers will often bring a sense of peace and help with communication and expression. Forget-me-not (*Myosotis arvensis*) can aid memory and help those who feel isolated and cut off from deeper levels of experience. Sage (*Salvia officinalis*) has violet-blue flowers that suggest it will be effective in the areas of the head and throat, and the leaves make an antiseptic gargle. The essential oil used very sparingly can help with certain types of headache. The flower essence helps to give a broader outlook on life and balances the mind.

# Double colour healing

Single colours are very effective healing and assessment tools. However, if two colours are used in combination, both the healing and the assessment capacities increase. In the last 30 years three systems have developed that make use of the double-colour technique for healing – AuraSoma, AuraLight and AvaTara. All consist of coloured oil floating on top of a different coloured water in clear bottles. Cards can also be used as double-colour healing and assessment tools. They may have windows of theatrical spotlight gels or stained glass, or be simply printed with blocks of colour.

With all colour combinations, the top colour represents the conscious, the present and the most apparent energies. The lower colour represents the underlying factors, the past or roots of the situation and associated unconscious issues.

## how to use a double-colour system

As with single colour selection, just pick the combination that appeals to you most. Your choice will reflect your current situation. Each of the colours is then interpreted through its correspondences. Try also selecting the combination you like the least, as this will reflect areas that may need a different kind of attention.

Sometimes several combinations may be chosen. The first choice can represent the roots of the present situation, the second choice can indicate the difficulties encountered, and the third choice can show the primary healing requirements.

▽ **Colour rarely appears isolated in nature. Combinations of colour build up complex and specific effects, affecting moods and thoughts.**

△ **Bottles of dual-coloured liquid capture the attention easily, regardless of any understanding of colour healing.**

## examples of double-colour selection

### Choice 1 – yellow over red – the roots of the situation

• Physically this could indicate the possibility of tension or digestive difficulties (yellow) with a need for activity or initiative (red).
• Emotionally this may show that fear or anxiety (yellow) is being fed by anger or passion (red).
• Mentally, there is a need for clear, logical choices (yellow) to begin new projects (red).
• Spiritually there may be a need to get to know yourself better (yellow) in order to become more secure and grounded in the world (red).

### choice 2 – green over blue – the difficulties encountered

• Physically there may be breathing problems (green), and some communication difficulties (blue).
• Emotionally, there might be a feeling of being confined (green) by ideas and beliefs (blue).

• Mentally, there is a definite need for space (green) to find peace (blue).
• Spiritually, there is a desire to go your own way (green) in a natural flow (blue).

### choice 3 – violet over turquoise – primary healing requirements
• Physically, there is a need to be in quiet and harmonious surroundings (violet) so

that you can settle down and just be yourself (turquoise).
• Emotionally, consider cutting away illusion and delusion (violet) to find where the truth is for you (turquoise).
• Mentally, you need to gain inspiration (violet) from your own resources (turquoise).
• Spiritually, there is a need to heal yourself in order to feel at one with life (violet) and be able to express yourself freely (turquoise).

## how double colours can heal
In a healing situation, once the choices have been made and discussed, issues often rise to the surface. Colour has a habit of bringing to the attention facets of life that have remained hidden. This gives an opportunity for healing. One way to bring healing is to have contact with the chosen combinations for a few minutes. If bottles are being used, they can be held or placed around the body.

◁ **Your choices can be held up to the light or close to the body, for the healing effect of colour to be absorbed.**

△ **Selection from a range of double-colours elicits deep levels of information about a person's needs and direction in life. The choice of bottle will be made on an intuitive level.**

The oil and water constituents of the bottles can also be massaged into the hands, feet or other appropriate places. If the combination is a light gel, it can be projected on to the body, or on to a wall to be looked at. The constituents of the combinations can also be introduced through diet, lifestyle or through your surroundings.

In the third example given here, the primary requirements were shown to be violet over turquoise. This could suggest spending quiet periods alone, and also introducing violet and turquoise items temporarily into the living space. Wearing two of the appropriate colours can be an immediate way to bring those energies into your life. This could be through single coloured separates or by wearing ties or scarves of the colours. Even such simple changes can have profound effects.

# Colour and shape

Philosophers and mystics have always been interested in exploring the origins of creation. Eastern and Western thinkers have traditionally used light and colour combined with geometric shapes to help define the forces of the universe in symbolic terms.

## sacred shapes

The science of geometry is the basic patterning of all matter in creation. In Classical Greece the philosopher Plato devised a system of representing the elements with coloured geometric forms, in an attempt to explain the building blocks of all existence, including spiritual realities. Platonic Solids define how to form physical matter, because they represent the only way atoms can pack together. Like the elements and colours,

energy interacts to form physical matter. The Platonic Solids, therefore, encapsulate our understanding of the universe.

At around the same time that Plato was working, Indian philosophers were also choosing different shapes and colours to represent the elements. They called the elements and their symbols tattvas, literally: those things that possess distinction.

Shape holds and defines colour, giving it solidity and presence, while colour imparts different qualities to shape. A viewer reacts differently to a blue triangle and a red triangle. A yellow circle feels different to a yellow square. The human brain's response to various stimuli has allowed the non-verbal language of symbolism to develop in every culture.

▽ A set of Platonic Solids cut out of clear quartz: (left to right) cube of Earth; octahedron of Air; tetrahedron of Fire; dodecahedron of Ether; and icosahedron of Water.

△ Shape as well as colour contains specific energies. These are harnessed especially in religious buildings to enhance the spiritual qualities of the surroundings.

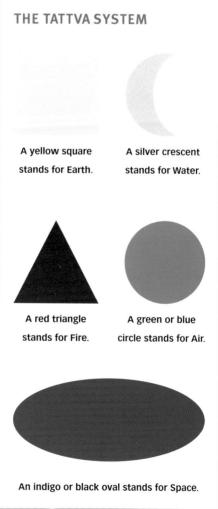

## THE TATTVA SYSTEM

A yellow square stands for Earth.

A silver crescent stands for Water.

A red triangle stands for Fire.

A green or blue circle stands for Air.

An indigo or black oval stands for Space.

Colour therapists such as Theo Gimbel and Howard and Dorothy Sun have introduced shape into their colour healing work. Theo Gimbel shines coloured light through shaped apertures on to the body to help restore balance to its subtle energy systems. The Suns assess their patients' wellbeing after asking them to choose from a range of coloured shapes based on the Platonic solids. This gives an accurate profile of both personality and situation. Similar assessment techniques are continuing to be developed as it becomes more widely understood that our instinctive choices of colour and shape can accurately indicate underlying factors in our lives.

Mary Hykel Hunt, a Welsh psychologist and colour worker, is in a unique position

## WHAT'S IN A NAME?

Ask a friend, colleague or family member if you can look at their name for colours and shapes. Sit quietly, thinking about the name, and intuit what colours and shapes seem to be present in it.

Let us imagine that the name you're thinking about is Kathy. You might feel that the name is made up of a three-dimensional blue rectangle (or double cube) followed by a red circle, a brown cube and a yellow crescent.

The three-dimensional rectangle or double cube represents Earth, coloured with the blue of communication. It suggests someone with practical communication skills. The cube again represents Earth, this time coloured brown for practicality and focus. This shows creative and nurturing skills put to practical use.

The circle represents Air, coloured red for activity. This activates or energizes communication.

The crescent represents Water, coloured yellow to show thought processes, anxiety and joy. This hints at the emotions that lie behind the practical activity, and suggests that there may be some problems with self-criticism.

△ **The forms of classical Indian architecture are precisely proportioned to reflect the elemental shapes of the tattvas, such as the crescent, square, cone and sphere.**

to explore the relationship between shape, colour and personality. From birth she has been synaesthetic, that is, her senses of sight and sound are combined so that she experiences colour and shape with each sound she hears. This has enabled Hykel Hunt to train others to explore the innate ability we all have of translating one sense into another. Hykel Hunt's workshops provide people with a whole series of symbols, similar to the tattvas, with which to intuitively explore the energy make-up of the world around them.

People's names provide a rich source of intuitive exploration. Hykel Hunt teaches how to intuit coloured shapes from the sound of someone's name and then to use those colours and shapes to discover the

skills and gifts of that person. The more you try to link colour, shape and sound, the more successful and confident you will become. Try the name visualization exercise in a group of people, and you will find remarkably similar results.

This suggests that people can successfully tap into their innate skills with a little practice and encouragement. It also backs up the findings of the Indian and Greek philosophers, who saw correlations and correspondences between colour, shape and human experience.

# Colour visualization

In Tibetan meditation practices, different aspects of energy are visualized as spheres of coloured light. Visual imagery of many sorts is a major part of Tibetan spiritual techniques, along with the use of breath control, sound and posture.

Complex visualizations take practice to achieve, but the focus required is itself of benefit, by taking the mind away from everyday concerns. In all visualization exercises it is important to remember that cinema-like clarity and detail are not necessary to achieve success. Simply reading through an exercise begins to create the right emotional picture.

## energy sphere visualization

The following exercise is designed to integrate the inner and outer worlds by bringing the colours of the directions into the heart. This leads to a balance of harmony

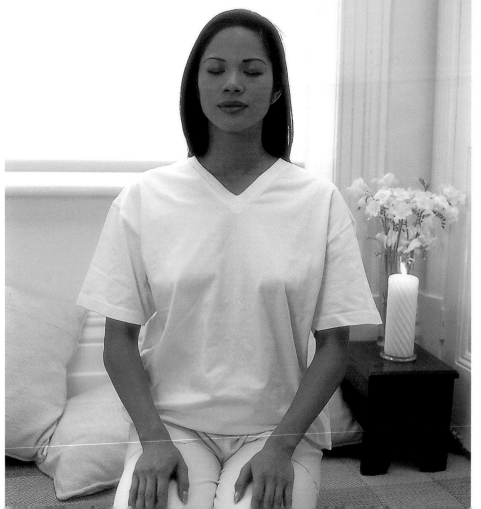

△ **Visualization is the natural function of the human mind to think in pictures.**

with one's surroundings and restores equilibrium in the body, mind and emotions.

**1** Sit in a comfortable position, facing the east. Imagine a deep blue lotus with four petals resting at its centre.

**2** In the heart of the flower is a luminous clear sphere of light, like crystal. It reflects the blue of the petals and represents the element of space (ether).

**3** Before the lotus is a yellow sphere, representing the east, the earth element.

**4** To your left, the north, is a green sphere, the air element.

**5** Behind you is a red sphere of the west, the fire element.

**6** To the right of you is a blue sphere of the south, the water element.

◁ **Visualizing specific colours around you, in the compass directions, then visualizing blue and white flowing through you, is exceptionally relaxing and healing.**

## rainbow breathing

This is a simple but effective way of bringing colour energies into your body to restore balance when there has been stress, or to identify which colour energies you are most in need of absorbing.

**1** Take a minute to relax and calm your mind with your eyes closed.

**2** Imagine the air around you is a rich, deep red. As you breathe in, your whole body fills with red energy. Continue breathing in the red light until you feel you have sufficient, then breathe out the red light through your feet or your spine, into the earth.

**3** Next, imagine the air becomes a vibrant, warm orange colour. Breathe in the orange energy in the same way. When you have

△ **The visualization of pink light has a calming, integrating and healing effect on yourself and your surroundings.**

△▽ **Imagining an object of the same colour as the one you are visualizing will help to create a clearer image. Look at a bright coloured flower and imagine yourself breathing in the colour.**

completed the process and breathed it out to the earth, continue with the other colours of the spectrum: yellow, green, blue, indigo and violet.

If you have need for a particular colour energy, concentrate on that visualization and take notice of how it seems to move around the body. Make sure the light goes to every part of your body by paying attention to areas that are difficult to visualize.

## protecting the heart of all things

This is a visualization exercise that is extremely valuable when we face difficult circumstances in our lives. It helps to remove fear, which is the cause of all other negative reactions, both from ourselves and from the people around us. Doing this exercise can also help to reduce anger, aggression, irritation and misunderstanding.

**1** Right at the centre of your heart chakra, in the middle of your chest, imagine a spark of bright pink light.

**2** Keep your imagination on that spark of

light strong and gradually see it radiating out through the body in a strong pink glow.

**3** The spark of pink energy is like a sun in your heart and its light completely fills your body and then continues to expand outwards in a pink halo of light surrounding everything around you.

**4** As it touches others, the pink star at their own heart sparks into life, so that the pink energy gets stronger the more people around you it contacts.

**5** At the end of the visualization, allow your attention to return to the pink star at your heart, as the surrounding colour fades gently away.

If when you begin the visualization, you see a different colour, allow that to be your focus. It may be more appropriate to the energy of the situation you find yourself in, even if you feel the colours you see to be negative or hostile.

# Colour in meditation

Colour is a very powerful tool in all meditation exercises because it has a profound effect on the nervous system, no matter what else may be happening on the surface levels of the mind. Here are two meditation exercises that use colour in different ways. When you use them make sure you are sitting or lying in a comfortable position, with no risk of disturbance or distraction.

## absorbing the lights of perfection

One of the main practices in Tibetan Buddhism is to visualize a teacher or enlightened being, such as a buddha, and absorb their enlightened qualities into one's own body in the form of coloured light. The nature or form of the visualized being is not as important as the confidence and faith of the meditator. The being represents all those who have taught us, looked after us, and wished us well in our lives.

The following exercise is calming and clarifying and helps to bring the energy of the mind into its natural state of relaxed quietness. It helps to establish a continual connection to your true nature.
1. Sit quietly for a minute or two. Consider all the teachers and spiritual beings who have inspired you with the qualities of clarity, compassion and truth. Visualize their presence in front of you as a glorious bright

▽ **Feel the coloured lights at brow, throat and heart dissolving all negativity and bringing clarity and peace.**

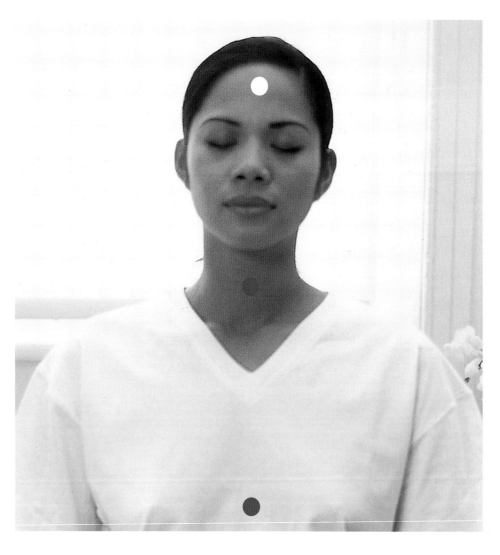

light suffused with translucent rainbow colours. Within the light is a figure representing all the wisdom of the universe.
2. From the forehead of the figure, a clear white beam enters your forehead and fills your body with light, cleansing all heaviness and negativity from your body.
3. Next, from the throat of the figure of light emerges a ray of ruby red, which enters your own throat. From there, it fills your body and cleanses negativity from your senses.
4. Now from the heart of the figure of light flows a ray of shimmering deep blue, entering your own heart and pervading your whole body, clearing away negativity from your mind.
5. As you have shared the purifying colour vibrations from the being of light, you have merged together so that now there is no distinction, no difference between your energy and the clear compassionate light of the universe.

## a tattva meditation

Using the tattvic shapes, the traditional Hindu symbols of the elements, can be an effective way to balance personal energies. Many variations are possible but the aim is to absorb the quality of each element and integrate it into the body.

For this meditation you need to focus on each tattva in turn or concentrate on those you feel need more balance. As you visualize the shape within your body, feel your inbreath entering the symbol, charging it with energy. As you breath out imagine it removing imbalance from that area.

Alternatively, you can place a representation of a particular tattva in front of you on a white wall. As you breathe naturally, imagine that you are breathing in the energy of the element represented by the colour and shape.

The yellow square of Earth sits with its base upon the base of the spine. It can be used when energy is low and there is a lack of motivation.

△ Gazing at an elemental tattva shape lets you understand the quality of energy of shape and colour and will balance the element in your body.

▷ Working with coloured shapes on card can be an intuitive way of selecting and balancing your needs at the moment.

The silver-white crescent of the Water element sits between the navel and the pubic bone within the top of the pelvis. Use it when there is indecision, excess of emotion or a feeling of heaviness.

The red triangle of Fire sits pointing downwards from the base of the ribcage towards the navel. It is useful to calm anger, irritation and exhaustion.

The blue circle of Air is in the centre of the chest. It will help focus concentration, reducing agitation and scattered thoughts.

The midnight blue or black egg of Ether or Space sits within the throat. It can soothe feelings of emptiness and uselessness.

# The chakra system

'In the body there are many kinds of channels, which are very extensive. The sage must understand them in order to understand his own body… Running transversely, up and down, they exist in the body joined together like a wheel, dependent on the life-force and linked to the breath of the body.'

*From the Shiva-Svarodaya Tantra, traditional Indian teaching on the subtle anatomy of the body.*

# What are chakras?

Over the last five thousand years, sages, philosophers and mystics have described the subtle energies in our environment and within our bodies in many different ways. Several systems have developed to explain them in the context of other philosophical backgrounds. However, it was generally agreed that wherever dynamic energies meet together in nature they form spinning circular patterns, or vortices. On a small scale this can be seen in tiny spiral eddies on the surfaces of streams and rivers; on a large scale in the movements of cloud systems that create cyclones and anticyclones.

The seers of ancient India perceived similar vortices within the energy of the human body. They described these in the Vedas, the primary source of all Hindu cosmology and philosophy, codified around 3000 BC. According to the Vedic seers, wherever two or more channels of subtle energy meet, there is a vortex, which they named 'chakra', meaning 'wheel'. Because these energy concentrations appeared to them to be funnel-shaped, multi-coloured and related to spiritual qualities, they became associated with the sacred lotus.

Where major energy flows coincide – on the midline of the body in the front of the spinal column – the seers of India saw seven main chakras that seemed to mirror both health and the spiritual state. These seven

△ **Wherever different streams of energy converge, a spiralling dynamic funnel, or vortex, is created, as in this cloud formation.**

chakras were like multi-dimensional gateways that would allow the individual to access different experiences and states of consciousness. The use of visualization, sound, chant, meditation and exercise to activate, cleanse and integrate these seven chakras became an important part of spiritual practice, especially in the Himalayan regions of India, Nepal and Tibet. Under guidance from an experienced teacher, each student was taught the appropriate methods to activate and integrate every part of the chakra system in a safe and balanced way.

Though everyone is likely to experience problems and energy stresses in different parts of the body and mind, our individual strengths and weaknesses are unique to us. In the same way, each chakra deals with particular areas of function, but the quality of the energy will vary from person to person. The skill of the teacher is to identify how to clear the energy pathways as the blocks reveal themselves.

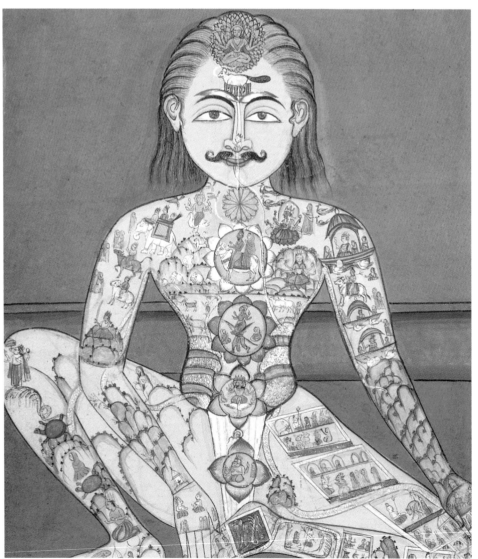

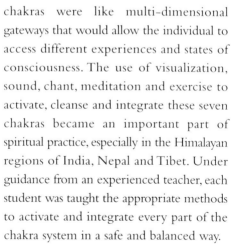

◁ **A depiction of the body's chakras and energy channels from an 18th-century Hindu manuscript.**

△ The spirals of nature mirror the vortices in the human body, which are formed when two or more channels of energy meet.

▽ The Vedic seers could perceive the structure of the cosmos and had startling knowledge of its true nature. In the same way, they were able to understand how cosmic energies manifested themselves within the human body.

## chakras today

Many of the original Vedic texts discuss the development of psychic skill and supernatural power that arises from spiritual exercises. This connection with the spirit world attracted the attention of 19th-century Western thinkers, many of whom had become interested in oriental mysticism. As movements such as Spiritualism and

Theosophy developed, the Vedas were translated into Western languages. These translations emphasized the development of the higher chakras, and the desire to go beyond or escape from, the bonds of the physical world. This bias echoed the trends of theosophical thinking, and usefully avoided what were viewed as embarrassing sexual techniques involving the three lower chakras. This false division into lower (or mundane) and higher (or spiritual) chakras misses the point that is continually reiterated in the original texts: that all chakras are of equal practical value.

Today our way of understanding the chakras is different again. Since the 1970s the seven chakras have been seen as fitting in with the other sets of sacred sevens, and have become particularly associated with the seven rainbow colours, with each chakra having its own colour. Although this is a modern departure it works very well, combining as it does an easy-to-remember colour code with the qualities and functions of each chakra. It is important to remember, however, that whichever system is used, classical or modern, it is really no more than a partial description of a complex set of energy interactions that make up the human mind, body and spirit.

# Chakra imagery

Whatever their correlation to physical structures within the body, chakras are entirely non-physical. The mind, rather than the sense organs, is the traditional tool for accessing, exploring and balancing the energy of each chakra. The main features of each chakra are described here as in the original Vedic texts, as they would be visualized by a meditator. Each chakra is symbolized by layers of imagery, including a particular animal, and a god and a goddess whose form and attributes encapsulate the inherent qualities that arise when the chakra is functioning in a balanced way.

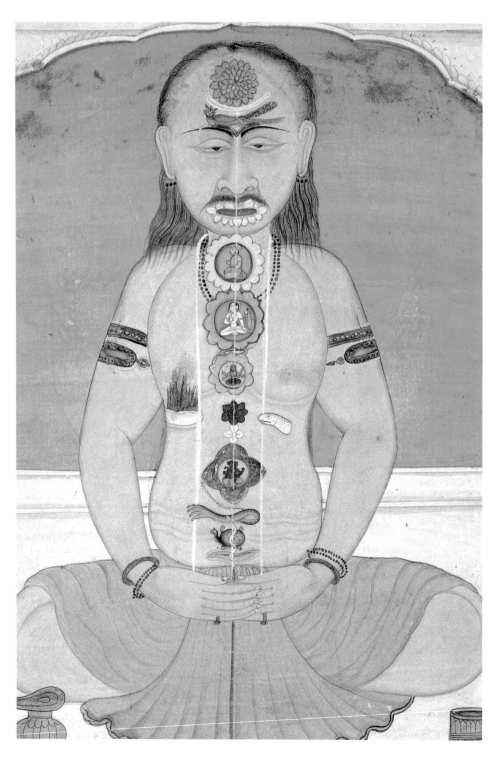

◁ **An Indian depiction of the chakras, each with their god or goddess depicted within.**

## muladhara

This is the base chakra and its name means 'foundation'. It has four vermillion petals around a yellow square. The yellow square represents the element of Earth and the petals represent the four directions: north, south, east and west. The animal form representing the base chakra is a seven-trunked elephant, associated with solidity and assuredness. The elephant's trunks represent the sacred sevens, the chakras, planets, colours, notes and behavioural aspects which each of us must work with in the world. On the elephant's back rests the bija, or seed, mantra – the sound that stimulates the energy of this chakra – Lam. The god and goddess images show attributes of fearlessness and stillness.

## svadistana

The sacral chakra, whose name means 'sweetness', has six red petals. It represents the Water element. The sacral chakra's animal is a crocodile, which represents its sensuous, watery and deceptively strong energy. On the crocodile rests the bija mantra Vam. The images of the god and goddess display peaceful emotions.

## manipura

The solar plexus chakra's name means 'city of gems'. Ten luminous blue petals surround a downward-pointing red triangle, symbol of the Fire element. The animal is a ram: headstrong and direct, his fiery nature controls the group of which he is the leader. The deities represent control over anger and control of energy. The bija mantra is Ram.

## anahata

The name of the fourth, or heart, chakra means 'unstruck'. Twelve deep red lotus petals surround a hexagram or six-pointed star of grey-green, representing the element

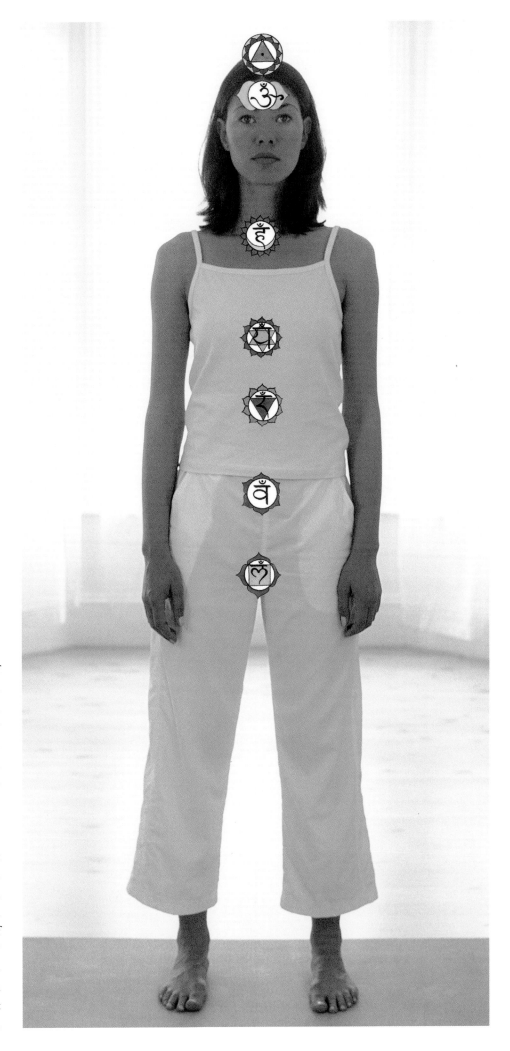

▷ The chakras are usually mapped in a vertical line running up the spinal column, corresponding to the physical structures to which they relate.

of Air. The animal is a black antelope, leaping with joy. It shows the sensitive, aware and curious nature of the heart chakra. On the back of the antelope rests the bija mantra Yam. The sound here controls breath and life-energy. The deities represent the arts and harmony in both inner and outer worlds.

## vishuddha

This is the throat chakra, and its name means 'pure'. It has a circle of 16 lavender or smoky purple petals enclosing a silver crescent and the white circle of the full moon. This represents the ether or space, where all the elements dissolve into their refined essence, akasha, the pure cosmic sound. The animal is an elephant, the colour of clouds. His single trunk represents sound and he carries the memory of all past knowledge. He carries the bija mantra Ham, which empowers his voice. The deities represent the union of the elements, dreams of inspiration and higher knowledge.

## ajña

The brow chakra's name means 'command'. It has two petals of luminescent pearly blue. Within a white column (the 'colour of light') is a representation of unified consciousness – a combined male and female deity. There is no animal here for the bija mantra, Aum, to rest on, so it rests on the finest quality of sound itself, known as nada. The goddess of this chakra embodies unconditional truth.

## sahasrara

The 'thousand-petalled' crown chakra is at the top of the head. It is sometimes described as formless, sometimes as a moonlike sphere above which is an umbrella of a thousand petals with all the colours of the rainbow. The bija mantra is the 'nng' sound, known as Visarga. This is the breath-like sound that ends all previous bija mantras. It rests upon the bindu, the first moment of creation in the relative universe.

# Physical correspondences

Because they cannot be seen by normal means, the chakras and the nadis – their related system of subtle channels – are represented by diagrams and other symbolic maps of the body. This is necessary to clarify the relationship between the subtle centres and the physical organs and structures with which we are familiar. However, mapping the chakras in this way can lead to a very static, inflexible and two-dimensional view of what is an elegant, dynamic and ever-changing interaction of energies.

Being non-physical, influencing matter but not consisting of matter, chakras are not bound by the laws of matter. In classical texts the chakras and nadis are considered to be expressions of consciousness. Time and

△ Chakras provide the underlying orderliness of our being. Those with clairvoyant sight see them at every level, from physical to most subtle.

▽ A diagrammatic view of the chakras helps to identify their physical correspondences, though it does not reflect their interactive nature.

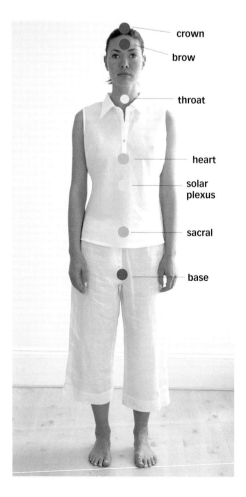

crown
brow
throat
heart
solar plexus
sacral
base

space, three-dimensional existence and scale have little relevance, except as a way to understand the chakras in familiar terms.

Around each chakra, echoing its function, are one of the main endocrine glands, a concentration of nerves known as a plexus, and concentrations of blood vessels and lymph nodes. There is some difference of opinion as to which physical system is related to which chakra, but most healers follow the correspondences described below.

## the base chakra

Located at the base of the spine, the base chakra is sometimes represented as a vortex with a downward opening. In some systems it is related to the testicles or ovaries, in others to the adrenal glands. Although physically a long way from the base, the adrenal glands reflect the survival instinct of this chakra. The concentration of nerves in this area is called the coccygeal plexus.

## the sacral chakra

The second chakra, sometimes called the sex chakra, is located in the lower abdomen, between the navel and the pubic bone. It is related to the sacral vertebrae in the spine, the sacral plexus of nerves and the sex glands – the ovaries and testicles. This chakra is associated with emotions and sensuality.

## the solar plexus chakra

The third chakra is located on the front of the body between the bottom of the ribcage (diaphragm) and the navel. It is concerned with personal energy and power and is associated with the adrenal glands and the pancreas. The solar plexus chakra is named after the complex of nerves found here and is connected to the lumbar vertebrae.

## THE LIMBIC SYSTEM

Deep in the centre of the brain lies a complex series of organs known as the limbic system. Within it, the pineal and pituitary glands control all the hormone systems of the body – in the same way that the crown chakra regulates the chakra system. Modern Vedic seers have linked each part of the limbic system with the functions and energies of the planetary influences in our lives: microcosm and macrocosm can exist at the level of neuroscience, as can the concept of the non-physical chakras.

▽ **The pineal (left) and pituitary, or master, gland (right) are very small organs that control the body's hormone-releasing systems.**

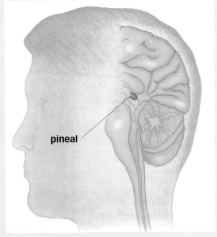

pineal

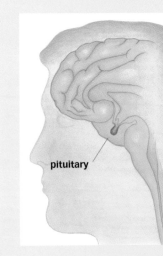

pituitary

unseen, subtle forces, or spiritual powers, that control the existence of physical matter.

Like seed crystals dropped into a saturated solution, concentrations of dynamic orderliness, or points of consciousness, act as a template for the accretion of physical matter and the development of the systems of the human body. The chakras can be understood as working in the same way as planetary bodies in a solar system. Each, by its placement and qualities, attracts free floating matter and maintains it in its orbit.

Seen as concentrations of consciousness or crystallized mind, the physical systems of the body cannot be separated from the subtler structures. The body, mind and emotions are all extensions of chakra function. Changes at one level will bring automatic changes at every other level. Dysfunction at the physical level is echoed in the function of the chakras, and stress in the chakras can be felt as discomfort at the level of mind, body or emotion.

## the heart chakra

The fourth chakra is the heart, located in the centre of the chest, associated with the thoracic vertebrae of the spine. The related gland is the thymus, a small gland above the heart vital for growth and the maintenance of the immune system. Two nerve centres are found here – the pulmonary plexus and the cardiac plexus. This chakra deals with love and relationships.

## the throat chakra

The fifth, or throat, chakra is located near the cervical vertebrae and the base of the throat. It manifests communications and creativity. The thyroid and parathyroid glands (which control the body's metabolic rate and mineral levels) and the pharyngeal plexus are found here.

## the brow chakra

The sixth chakra is the brow, located in the centre of the forehead. This is linked to the pineal gland that maintains cycles of activity and rest, and to the carotid plexus of nerves. The brow chakra directs intuition, insight and imagination.

## the crown chakra

The seventh chakra, the crown, is located just above the top of the head and influences all the higher brain functions. It is connected to the pituitary, the gland that controls the whole endocrine (hormone) system. The entire cerebral cortex is influenced by this centre. The crown is associated with knowledge and understanding.

## subtle forces

The modern study of embryology has yet to uncover the mechanisms by which original cells, which are identical and undifferentiated, migrate to certain places in the embryo and begin to form specialized organs. In complementary medicine and the holistic philosophies of non-Western cultures, it is the

▷ **The endocrine glands maintain hormone balance in the body. Energy levels, emotional states and reactions to external and internal conditions are under their direct control. They can be seen as representatives of the chakras at a physical level.**

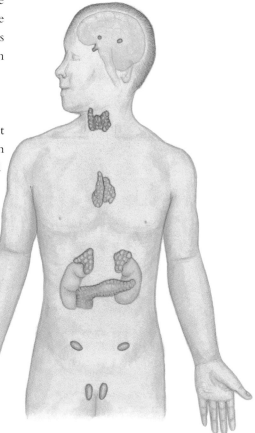

# Cycles of nature

In the original Indian texts the chakras are related to a series of milestones in life. Each chakra and its function represent a stage of development and growth. Each stage can be seen as a time in which certain skills are developed. The precise shift from one stage of development to another will vary from individual to individual. The stages may overlap, but in some cases, where stress or trauma disrupts the chakra energy, this may create an underlying problem for subsequent growth. If one function remains underdeveloped, all the others dependent on it will have a built-in dysfunction.

## conception and birth

The base chakra relates to the creation of the physical body, so it represents a stage of growth that begins at conception and continues until around the age of one year. The immediate, powerful energy of the base chakra is evident in the speed of growth and the primary need to survive. An infant during this time is dependent on others for its food, warmth and shelter. This period helps to anchor the individual into the physical world.

## the developing baby

The sacral chakra begins to activate consciously at about six months and its effects last to around the age of two years. The feedback in this time comes from pleasure and gratification. The distinction between the child and the mother begins to become more apparent. Being given space to explore existence without negative reinforcement or verbal reprimand helps to build confidence in being a separate individual.

▽ **All chakras are present in the growing child but during natural development energy focuses at certain centres.**

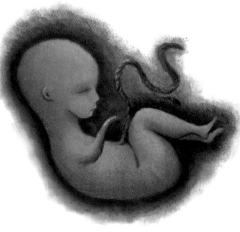

◁ **From the moment of conception, consciousness coalesces around the energy of the chakras. The primary needs of survival and nutrition are the first focuses of each new life.**

◁ Play exercises all the chakras, no matter what the age: it fosters a sense of security, energy, a desire to explore, confidence, ability to relate to the world, self-expression and imagination.

## the small child

The onset of the activity of the solar plexus chakra is commonly referred to as the 'terrible twos'. It starts at around 18 months and lasts until the child is about four years old. This is when language develops, together with an understanding of the passing of time. Maintaining the balance between freedom and discipline is crucial at this age. Lack of restraining discipline creates an overpowering, egotistic child, whereas too much control will stop any sense of autonomy developing.

## the child

The heart chakra covers the period from four to seven years and is characterized by relationships outside the immediate family. Relating helps to build self-esteem and self-acceptance. If love and relationships are always seen as being conditional – that is,

▽ Shared, cooperative creativity flourishes when the sacral and throat chakras have developed in a balanced way. Problems can arise if other chakras do not work in harmony.

having an emotional price-tag attached – the underlying feelings of guilt and grief caused by not receiving enough love can create great difficulties through life.

## the pre-pubescent

The development of the throat chakra between the ages of seven and 12 marks the beginning of the stage of self-expression. If the lower chakra energies have been integrated to a reasonable extent, confidence can be gained from a firm emotional base. Through the throat chakra, this is given back to the community and family, sometimes in plays and perfomances.

## the adolescent

The brow chakra covers the adolescent years, when the young person should be encouraged to reflect on the patterns in their own and others' lives. This is the first of several key stages when it is possible to re-invent and readjust the role that an individual sees themselves playing in the world.

## the adult

The crown chakra becomes active between 20 and 27 years, as the individual fully reacts and interacts with the world. Sometimes this stage stays dormant, because it relates to questions like 'Why am I here?' and statements like 'There must be more to life than this.' These issues may never be looked at. On the other hand, the action of exploring them may be the beginning of a radical change of life and work. Having gone through a whole cycle, the

process begins again with the base chakra. Just as, in musical scales, each octave returns to the start note, the chakra cycle can repeat many times in a single life. The fact that this cycle renews itself periodically gives us opportunities to heal and repair ourselves. This enables us gradually to strengthen the energy within our chakra system and express more of our potential.

▷ As adults, we pass through successive cycles of the chakra system, continuing our own spiritual growth while also perhaps fostering the development of children.

# Nadis, kundalini and minor chakras

The seven main chakras are only part of a much larger complex of subtle energies that make up the individual human being. For example, there are many other chakras throughout the body, all of which are expressions of different kinds of consciousness and energy. The physical disciplines, such as hatha yoga – the use of

▽ **This traditional image, called Sri Chakra, is a schematic representation of the main energy components of the human body.**

specific postures to encourage spiritual development and health – and mudra – the holding of specific hand positions – have developed to make use of the energy of these smaller chakras and the channels that link them together.

Surrounding each chakra are the main channels of energy, called nadis, that flow from the centre and interact with the rest of the body. Nadis are related to some aspects of the autonomic nervous system, and also to the meridian channels identified in traditional Chinese medicine, but they are of a much finer subtle substance.

There are said to be, in total, 72,000 nadis. Fourteen are named and described in detail, and of these three are of prime importance: the ida, the pingala and the sushumna. These three main channels run

▷ **The Sushumna is the central channel from which the chakras emerge. Weaving from side to side are the Ida and Pingala, the sun and moon channels.**

parallel to the body's physical axis of the spinal column.

The sushumna is the central channel, and the most important. This is the channel that yogis seek to cleanse and into which they direct energy to achieve realization. As the Tibetan teacher Lama Sangwa said: 'By causing the winds (pranas) and subtle drops (elements) to enter into the central channel, bliss arises and the body itself becomes the source of enlightened awareness.'

Ida, the left channel, carries a lunar energy that is nourishing and purifying.

▷ **The caduceus represents the Staff of Hermes, the Greek Messenger of the Gods. It was adopted as the symbol for healing and bears a striking resemblance to the three main nadis of the human body.**

△ The lotus petals round each chakra represent the nadis that distribute that chakra's energy through the body. Each chakra and nadi are expressions of the individual's core life-energy held within the three central channels.

## NADI SODHANA

Purification of physical and subtle energies in the body helps to clear the nadis, strengthens the chakras and begins to free up the primal energy of kundalini. A safe, well-balanced exercise for this is a breathing exercise (or pranayama) known as nadi sodhana. This exercise helps to balance the energy in the left and right channels (ida and pingala) and is calming and relaxing.

**1** Sit comfortably with a straight spine. (If sitting in a chair, plant your feet flat on the floor.) Tuck your chin in so that the back of your neck is straight. Sit for a moment with your hands on your knees and calm your body and mind.

**2** With the right ring finger, close off your left nostril by gentle pressure to the fleshy part and inhale slowly and deeply through the right nostril.

**3** Now use your right thumb to close the right nostril, releasing the left nostril, breathing out through the left nostril, slowly and deeply.

**4** Keep the right thumb in place and now breathe in through the left nostril. At the end of the breath, close the left nostril with the right ring finger again.

**5** Now breathe out slowly through the right nostril.

**6** Repeat the whole sequence of breaths ten times.

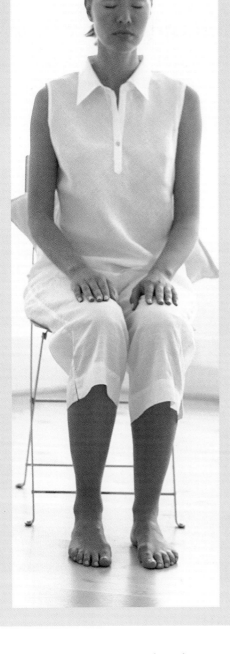

Pingala, the channel on the right side of the sushumna, is said to carry solar energy. The three channels are sometimes represented as running parallel to each other, while in other depictions the solar and lunar channels are seen weaving between the chakras until all three meet at the brow chakra.

The fundamental life energy of the individual is thought to reside in a quiet state within the base chakra. This force is called kundalini, which means 'coiled up'. As the chakras and their nadis are cleansed of stress and other energy blockages, more of the kundalini energy is able to move freely through the body. As this energy is pure consciousness, its awakened state can create various degrees of realization or enlightenment in the individual.

Many of the main chakras located on the central channel have smaller associated energy centres. For example, the muladhara at the base of the spine has related centres at the groin points, the knees and the soles of the feet. All these minor chakras help to ground and balance the physical energies. The heart chakra, anahata, has a smaller chakra inside it, which is represented as having eight petals. This is the spiritual heart, the anandakanda, whose eight channels represent the emotions.

# Chakras in other therapies

Although the chakras are non-physical, they influence physical functioning. Their subtle channels, the nadis, interface with many systems, both energetic and material.

The original theory of the chakras was holistic. It set out a coherent system of psycho-spiritual development that automatically included the health and wellbeing of the physical body. Blocks and stresses caused by ignorance and inappropriate belief systems were believed to produce physical illness and spiritual suffering. Nowadays, complementary and alternative therapies are again seeking to work with a unified holistic vision of the human being. For this reason, integrated and self-contained systems like the chakras are again becoming useful models for healing.

## yoga

Followers of the original Indian spiritual traditions worked with the chakra energies through physical exercise. Hatha yoga

▽ **Hatha yoga is effective because it directly influences the chakra system. Holding a posture ensures that the nadis, the chakras and the muscles all work to bring specific functions of the system into balance.**

positions (asanas) are designed to tone the physical body and stimulate the chakras and their nadis. They will do this automatically, though it is useful to follow a sequence of asanas that works through each of the chakras in turn.

## sound

Used to restore balance to the body, sound therapy is often focused on the chakras. Each area of the physical system is made up of different densities of tissue and hollow cavities. Sound, either produced externally by a therapist or internally by the patient, resonates with different areas of the body according to the tone that is being made. Blocks in the emotions, the physical body and within the chakras can be loosened and released very effectively by sound. Resonant instruments such as didgeridoos, tuning forks, bells, gongs and singing bowls can all be placed close to chakra points.

Toning, which uses the resonant voice to make particular sounds, is also commonly used to release blocks. For example a resonant 'mmm' sound vibrates the bones of the head and the brow chakra, while an open 'aaah' sound relaxes the diaphragm and energizes the solar plexus.

△ **Sound vibrates the physical structures of the body, and its subtle qualities also help to balance or clear the chakras and nadis.**

▽ **Colour therapy harnesses light, the subtlest of all physical energies. Specific colours can be used to help energize and heal particular chakras.**

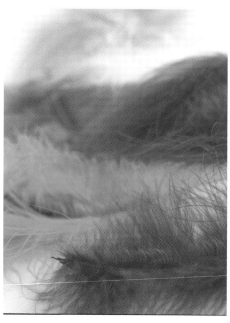

## colour therapy

The original yogic exercises placed great emphasis on visualization. This often involved building up exact and powerfully coloured shapes and patterns, each of which created specific changes within the brain function and caused energy channels to activate around particular chakras.

Today colour therapy offers healers a valuable way of working directly with chakras. There are many ways of introducing colour into the human energy system. Shining coloured light directly on the chakra, over the whole body or through the eyes all create physical, emotional and mental changes. Visualization and imagination techniques involving colour are also often used. The body affects the mind and the mind affects the body, and as the ancient yogis and seers of all cultures discovered, energy flows where the attention of the mind is directed. This energy is the same as prana, or life-energy, so naturally it can be effective in bringing health to an area needing attention.

△ Even therapies that do not specifically focus on the main chakra points have a profound influence on them. Any release of stress takes the burden off the chakra system as a whole.

▽ **Crystal therapy uses the combination of colour and resonance – the energy unique to each type of stone – to rebalance the chakra centres.**

## crystal healing

In crystal healing the seven main chakras are often the primary areas of stone placement. The organized structure of natural minerals has been found to have a beneficial and quick-acting effect on balancing the chakras. After an initial assessment, during which the quality of energy in each chakra is determined, stones are placed on and around each centre. The stones very often follow the Western colour correspondences, so that red stones will naturally enhance the qualities of the base chakra, orange stones those of the sacral chakra, and so on. From this starting point the therapist can modify the approach to release stress and correct under- and overactive chakra states.

## healing by touch

Spiritual or hands-on healers may focus their healing attention at chakra points where they sense energy flowing with a significantly greater or lesser intensity than elsewhere. Because chakras are energy gateways that allow a flow of energy both inwards and outwards, they are natural focuses for a great many developing types of holistic therapy.

# Discover your own chakra energy

Chakra energies are forever changing, interacting, balancing and rebalancing. From hour to hour and minute to minute as our activities alter, we move from concentration, to remembering, to physical coordination skills, to relaxing. As we do so, different chakras become more or less dominant. As individuals we each have a predisposition to certain chakras being more dominant than others. If we enjoy physical activity and have a practical, hands-on job, this will focus our energies at the first and second chakras. On the other hand, with an occupation that focuses on organizational skills and ideas, the solar plexus and brow chakras will inevitably become more significant.

Our life circumstances also alter the flow and interactions the chakras have with each other and with the environment. For example, if we are naturally comfortable working in socially complex interpersonal relationships – a heart chakra state – and then have to spend time where there is little chance to interact with others, or where our relationship skills are not valued, then this inevitably requires us to 'change gear' and focus our chakra energies in different ways. If we can identify the chakras that need

▽ **Give yourself time to think about the questions before you choose your answer.**

balancing, we can help ourselves a great deal in our journey towards our full potential and wellbeing.

Chakra dominance is not in itself a problem. However, where a major imbalance occurs, one or more chakras begin to take over the roles more properly belonging to others. This overburdens the dominant chakras and atrophies the others. We can survive for a long time in this false equilibrium, but it is like having a toolkit where only the hammer is used whatever the job. Often it is an accumulation of stresses and trauma in a chakra that reduces its effectiveness. If this is not remedied the system will naturally compensate by diverting energy to areas that are still working. This is the state of false equilibrium that most people cope with in their lives.

## the questionnaire

In the following questionnaire there are seven options open to you for each question posed. Jot down the number of each reply on a sheet of paper. Pick more than one choice if it seems appropriate.

Now see how many times you recorded each number. Each refers to a chakra: 1 the base chakra, 2 the sacral chakra, 3 the solar plexas chakra, 4 the heart chakra, 5 the throat chakra, 6 the brow chakra and 7 the crown chakra. If you look at your score, you will be able to see which chakras are dominant for you.

For example, if you have two answers of number 1, two of 2, six of 3, two of 4, three of 5, one of 6 and three of 7, you will see that the third chakra, the solar plexus, is dominant. This is where most of your energy is focused. Although dominant, the solar plexus chakra needs the most attention and healing. Chakras 1, 2 and 6 (base, sacral and brow) have little focus of attention, so they too, may need healing and energizing.

▷ **If some of your chakras are overburdened your system will not be functioning properly.**

# THE QUESTIONNAIRE

**1** Which area(s) of your body concern you the most?
❶ feet and legs
❷ between waist and hips
❸ waist
❹ chest
❺ neck and shoulders
❻ face
❼ head

**2** Which area(s) of your body do you dislike?
❶ feet and legs
❷ between waist and hips
❸ waist
❹ chest
❺ neck and shoulders
❻ face
❼ head

**3** Which area(s) of your body are you proud of?
❶ feet and legs
❷ between waist and hips
❸ waist
❹ chest
❺ neck and shoulders
❻ face
❼ head

**4** Which area(s) of your body are affected by major health issues?
❶ feet and legs
❷ between waist and hips
❸ waist
❹ chest
❺ neck and shoulders
❻ face
❼ head

**5** Which area(s) of the body are affected most by minor health issues?
❶ feet and legs
❷ between waist and hips
❸ waist
❹ chest
❺ neck and shoulders
❻ face
❼ head

**6** Which colour(s) do you like the most?
❶ red
❷ orange
❸ yellow
❹ green
❺ blue
❻ dark blue
❼ violet

**7** Which colour(s) do you like the least?
❶ red
❷ orange
❸ yellow
❹ green
❺ blue
❻ dark blue
❼ violet

**8** Which are your favourite foods?
❶ meat/fish/pulses
❷ rice/orange fruits
❸ wheat/yellow fruits
❹ green fruit and vegetables

**9** Which sort of exercises or interests attract you?
❶ fast action
❷ dancing/painting
❸ crosswords/puzzles
❹ anything outside
❺ drama/singing
❻ mystery/crime novels
❼ doing nothing

**10** What sort of people do you look up to or admire?
❶ sportspeople
❷ artists/musicians
❸ intellectuals
❹ conservationists
❺ speakers/politicians
❻ inventors
❼ mystics/religious figures

**11** What sort of person do you think of yourself as?
❶ get on with things
❷ creative

❸ thinker/worrier
❹ emotional
❺ chatterbox
❻ quiet
❼ daydreamer

**12** What emotions do you consider are uppermost in you life?
❶ passionate
❷ easy-going
❸ contented
❹ caring, sharing
❺ loyal
❻ helpfully distant
❼ sympathetic

**13** What emotions do you have that you would like to change?
❶ temper
❷ possessiveness
❸ confusion
❹ insecurity
❺ needing things to be 'black or white'
❻ feeling separate from others
❼ not saying 'no'

**14** If you get angry, what is your most common reaction?
❶ rage/tantrums
❷ sullen resentment
❸ get frightened
❹ blame yourself
❺ keep quiet
❻ withdraw
❼ imagine nothing happened

**15** What are you most afraid of?
❶ dying
❷ lack of sensation
❸ things you don't understand
❹ being alone
❺ having no-one to talk to
❻ losing your way
❼ difficult situations

**16** Which of these describes the way you prefer to learn?
❶ fast
❷ slowly
❸ quickly but forget
❹ through feelings
❺ by rote
❻ instinctively
❼ can't be bothered

**17** What best describes your reaction to situations?
❶ enthusiastic
❷ go with the flow
❸ think things through
❹ see how things feel
❺ ask a lot of questions
❻ see the patterns then act
❼ drift along

**18** If you are criticized or reprimanded, what is your usual response?
❶ anger
❷ resentment
❸ fear
❹ self-blame
❺ verbal riposte
❻ think about it
❼ denial

**19** How would you describe your favourite books, films, video games?
❶ combat action
❷ art
❸ skill, intellectual
❹ romances
❺ courtroom dramas
❻ detective stories
❼ spiritual or self development

**20** Which category best describes your friends?
❶ competitive
❷ creative
❸ intellectual
❹ loving
❺ idealistic
❻ rebellious
❼ spiritual

# Chakras of manifestation

Once you have completed the questionnaire on the previous page you can use the following chapters to find appropriate ways to heal and balance the chakras that need attention. This chapter covers the first two chakras, the base and the sacral. They ensure the stability of the individual at every level of body, mind and spirit.

# Base chakra – foundation of energy

Matter requires stability and structure in order to exist. Energy must be organized and maintained in the face of all sorts of opposing forces in the universe. The force of gravity is the energy of compression and its focus is the basis of the first chakra, located at the bottom of the spine. This is the rock upon which the whole of the chakra system, the subtle energies and the physical body rely, and without which disorder soon arises.

The Sanskrit name for the base chakra is muladhara, which means 'root'. The foundation of our life is the physical body

▽ The muladhara chakra ensures our physical existence, nourishing and energizing the whole chakra system.

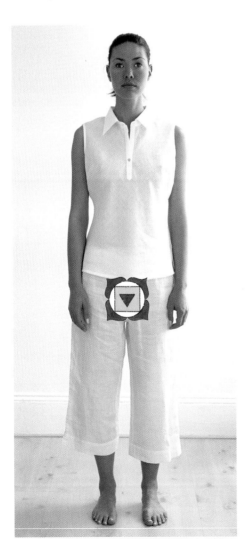

△ Placing too much value on thought processes, of knowing rather than feeling, can create an imbalance that isolates us from the planet.

and its ability to use energy to sustain itself. Survival is the key activity of the base chakra, which deals with life at the level of practicality. The base chakra is the closest energy centre to the Earth and it links us to the planet itself.

## head in the clouds

The base chakra is what links 'us' – the consciousness sitting up there in the head commenting on everything that's going on – with our bodies. Many ancient cultures saw the mind or soul as located in the heart. The West puts emphasis on the head, the seat of the rational thinking mind, and often views the body as an awkward nuisance. With such a dissociation, the natural connections with physical reality and the sense of being a part of creation can be lacking. This induces a false sense of detachment, disinterest or even disdain, where nothing is truly valued and nothing is appreciated. Life can quickly become dull and meaningless.

△ Our sense of self, and desire to live, are the hidden roots of our existence; this is the ground of our being that sustains us constantly.

## reactions

The base chakra relates to physical solidity and support, especially to the skeletal structure of the body and its flexibility. It is no use having a strong physical base if there is no flexibility. In order to survive any sort of stress, body and mind must be responsive. In an emergency, we must react quickly in an appropriate way, resisting or giving way as necessary. This instinctive feel for survival is the 'fight or flight' response of the adrenal glands just above the kidneys, which are responsible for preparing us for rapid action when faced with the threat of danger.

Like the adrenal glands, the base chakra has a relationship with the circulatory system and the blood supply. It also influences the skeletal muscles of the arms, legs and torso that allow us to move through the world. The base chakra is linked to the colour red and is responsible for maintaining the body's heat – the core temperature that allows chemical reactions to take place in the cells at the correct rate.

◁ Both the inability to sustain energy levels and the need for continual excitement or stimulation can indicate imbalance in the base chakra.

## TO ENERGIZE THE BASE CHAKRA

Exercising the sense of touch, attending to practical matters, gentle movement and exercise can help to energize and re-connect us to the base chakra. Any of the following will help:

• A warm bath.
• Massage, aromatherapy or reflexology.
• Walking, running, jumping or stamping the feet improves the circulation, co-ordination and our link to the planet.
• Eating, especially high protein foods. Taking a good mineral supplement may also help. A shortage of zinc is one of the commonest causes of 'spaciness' and lack of mental focus.

▽ Any activity, such as bathing, that emphasizes physicality and stimulates the senses – especially smell – helps to balance the base chakra.

Imbalances in the base chakra can show up in many ways. Characteristic symptoms include a chronic lack of energy, with exhaustion following even slight exercise, problems with stiffness and painful movement, particularly in the hips, legs and feet. When poor physical co-ordination or poor circulation (a tendency to have cold hands and feet) is present, the base chakra is worth looking at.

The base chakra may also need healing and energizing when someone is uncomfortable with their body. This can lead to a sense of confusion or unreality and may show in a lack of drive or motivation and an aversion to getting involved in practicalities or physical exercise. Conversely, an imbalance in the base chakra can also cause excessive tension or excitability, with a continual need for stimulation.

# Base chakra – seat of passion

The emotional responses that are associated with the base chakra express the need to ensure personal survival. They tend to be direct, explosive and strong, yet once satisfied, they will dissipate immediately. Young babies, in whom the base chakra is dominant, clearly demonstrate these qualities. They will express themselves forcefully and loudly whenever they are hungry, tired or uncomfortable, yet will fall asleep quickly once satisfied.

## fear

Whenever there is a sense of loss of control or powerlessness, the base chakra energies and our survival instincts are activated. The fiery emotional states of anger, assertiveness and aggression all arise from one fundamental cause, and that is fear. Fear begins as soon as it seems that there is a loss of control, or a sense of being trapped. A dramatic response is still a biological necessity in some cases, but unfortunately as life has become more complicated, it is much less possible to feel that we are really in control of our own existence. Television, for example, presents us with events from all over the world over which we have no control, and yet we experience them emotionally and our bodies automatically

▽ **The innate survival instincts of the base chakra automatically activate whenever we feel threatened or powerless.**

respond as if we were actually involved. Our means for survival – food, water, heat, light and money – are all supplied to us by others. In these circumstances it is quite easy to become habitually fearful. This usually manifests itself as stress, which is an increasing inability to deal with changing situations in a flexible, creative way. Depending on the personality, stress and fear will show as either withdrawal – like a trapped animal hiding in a corner pretending not to be there – or aggression, in which case even those offering help will be perceived as a threat and attacked.

Remaining in a constant state of alert drains the body's energy and makes it more difficult to respond effectively when real danger presents itself. This can cause an emotional burn-out, which makes it impossible to become excited or motivated by anything.

▽ **The physicality and immediacy of passion easily bypasses the rational mind. It is energy that must be expressed immediately.**

## releasing energies

There may be times when you feel the need to release an excess of base chakra emotional energy. There are several ways to do this. A simple and effective method, and a good way to begin, is to describe your strong feelings in writing, without judging them or censoring them. When you have finished writing your account, burn everything that you have written. This is the important element. The content of your writing is not important – it merely serves to let go of the excess energy.

When you are feeling the effects of withdrawal from emotional involvement, routine physical activities such as gardening, washing and cleaning can be helpful. Running, drumming, or dancing to music with a strong rhythm will keep the energy circulating and prevent a build-up.

It is a lot easier, however, to release an excess of base chakra energy, than it is to build it up if it is lacking. Poor motivation is one of the main features of insufficient energy in this chakra.

△ **Strong feelings initiated by the base chakra should not be held on to. Writing the feelings on a piece of paper and then symbolically burning them in a fire can help to release them.**

▽ **Channelling strong feelings into a simple, constructive activity, however mundane, helps to take the pressure off and regulates the safety valve of the base chakra.**

## passion

Lust, physical passion and sexual excitement are complex emotions. They all involve many different chakras. But it is the motivation to ensure survival of the species that underlies immediate physical attraction, and this is associated with the base chakra. In this capacity the base chakra functions at many levels, promoting circulation, excitement, instinct and spontaneity and helping us to focus on the physical body in the present.

Imbalance within the base chakra can show as a build-up of strong emotions, which may then be released inappropriately or excessively. There can be a tendency to selfishness and a lack of concern for others, or a total denial of the emotions we are actually experiencing, especially anger. Lack of assertiveness can also indicate difficulties in this area.

# Base chakra – the pioneer

The base chakra gives the energy and motivation needed to make good use of whatever resources are available. One of the main functions of the base chakra is to solidify, to make real. This includes the realization of dreams and the maintainance of energy levels within the body.

In order to survive, the human race learned to be very good at inventing and making new tools and creating new technologies. The base chakra is essential in the manifestation of any idea, dream or concept. Without its down-to-earth energy, it doesn't matter how wonderful our inspiration is or how useful a new invention may one day prove to be. The base chakra will find whatever is solid and viable in the most ephemeral concept and enable it to be made manifest and useful.

## action

The desire to act, to move, to do, is an expression of the powerful energy of the base chakra. This energy is an absolute prerequisite for any new venture or project. Creativity, though, involves nearly every one of the main chakra centres in some way. Acting only by itself, the base chakra would be likely to 'make do' with the first thing it came up with and might well completely destroy it if it did not work right away.

Complete involvement in the practicality of making something new is a characteristic of this energy. The need is to see something coming into existence through personal skill

△ Whatever the drive of the base chakra may be, without sufficient food to sustain the physical body, nothing will be achieved.

▽ Surviving in dangerous situations puts our attention on physical skills, our senses and our feeling of being alive – all base chakra qualities.

and effort. As soon as it is there, taking its place in the real world, the job of the first chakra is done, and unless supported by other energies, the creator will become quickly distracted by another new project.

This short-lived burst of energy can be useful in an appropriate context. For example, people with the dynamic skills associated with the base chakra are happy to create possibilities but content to let others work on the fine details. They are not interested in keeping total control, so allow space for others to follow in their work.

## going boldly...

The base chakra energy is the pioneer, always willing to go where no one has gone before and to do things that have never been done. In a balanced base chakra there is the energy, confidence, know-how and dexterity to survive and thrive in the moment-to-moment exploration of new territory. Exploring, mountain climbing, white-water rafting, and all other activities where people voluntarily put themselves in a completely self-reliant situation, engage with the survival instincts of the base chakra.

When base chakra energy is excessively dominating, however, only experiences that are life-threatening are enjoyed, and only the making of new things is important, not the uses to which they are put; 'doing' becomes the only comfortable state and 'being' is intolerably boring. Such states may arise from habit patterns that develop when there is actually a significant underlying lack of security. People with this problem feel the need to keep busy, which is often an attempt to disguise a sense of emptiness, a huge void that seems to threaten the existence of the individual.

The energy of the base chakra is one of concentration and gravity, so a feeling of vacuum, completely free from solidity and form, unable to be held or defined in any

▽ **Base chakra energy initiates new projects but by itself will soon become distracted. We need other chakras to support and sustain our enthusiasm through to completion.**

### SELF-PARENTING

This exercise helps to resolve some of the earliest memories and concepts we have around feelings of security and self-identity. It can help to release stresses held within the base chakra.

**1** Settle yourself in a quiet, dimly lit room. In your imagination take yourself back to the moment of your conception. How would you like it to have been?

**2** Move forward in time and see yourself as a baby in the womb, as a newborn child and as a young child. Imagine at each stage that you are happy, content, comfortable and as secure as you can be. Feel that sense of security throughout your body.

**3** Sort out a daily routine that allows you more time to fulfil all your personal needs in every possible way. Try to follow that routine for a day, then a few days, then maybe a week. Allow the process to become a natural part of your routine, and feel the benefit of this self-parenting.

way at all, is completely alien to it. This feeling of emptiness often arises in situations where something established and apparently solid (a state the base chakra understands very well), becomes subject to change, death or decay. As change is the only constant in our lives, it is difficult for us to deal with the times when we feel our very foundations have been removed. Everyone will cope in different ways with such a situation, but it can be helpful to watch ourselves to ensure that our chakra energies, and the various activities they reflect, remain as evenly balanced as possible. Getting stuck in one chakra state will only lead to energy collapse sooner or later.

Base chakra imbalance at the mental level can show as obsessive focus on one thing to the exclusion of everything else, or else as a rigid and materialistic outlook that usually also masks deep insecurities about personal survival issues. People who are interested in only new and risky or dangerous ventures, or who show the opposite trait of being completely lacking in practicality, disintegrating into confusion when faced with practical projects or being unable to complete anything, might benefit from work with the base chakra.

# Base chakra – the fortress

The spiritual purpose of the base chakra is the protection of individual integrity. The base holds together the fabric of the personality and is the very real foundation for every spiritual discipline. This energy centre is the place where the ladder to heaven rests. Unless that ground is completely solid in every respect, little else of true value will be accomplished.

## anchor

The base chakra must be well balanced in order to anchor and make use of spiritual energy so that it can be of value to us here and now. The more someone works with spiritual growth and development, the more vital it becomes to anchor those energies. We are adrift in an ocean of different energies, physical, electromagnetic and subtle. Some are obvious to the senses, like those that create the weather. Others are more subtle, such as the electromagnetic fields that cover the planet from both natural and artificial sources. Each of these energy fields has the potential to disrupt the way we function if it bombards us with a

▽ **Without the grounding influence of the base chakra our system would be constantly upset by the changing tides of energy around us.**

### THE WARRIOR

This yoga posture stabilizes the base chakra. You may be surprised at how much heat this static posture generates. Remember to breathe normally while you are doing it.

**1** Loosen your clothes and take off your shoes and socks. Spread your feet apart, to make a triangle of equal sides with the ground.

**2** Stretch your arms out to the sides, and rotate your left foot outwards. Bend your left knee, keeping the right leg straight. When you reach a position where you could be sitting on an imaginary chair – stop.
**3** Hold the pose for as long as is comfortable, then return to standing.
**4** Repeat to the right, holding the pose for the same length of time.

vibration that is stronger than our own. This is the process called entrainment, where an energy with a strong coherent pattern begins to make weaker, more disorganized energy fields vibrate at its own frequency.

Taking the analogy from electricity a little further: if we do not have an effective way of earthing outside energies, static will build up and begin to interfere with our own 'signal'. The base chakra is that lightning rod, that earth cable, which prevents unwanted energy signals from destroying our equilibrium.

One indication to look for that suggests a spiritual imbalance in the base chakra is an 'otherworldliness', a loss of awareness and

▽ The solid form and orderliness of the mineral kingdom reflects the nature of the base chakra. Dark-coloured crystals naturally ground and centre our own energies.

interest in the real world and in practical survival issues. There may also be a lack of discipline, an unfocused attitude, wishful thinking and fantasizing or a dissociation from the body and its requirements, often accompanied by a desire to escape physical incarnation. People with a weak base chakra may be easily swayed by their impressions, lack the ability to discriminate between viewpoints and belief systems, or receive psychic and clairvoyant messages over which they have little or no control. A lack of grounding can create hyperactivity, restlessness, the inability to settle, and very volatile emotions.

Grounding and earthing restores the natural flow of energy to and from the base chakra, and visualization is helpful. With your feet firmly on the ground, imagine tree roots extending down and out from where you are touching the ground. With each outbreath imagine the roots growing deeper and more firmly into the earth. With each inbreath, allow the sustaining energy of the Earth to flow through your whole body.

△ The purpose of meditation is to let go of all excess activity in the mind, emotions and body in order to experience the world as it is – not to escape from reality.

▽ Dancing and drumming have been used for millennia as a means to attain spiritual states. Energizing the base chakra, and all other chakras in turn, strengthens the body and spirit.

# Sacral chakra – the pleasure principle

The sacral chakra is the second energy centre. It is located in the area below the navel and above the pubic bone, at the front of the pelvis. Physically this chakra is involved with the organs of the lower abdomen – the large intestine, the bladder and the reproductive organs.

Detoxification is one of the key functions of the sacral chakra, at every level, from the physical through to the spiritual.

▷ **The sacral chakra is the reservoir of our life energy, from which energy, or chi, is channelled or directed through the rest of the body.**

▽ **The sacral chakra, located in the area below the navel and above the pubic bone, is the second energy centre.**

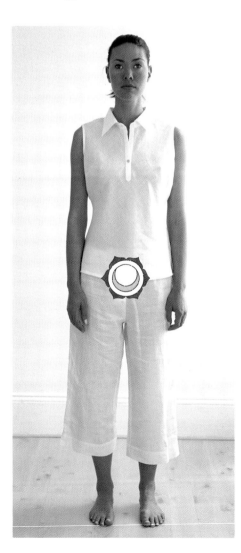

Traditionally this chakra is connected with the element of water and has its characteristics of flow, cleansing and movement. The symbol of the chakra is a white, blue or silver crescent, which is also a reminder of the moon's influence on all things watery, including the ebb and flow of the emotions.

So while the defining characteristic of the base chakra is the element of Earth, representing solidity, focus and the structure of the skeletal system, the sacral chakra represents the polar opposites of these: flow, flexibility and the emptiness or hollowness of the body's organs – bladder, intestine, womb and so on.

The whole pelvic region is shaped like a bowl, in which the energy focus of the sacral chakra lies. The pelvis is shaped to support the legs and the many different muscles that control their movement. Any strain or tension here can create a whole range of symptoms, from lower back pain, irregular or painful menstruation, constipation and sciatica to problems with fertility, impotence and fluid balance in the body.

Any disease state that features poor balance of fluids or flexibility will correspond to an imbalance within the second chakra. Water

▷ **Belly-dancing is an ideal activity to balance the sacral energies. It strengthens the pelvic and abdominal muscles and it encourages flexibility.**

△ **The sacral chakra is associated with the energy of the moon and with the emotions and fluids of the body.**

absorption is an important function of the large intestine, while control of the mineral and water balance in the blood is regulated by the kidneys. If the functions of these areas are impaired, the balance of chemicals in the body is upset, and it becomes more difficult to eliminate toxins and waste products, which effectively poison the body.

It is the job of the sacral chakra to keep things moving. Any rigidity of the joints, such as in arthritis and other similar conditions, can also reflect unbalanced energy at this centre.

## balance and flow

The area of the sacral chakra within the pelvis is also our centre of gravity. It rules our sense of movement and balance, and gives grace and flow to our activity. It is the reservoir of what the Indians call prana and the Chinese call *chi* – the life-energy that infuses every living system, the subtle substance within the breath that is so important in the spiritual disciplines of the

△ **The slow, graceful, physical movements of Tai Chi and Chi Kung stimulate the flow of *chi*, which is visualized as a subtle substance with a consistency and speed of flow similar to honey.**

East and in the martial arts that developed among the elite monks of the Hindus, Buddhists and Taoists.

Today the West is familiar with the disciplined exercises of Tai Chi and Chi Kung. They have developed over thousands of years as an effective way to control and direct the flow of the subtle force of *chi* through the body and even beyond, into the environment. One of the main centres for gathering and distributing *chi* is known in Chinese as *tan tien*. It is equivalent, though not identical, to the sacral chakra. The same place is called the *hara* in Japanese, the centre of the life-force. From this reservoir *chi* can be channelled and directed through the rest of the body to maintain health and give great amounts of strength and endurance, or to open up states of awareness.

It is only from a flow outwards from ourselves that we can begin to explore and experience the world that is not us. Remaining centred and solid within the security of the base chakra, our awareness can reach beyond the immediate, stretching out a curious hand to things just beyond our grasp. Movement and curiosity is required. The grace and balance of the sacral chakra's smooth flow of energy helps us succeed. Here we begin to experience the energy of the world around us.

## WU CHI

One way of energizing and balancing the sacral chakra is to take up belly dancing. Another is to perform this standing posture exercise, called wu chi in Chinese. Begin by holding the posture for between two and five minutes, then increase the time gradually.

**1** Stand with your feet apart, directly under your shoulders.

**2** Let your hands hang loosely by your sides and allow your shoulders to drop.

**3** Imagine your whole body is hanging by a thread attached to the top of your head, suspending you from the ceiling.

**4** Allow yourself to relax, making sure your knees are not locked. Breathe normally.

Watch as you become aware of the tensions in your muscles and the internal chatter of your mind. Let them go.

# Sacral chakra – feeling the need

The emotional level of the second chakra is reflected in its watery nature. Its activity is focused on flow, movement and exploration of the surroundings. Its motivation is enjoyment and pleasure and its reward is sensation – the invigoration of the senses.

The whole of life at the earliest stage of development revolves around feeling secure and well-fed. This is the level of the base chakra: making sure that survival is assured. Once these primary needs have been met, the priority is to explore the potential of the body through play, and to explore the surroundings using all the senses. This is where the sacral chakra comes in – any young animal playing is behaving under the influence of this chakra.

## brain works

Experiments carried out to map activity in the brain show clearly that the first nerve pathways to be established directly after birth serve the parts of the brain where pleasure is registered. This helps the learning process of the infant, because it reinforces actions

△ Spontaneous enjoyment of experience, exploration of the senses and play are all characteristics of the sacral chakra, stimulating our ability to learn and develop as individuals.

▽ In the animal world there is no distinction between playing and learning. Play leads to the development of skills for survival and a more successful life.

that are more likely to be beneficial, rather than those that are more likely to cause damage, pain or suffering.

The parts of the brain concerned with registering pleasure – called the limbic system – also directly affect the hypothalamus. This small organ deep in the centre of the brain controls the hormone system and the activity of the autonomic nervous system – the involuntary processes that maintain balance in the heart rate, breathing and blood pressure.

## enjoyment

Happiness and enjoyment are important factors in maintaining the smooth running of the individual. They have been built into our awareness to encourage us to stay in harmony with ourselves and the environment. The sacral chakra maintains

## BADDHA KONASANA

Hatha yoga helps the flow of life energy and increases physical flexibility and resilience. This exercise, baddha konasana or the cobbler's pose, encourages energy flow in all levels of the sacral chakra.

1 Sit on the floor, bending your knees and keeping your back straight.
2 Turn the soles of your feet to face each other.
3 Place the fingers of both hands over your toes.
4 Allowing your knees to fall outwards, draw your feet in towards your body. Don't try to force your knees nearer the floor. The more you relax your pelvis, the more the muscles will allow the knees to fall.
5 Stay in this position for a few moments before relaxing.

this flow of communication between body and mind through sensation and emotion. In order to be most effective, the mind has to be aware of subtle changes in the feelings. Very often vague intuitions and 'gut' feelings are dismissed by the conscious mind because they are not precise enough. It is possible to educate the conscious mind to take notice of the flow of feelings and the energy fluctuations of the sacral centre, making us much more sensitive and responsive to what is going on around us.

Flowing in harmony with our own energy and with our surroundings requires a level of flexibility as well as the ability to change focus – to let go, when necessary, of things that are no longer useful or helpful to us. An imbalance in the sacral chakra often arises when for one reason or another we become fixated on something that we refuse to admit to ourselves is actually inappropriate or unrealistic.

Indications that the sacral chakra is out of balance can be emotional over-sensitivity or an unhealthy emotional dependency on someone else. Very often this includes intrusive behaviour and a failure to respect normal boundaries. At the opposite extreme there may be rigidity, with a lack of physical or emotional flexibility. Repression of feelings, a fear of sensuality, sex, pleasure or enjoyment, as well as guilt over feelings and desires, all indicate sacral imbalance that can result in frustration and bitterness.

▷ **Adults who display sacral chakra imbalances may well have experienced a lack of close physical contact as young children.**

# Sacral chakra – the artist within

The sacral chakra is located right in the centre of the womb area. It is thus related to fertility, giving birth and all other aspects of creativity. Creativity at the sacral chakra level is to do with manipulation of the senses and the world. At the orange level of the second chakra the process is very personal. It is a spontaneous mechanism to keep energy moving, to avoid the build-up of stress. The complementary blue chakra, the throat, is also related to the creative process but as a means of external expression, a way of communicating.

## the nature of stress

Stress is commonly understood to be the accumulation of difficult and negative circumstances. In fact it is any stimulus, good or bad, enjoyable or painful, that throws the body out of balance to such a degree that it is unable fully to return to its previous equilibrium. It is a widely held belief that creativity can be stimulated by stress, and that true art therefore requires suffering. This is really a misunderstanding of the processes that are controlled and directed by the sacral chakra.

The accumulation of physical stress in the muscles and organs of the body, and emotional and mental stress in the subtle

▽ The flow of the emotions is experienced like the tides of the sea, changing from hour to hour. Any activity, such as making music, can quickly alter emotional states.

△ It is the activity of a creative act that is important in stimulating life-energy, not the quality or permanence of the end product.

bodies and chakras, creates a breakdown in the natural movement and flow of life-energy. This rigidity, if allowed to build up unchecked, leads to atrophy and eventually to death. Old age can be seen simply as this process of accumulating stress. Indeed old age is a relative term – some people who have hard, unforgiving lives look old at forty, while others, who are flexible and happy despite the hardships they have endured, look radiant at eighty.

Stress initiates survival drives, which are first chakra functions. But the trouble with stress is that if it is not dissipated quickly by 'fight or flight' responses, a different approach is needed. The more creative, flexible energy needed to give the right response is provided by the second chakra.

△ **Creative activity explores the flow of mind, body and spirit as they focus on one object. Successful art communicates this life-energy whatever the technical skills of the creator.**

## flowing energy

Life-energy is like a stream, it must keep moving. Once it stops moving, a stream is no longer a stream. Likewise, life-energy that is blocked stops being life-giving. The sacral chakra helps to ensure the supply of life-energy available to us by keeping the flow in motion. Where stress creates blocks and rigidity the sacral chakra creates opportunities for life-energy to move around them, much as a stream will divert its flow to move around a build-up of debris in its path. Creative activity is like this diverted stream of energy, restoring the quality of flow back into the systems of the body.

The sacral chakra often initiates creative activity as a way of finding new solutions to intractable problems. This is a sense-based process of feeling the way to solutions, rather than a conscious, rational assessment and analysis of the situation. The process can begin when stress levels are high enough to stop normal activity. There is an impasse and at that still, quiet moment, some small unconscious act, such as doodling, grabs all the attention and focuses the flow of life-energy into the creative process. Depression and despair may sometimes precede creativity, but once begun, the process of release is like an increased force of water, strong enough to wash the accumulated debris of stress aside, restoring a natural flow of life-energy.

Creativity is the natural state of life-energy and it restores life to a natural balance. Successful art, beautiful design and skilful craftsmanship are exhilarating and life-supporting because they embody this flow of life-energy. Creativity should never be seen as the domain of the expert and the specialist. We all have a sacral chakra, which is the womb of creativity, within us. If we let its energy flow naturally, everything we do will be an expression of the joyful creativity of living.

# Sacral chakra – healing the wounds

chakras of manifestation

The sacral chakra is the focus of our experience of pleasure and also the first place that experiences any kind of pain. Wherever trauma and pain may be in the body, they are registered in the second chakra. Pain is also held there if the trauma the pain creates is not released. Any shock to the system breaks the usual flow of our

▽ The effects of an accident or shock can last well beyond the actual event, colouring our lives for many years.

life. For example, the memory of an accident often gets stuck in the mind, where it is relived continually.

The sacral chakra is primarily affected for two reasons. First, the life-energy or *chi* is tightly gathered in this area of the body, so any threat to it causes turbulence and upset here. Second, it is the function of the sacral chakra to maintain the flow of life, which helps to remove the fragments of trauma locked within the different systems of the body.

**EMOTIONAL STRESS RELEASE (ESR)**

One of the most effective ways to release stress is to lightly touch the frontal eminences of the skull. These are two slight bumps above the outer edge of the eye at either side of the forehead. While stress is being released a slight irregular pulsing can often be felt at the eminences, which dies away once the process is complete.

**1** Lightly hold the fingertips to the frontal eminences of the skull, or hold a hand across the forehead to catch both points easily.
**2** Turning your attention to the stressful event will now automatically begin to release the accumulated tensions. It is not necessary to relive each event in detail, though often this occurs automatically. Strong feelings and emotions, as well as physical reactions, may surface while these points are being held.
**3** As long as the process is allowed to complete itself, the body quickly and effectively releases the frozen memories once and for all.

▷ **Stress becomes physically locked into the body as well as into the chakras. Intellectual understanding of a trauma alone is not always enough to remove it.**

## shock release

Emotional and mental shock can heal like broken bones, but scars may last for a long time, subtly affecting how we think and feel. Each event distorts or locks away energy that we need for our everyday lives. It takes a lot of psychic energy to separate memories of pain from our awareness and, like unwanted baggage, they load us down.

There are some very effective ways to help the sacral chakra release and let go of trauma and shock without the need to go through the pain of reliving the event. Counselling methods and psychological examination of trauma have been shown sometimes to increase, not decrease, stress levels. This is because the practical release of stress is a priority of the body, not simply an intellectual understanding of how the stress has been affecting behaviour. The sites, such as the sacral chakra, where the actual stress is located, need to be re-integrated into the present before the imbalances can be released effectively. One way to do this is to try the Emotional Stress Release exercise on the opposite page. It is important to remember that memories, particularly painful ones, tend to be stored with other memories that are in some way related. Releasing stress that initially appears to be caused by a minor event may be an opportunity for the body to let go of many other stresses that deal with a similar scenario or emotion.

An upset digestive system, particularly constipation, can indicate that stress and trauma are interfering with normal functioning. There may be an inability to become emotionally involved with life and to enjoy it. Emotional volatility and a tendency to aggressive behaviour or tearfulness at the slightest provocation are other signs of problems. Inability to let go of a stressful event, so that it preys on the mind, shows that this chakra is blocked, as does suffering from an increasing number of infections and illnesses.

### CRYSTAL RELEASE

The sacral chakra can be supported in its release of stress by using a particular layout of crystals. You will need three clear quartz crystals, together with three moonstones or three rose quartz crystals.

1 With the three clear quartz crystals make a downward pointing triangle below the navel. If the crystals have points, these should point outwards.
2 Below these crystals and above the pubic bone, make an arc of the three remaining stones.

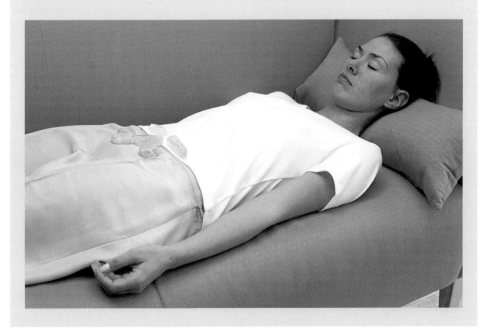

# Chakras of relationship

The third and fourth chakras are at the solar plexus and the heart. They begin to integrate our energy with the environment and the people around us. Growth always involves expanding into new areas, so the skills of recognizing potential dangers and establishing a place of personal power are essential.

# Solar plexus chakra – the organizer

The solar plexus, the third centre, is considered as a single chakra, but is, as the word 'plexus' suggests, a fusion of many different energies. Midway between the ribcage and the navel, it also corresponds to the lumbar vertebrae in the spine. The physical attributes of the solar plexus chakra fall into three main areas: the digestion, the nervous system and the immune system.

## digestion

The process of digestion and assimilation of nutrients is vital to sustain life. The organs linked to the solar plexus are the stomach,

▽ The solar plexus chakra, below the ribcage, is the main organizing principle affecting all parts of the body and mind.

△ The solar plexus chakra is associated with the element of Fire, not only because it creates physical heat in the body, but also because it takes raw materials and transforms them.

liver, gallbladder, pancreas, duodenum and small intestine. For digestion and the assimilation of nutrients to be successful, all these organs have to work in harmony. This involves a series of chemical reactions using a great many different catalysts. From the alkaline enzyme-rich saliva in the mouth, food moves to the acidity of the stomach. Here it is churned, thoroughly mixing the natural acids and enzymes. It then passes into the duodenum, where bile from the liver, via the gallbladder, begins to break down fats, and more enzymes from the pancreas begin to act on sugars and carbohydrates. As the mixture moves through the small intestine, the valuable nutrients from the food are absorbed through the wall of the intestine into the bloodstream. Failure to digest food efficiently means that nutrients are not absorbed.

▽ The solar plexus chakra is often referred to as the fusebox of the body. In this area are large concentrations of nerve tissue that, if disrupted, can affect the whole nervous system.

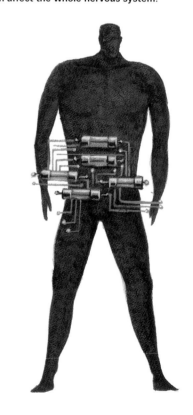

▷ If the ability of the body to recognize nutrients is impaired, so that absorption does not take place, eating healthily will make little difference.

## immune system

The immune system works like a library or a computer. It stores and categorizes information about everything the body encounters. For instance, on meeting a virus, the body recognizes it as an enemy and activates the defence mechanisms to fight and overcome the infection. If the body later encounters the same virus again it has the information to prevent a serious invasion.

Problems with this identification process often show up when the body reacts to harmless or even beneficial substances as if they are dangerous. This is experienced as allergy or intolerance. The opposite malfunction happens when the body harbours an infection for a long time because it fails to recognize its presence and so neglects to fight it at all. Difficulties also occur when the body fails to recognize its own enzymes, hormones or neuro-transmitters, and sometimes there is an inability to recognize minerals and vitamins that should be absorbed by the small intestine. These problems surface as deficiencies but do not respond to increased intake because the problem is not lack, but a failure to recognize the substance.

The solar plexus chakra is put under great pressure by the way we live today. Its physical functions are strained by the types of food we eat, the pace of life and new toxins in our environment. It is not surprising that many of the diseases in our society today are a sign of some dysfunction in the solar plexus chakra.

### ARDHA MATSEYANDRASANA

This exercise, the spinal twist, tones the whole of the solar plexus. The more upright you keep your spine, the easier it is to twist.

**1** Kneel down on a blanket or thick mat, resting on your heels. Slide your buttocks to the right of your feet. Lift your left leg, so the left foot is across the right knee.

**2** Shuffle your bottom around to get comfortable and to keep your spine straight. Bring your left arm round behind you, resting your fingers on the floor to steady yourself. Bring your right arm to rest on the outside of the left leg, the elbow bracing against the knee. Breathe in, then as you breathe out, lift your spine and twist round to look over your left shoulder. Breathe normally.

**3** When you feel ready to release the pose, breathe in, then as you breathe out, unwind yourself. First bring your left arm back around to the front and follow its movement with the head, naturally straightening the spine. If you are unable to stretch into the full twist, simply hold the knee instead of bracing it with an elbow. Repeat on the other side, mirroring the steps.

# Solar plexus chakra – sun of contentment

The solar plexus chakra is often identified with the element of Fire. Our emotional reaction to fire is two-fold. Fire gives warmth and comfort but brings fear and terror when it gets out of control. This echoes the emotional breadth of the solar plexus chakra.

△ **The unknown cannot be controlled because there is a lack of information. The mind becomes anxious and fearful.**

## fear

The key negative emotion that spawns all others is fear. It can become an underlying emotion that drives other everyday emotional reactions. Fear arises in any situation where the outcome seems beyond the capacity of the mind to determine, and there is an inability simply to relax. The mind conjures up limitless scenarios and gets locked into self-defeating thought processes of 'what if…'

Fear can escalate into terror or subside into anxiety in any area of life. Issues

◁ **Threats and rules that restrict our natural exuberance easily block the solar plexus chakra.**

### VISUALIZING THE SUN

Use this visualization exercise to invite warmth and joy into your life. This is a good exercise to do if you have feelings of unease or fear that you want to dispel. Using the positive aspects and strength of the sun you will create a feeling of security and contentment.

**1** Sit or lie down comfortably. Wrap a blanket around you if the day is cool. Breathe in, and as you breathe out, allow yourself to relax. Imagine a sphere of golden light beginning to form between your navel and the bottom of your ribcage. Imagine this sphere is also giving off a comfortable warmth. Allow the sphere to grow until it enfolds the whole of your body.
**2** Stay still for a few minutes, allowing the light and warmth to fill every part of your body. Imagine the sphere shrinking back until it is the size of a tennis ball. Allow the small sphere to sink into your abdomen, before shrinking down to the size of a pea. Let the imagery dissolve. Bring your attention back to everyday awareness.

◁ When the solar plexus chakra is functioning well, we are able to accept happiness in our lives. We can feel and appreciate joy in the simplest of situations.

concerning personal power are part of the solar plexus function. As children we were subject to the guidance of our parents, relatives and teachers, all of whom we related to and possibly still relate to, as figures of authority. If people in authority use their dominant position to force us into habit patterns that take our personal power from us, the solar plexus chakra becomes effectively blocked. Failure to accede to this dominance is often met by criticism and punishment. Subsequently we may feel shame for this lack of compliance. Shame prevents us from working with the solar plexus chakra at the emotional level, and this drives us into interacting with the world primarily through our thoughts.

## healing

In this area, healing can be approached in several ways. Allowing things to be as they are, rather than trying to control events, helps to remove fears. Expressing the Fire energy as anger helps to link the solar plexus with the sacral and base chakras.

People who experience a lot of anger often live so much in their minds that they do not realize how angry they are, especially with regard to authority figures who have dominated and disempowered them. Shame can often be recognized in internal conversations that replay critical comments from the past. Here the mental criticism, which effectively acts in the same way as a curse, needs to be neutralized by formulating an imaginary response from an adult standpoint.

◁ The shame that might be felt from past humiliation by an authority figure can be neutralized in the present by visualizing the situation, changing the balance of power, and bringing the authority figure down to his or her proper size.

# Solar plexus chakra – the librarian

Working at the mental level, the solar plexus chakra is one of the most powerful tools we have at our disposal to create our personal circumstances – our own heaven or hell. Sages and philosophers have known for thousands of years that personal belief systems, the thoughts by which we recognize and understand how the world appears to work, are of critical importance to our wellbeing.

## recording

Like a librarian or custodian, this part of our 'body-mind' catalogues and files away experiences and information for reference and retrieval when it is required. To carry out this organizational task efficiently it is necessary to be able to identify things clearly and accurately, to label them correctly, to file them in the right place and to cross-index where necessary.

Failure to store information properly results in many difficulties. Confusion and fear often arise from false identification.

△ Memory has been shown to be a function of the whole brain (rather than specific areas). In order to retrieve memories, communication within the brain needs to be efficient.

Incorrect filing also creates confusion, learning problems and difficulties in retrieval (remembering). Inability to introduce cross-referencing severely limits the ability to integrate experiences.

If we are forced into certain learning situations before the solar plexus chakra, our personal librarian, is mature enough to cope, blocks occur around the issues involved and we develop negative belief systems about them. These beliefs will affect the way in which we interact with the world around us and create disharmony in that

◁ Concentration, analysis and effective study all rely on the balanced functioning of the solar plexus chakra.

## MEMORY GAME

This game has many variations in different cultures. It exercises all aspects of the solar plexus chakra at the mental level – recognition, identification, categorization, recording and recall. This exercise can be repeated, preferably using different items. If you reach 25+ items you are doing very well. It is important that even if you can remember only five or so items, you do not get annoyed or disappointed with yourself. Practice improves scores. It is up to you how honest you are with yourself when doing this exercise.

**1** Find around 30 small items and place them on a plain background. Cover the items with a cloth.

**2** Collect a pen and paper. Uncover the items and look at them for not more than three minutes.

**3** Cover the items with the cloth again. Write down as many items as you can remember.

relationship. Stresses build up and unless action is taken to correct the inaccurate beliefs, it usually results in physical, emotional and mental difficulties linked to the solar plexus chakra. If we are unable to identify events clearly, our capacity to judge, weigh up alternatives and make decisions becomes very limited.

◁ **The solar plexus chakra controls our ability to identify problems and find solutions to unlock our understanding**.

## learning

In any learning situation, the information that needs to be learned has to be identified as such so that it can subsequently be catalogued correctly. Inability to learn or study may be the result of forced or inappropriate learning situations in early life. Stresses once created here will be remembered by the body-mind every time a similar situation arises. If the stress around the events can be released, new learning strategies can emerge.

# Solar plexus chakra – know thyself

The solar plexus chakra at the spiritual level applies its energies to defining the boundaries of the self – the individual. The challenge at this level is to gain wisdom and insight into the true nature of the self beyond the everyday level of the persona.

It is not possible to define who you are unless you can also identify who and what you are not. Here the discrimination and judgment of the mental level of the solar plexus is brought to bear on the inner self. When you know who you are, you can start to understand your place in the world.

When we shine the clear light of understanding on ourselves, the first thing we tend to notice is faults and problems that have apparently been created in us by others. But as we look more closely, the need to blame others for the predicament in which we find ourselves recedes. We begin to realize that the only way forward is to transform the way we judge ourselves

△ It is necessary to turn our attention away from outer stimuli if we are to see ourselves clearly.

and others. A major sign of progress along the path to wisdom is accepting that the world owes you nothing and that you are no more important than anything else.

Solar plexus issues often arise from how we perceive ourselves in terms of our personal power. If, through experiences with overbearing authority figures, we have been led to believe that we are clumsy, stupid, worthless or bad, our whole relationship to the world will reflect this. We will feel powerless and prone to failure because of our perceived 'faults'. Similarly, if we come to believe that we are superior to other people, our actions will reflect this and there will be a tendency to ignore the wisdom of

◁ In nearly all spiritual philosophies the wisdom of the Self has been compared to the light of the sun. The perfect clarity of the solar plexus chakra clearly illuminates everything for what it is.

others and forget our own shortcomings or failures. In both situations, current events or circumstances might be identical but the powerless focus on failure, while the powerful focus on success.

Looking with the spiritual discrimination of the solar plexus chakra, both of these viewpoints have been created by incomplete information. Our own interpretation of reality is coloured by other people's eyes, minds and emotions. It is the job of the solar plexus chakra to realize at a spiritual level that all such judgments are limited and ultimately false. Our view of ourselves and others is no more substantial than clothing or masks.

Solar plexus energy can best be employed as power to do something, but very often slides into power over others. This turns into a competitive race, where we try in all sorts of ways to be better than others – more wealthy, more intelligent, more happy, more spiritual. If the energies have been distorted by bad experiences, we become more hard-done-by, more lonely and so on.

Allowing the solar plexus an opportunity to shine with the clarity of the sun encourages a broader perspective where these false judgments can begin to be seen as the ephemeral shadows they really are.

▽ **Embrace and accept yourself in the same way as you love and appreciate your closest friends.**

## MEDITATION WITHOUT FORM

This is one of the easiest, though some say also the hardest, ways of beginning to perceive the boundaries between your everyday self and the finer levels of your whole being. It is sometimes called meditation without form, and uses only the breath as a focus. Because you are always in the present during this exercise, if there is a sudden noise you should not be startled at all. But if you have disappeared into your thoughts or imaginings, away from the attention on your breath, you will find external noises quite disruptive. Begin by doing this for five minutes. As you become more practised, gradually extend the time to 20 minutes.

Sit in a comfortable position, upright but relaxed. Place your hands in your lap, the right resting on the left. Close your eyes partially, so that light still enters but no clear image can be seen. Leave your mouth slightly open and rest the tip of your tongue on the roof of your mouth, just behind your teeth. Turn your attention to the movement of your breath as it enters and leaves your body. Don't think about your breath, or try to control it, just keep your attention on it. When you become aware that your mind has wandered and you have been thinking about something else, gently bring your attention back to your breath and continue.

# Heart chakra – embracing the world

The heart chakra is located near the centre of the breastbone or sternum. The physical organs and parts of the body linked to this chakra are characterized by their actions of expansion and contraction, drawing in and pushing away.

## physical attributes

The heart, with its rhythmic expansion and contraction, is the powerful muscular pump that sends oxygenated blood to all parts of the body. By its movement, the diaphragm, the powerful muscle below the lungs, creates changes in pressure, allowing us to breathe in fresh air. As the diaphragm contracts, the

▽ **The heart chakra is at the centre of the main chakras and is the balance point for the system.**

△ **The heart chakra governs our interactions as we reach out to touch and embrace other people.**

outbreath expels carbon dioxide from the body. The lungs are composed of tree-like air ducts that bring air into contact with the bloodstream. The blood picks up oxygen from the air, releasing back into it carbon dioxide and other waste products as it returns from its journey through the body.

These processes of expansion, interchange and contraction are reflected in our relationship with the world. The heart chakra regulates our interaction, making sure that we become neither too involved nor too remote from the world around us. The relationship is in constant motion: if it stays stationary all balance is lost. Reaching out and physically touching helps us to gather information. As we gather information we respond and begin to relate.

The action of the arms can be one of enfolding, enclosing, embracing and absorption. Equally, the arms can defend, push away and protect. The degree to which we keep the physical balance between what is outside us and our inner being is often reflected in the way we hold our upper torso and arms. Tension and rigidity suggest stasis and defensiveness. A relaxed stance and flowing movement not only shows ease with the world, it reduces the stress levels on the heart and lungs.

▽ **Arms and hands are the executors of the heart chakra energy. They reach out to hold or ward off the world around us.**

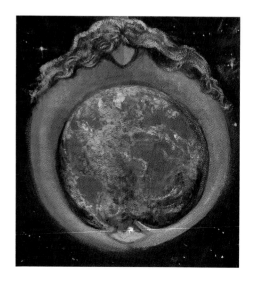

## GOMUKHASANA

This exercise extends the muscles and cavities of the chest and stretches and energizes the shoulders and arms. If your hands do not meet, hold a piece of cane or wood 25–30 cm (10–12 in) to link your hands instead.

**1** Kneel on a blanket or mat, sitting back on your heels. Stretch both arms out in front of you.

**2** Raise your left arm over your head, bending it at the elbow so the left hand rests near the top of your back.
**3** Sweep your right arm round to the right side, bending it at the elbow, sending the right hand up your back.
**4** If your hands meet, lightly clasp your fingers, otherwise hold each end of the piece of wood.

**5** When you have a grip on your hands, or the wood, take a breath in and bring your hands closer together, expanding your chest. Breathe normally. On an outbreath, loosen your grip then repeat, starting by raising your right hand above your head and mirroring the above stages.

# touching others

The art of balance is a theme that runs through all levels of the heart chakra. The element associated with this chakra is Air. Air flows from areas of high pressure towards areas of low pressure, always seeking a state of equilibrium. Likewise, the heart chakra continually strives to bring balance between external stimuli and internal emotions.

## love

The experience of love is characterized by the flow of emotion. Falling in love is a wonderful, scary experience, but for every falling in love there is a falling out of love. Unless we accept this natural balancing mechanism, falling in love can become a fearful experience because of the inevitable grief and abandonment that accompanies falling out of love again. Understanding that ebb and flow happens from day to day, from moment to moment, eases any temporary sense of loss. Trying to hold on to any fluid emotional state like love will lead to an obsessive, possessive attachment reminiscent of an imbalanced sacral chakra response, or that of a four- to seven-year-old child.

△ **Keeping the balance between personal needs and the needs of others is the function of the heart chakra.**

## acceptance

A balanced and coherent heart chakra is shown in the ability to accept ourselves, other people and all sorts of situations. Without a real self-acceptance there is no

▽ **The importance of unconditional love is never greater than in a parent-child relationship.**

way that we are able to tolerate the foibles and faults of others. When we feel comfortable in ourselves, with all our faults, we are less likely to be insecure or threatened by those who, through their own envy, jealousy or lack of self-worth, try to dominate or control everything and everyone around them.

## relationships

Any relationship can be heaven or hell. In a balanced relationship, each person has autonomy, but both also share. In relationships that are unhealthy, love is conditional to the point of being a weapon used to coerce the other into behaving or responding as required. Phrases like 'Well, if you really loved me you would…' and 'I'm doing this because I think it's good for you and I love you…' make a relationship one-sided. Many of us experience this threatened withdrawal of love as small children, and until our heart chakras become truly balanced, we may continue to play out the same pattern on our own children, family and friends.

## BALANCING A RELATIONSHIP

This visualization exercise can be helpful in sorting out a difficult relationship, or in finding solutions to problems in relationships where one partner shows an unhealthy dependence on the other. It encourages a personal sense of space and helps you to reach an acknowledgement of the qualities of the other person. You can repeat the exercise as often as you feel it is necessary.

**1** Set aside some quiet time when you are unlikely to be disturbed. Sit in a comfortable position, in a chair or on the floor, with an empty cushion or chair placed near you. Close your eyes, breathing slowly and calmly, and settle yourself.

**2** Once your breathing has slowed and you are feeling calm, start to visualize a cylinder of gold light shining all around you, reaching down into the ground and rising up above your head.

**3** On the other cushion, or in the empty chair, visualize the person with whom you have a relationship that needs to be rebalanced.

**4** As you visualize the person sitting near you, recognize the qualities in them that you feel are causing difficulties between you in your relationship. Recognize, also, all the qualities in them that you appreciate or admire.

**5** Visualize a second cylinder of gold light surrounding the other person. In your mind's eye, visualize both of you sitting within your own separate cylinders of gold light. If you notice any stray threads of light connecting the two cylinders, allow them to dissolve. Become aware of the space between you and the other person. Slowly return to normal awareness.

# Heart chakra – freedom to be

Most people are aware that their physical appearance and attributes are inherited through their genes from each parent. It is not so well recognized that we also inherit many of our thinking patterns in the same way.

## inheritance

Dominant beliefs, especially negative ones, can be traced through several successive generations. If we remain tied to these beliefs we never discover who we are and independence is never really achieved.

Following the rules drawn up by someone else gives us guidelines and lists of what we 'should' or 'ought' to do in order to develop a sense of duty and responsibility. These rules may have been enforced in some way, to mould us into the person the maker of the rules had in mind. This process can create, for the most part, a very harmonious society in which to live.

In some work situations, especially those dealing with emergency services, following the rules becomes a survival issue. While everyday life does not have that sort of intensity, for some people 'following the rules' remains an absolute necessity. This type of thinking has a robotic quality, producing people whose interaction can only follow a set formula or etiquette.

## values

As the heart chakra matures, the individual starts to examine the rules to see whether they are really valid. Repression and restriction becomes intolerable. Outright rebellion may seem to be the only way to break free of the suffocating pattern. Society as a whole does not deal kindly with people

◁ **In modern urban society the individual is moulded to fit in with a required role. Personal freedom may be exchanged for rigid order.**

who question the consensus: this stage of individualization can thus be a lonely journey. The best outcome is the development of a personal set of values and ethics by which to live, which may be based on the old rules, but come from a fresh, up-to-date perspective with a personal relevance. It has been said by philosophers that there is no freedom without discipline. When a balanced state of individual self-discipline is achieved, self-acceptance and freedom become possible.

In many cultures, such as classical India and China, it was accepted that at some stage of life a removal from the rigidity of normal society was a natural phase of personal development. Usually this occurred in later life, when family responsibilities were no longer an issue. Individuals could concentrate on spiritual disciplines or remove themselves to remote spots to perfect skills of poetry or painting. In most cases, the rebellious can find alternative societies where they feel free from control, although every group imposes its own rules and taboos, which offer the kind of orderly balance the individual needs. This clearly demonstrates that restrictions are a burden only when they do not offer a balance to the unique heart chakra needs of each of us.

△ **Expansion, growth and freedom are all pre-requisites for a healthy and mature heart chakra.**

Whatever the rules and regulations of a society may be, those who are openly rebellious become primary targets for the criticism of the group. Today's behaviour censors are the tabloid press, who rely on the unusual behaviour of individuals to sustain their demand for interesting stories. At the same time, the media tend to take a tribal stance, rejecting new concepts and unique insights in favour of the establishment viewpoint. There are always, though, small groups and individuals on the edge of society who are prepared to explore new balances and create new patterns.

▽ **Chains, restraints and restrictions are only recognized as such when the individual grows beyond the need for them. Before this point they offer security.**

## INDIVIDUAL OR INHERITED BELIEFS?

If you want or need to begin to de-programme yourself from values that are not yours, this exercise may help.

**1** Take time to think about, then list on a sheet of paper, beliefs that begin with 'I should...' Add to your list over a period of a week or so, then don't look at it for a week. Look at the list – seeing if you can identify any of the statements with older family members, teachers or partners. If you do notice any links, ask yourself if you honestly believe the statement. Reflect on the relevance of the other statements you have made to your present life. Cross out those that no longer apply.

**2** Copy out a list of the remaining statements, then leave them for another week. Repeat the self-questioning process. If there are any statements left on the list, they may highlight key issues that need dealing with or healing. They could also show you some of your present key values.

**3** A similar exercise focuses on your wishes. Make a list beginning 'I want...' Be completely honest and open with yourself. This has nothing to do with judging what is good or bad. Neither should you exclude things that seem to be unlikely, impossible or silly. Acknowledging your drives and ambitions, your daydreams and fantasies in this way can release many hidden levels of stress from your heart chakra and may allow your conscious awareness to move in a direction that is more self-fulfilling.

# Heart chakra – following the heart

At a certain point in the development and maturing of the heart chakra there is an opportunity to see yourself and the rest of the world from a very different perspective. This new view of the world can present some discomfort if the inherent patterning has always been to look outside yourself for confirmation and verification of your own worth. The realization dawns that while you can care, love and share with others you cannot live their lives for them or live your life through them. It can also be a very lonely moment when you realize that others cannot live your life for you either. They can love you, advise you and commiserate with you, but in the end, everyone is responsible only for themselves. Everybody has their unique direction in life.

△ **The heart chakra allows us to expand and grow in power while keeping harmony with the Earth and everything around us**.

## balance

If we are able to accommodate the paradoxical themes of the heart chakra, we can follow our own path while allowing others to follow theirs. The saying: 'If you love somebody, set them free' encapsulates the energy of a fully functional heart chakra. No matter how much you have shared with, taught, sacrificed for and loved someone, letting them be themselves is the greatest gift you can give. This releasing of the other person allows any possessiveness, misplaced sense of responsibility or dependence to disappear, and enables both of you to grow.

## compassion

When you are able to achieve some sort of balance between yourself and everything outside yourself, the way opens for a special mix of compassion and caring. With this balance comes the understanding that, although the boundaries between the self and the world needed to be clear to get to this point, when you arrive there are no boundaries. This is not a sacrificial relationship with the world, but a complete openness and acceptance of it. In order to progress as a spiritual human being, avoiding

## BALANCING THE INNER AND OUTER WORLDS

This exercise helps to balance your relationship with the world and can be extremely calming. Sit or lie down in a comfortable position.

**1** Breathe in then, as you breathe out, allow your body to relax. Visualize a flower giving off light at your heart chakra. Stay with that flower for a minute or two, feeling its energy and presence. In the centre of that flower, visualize the whole Earth.

Imagine the light of the flower filling the whole planet with incredible joy. Allow that joy and light to fill all of you too. Let that energy reach every single part of you, clearing away all negativity.

**2** After a few minutes, bring your hands together over the heart chakra in the centre of your chest. Feel the energy under your hands and allow your hands to release that energy by slowly returning them to their original position lying in your lap.

Visualize the Earth at the centre of the flower at your heart chakra, melting into the flower and then the flower melting into your heart. Stay with this thought for a moment before slowly returning to normal awareness.

▷ **At its spiritual level of function the heart chakra directs us along our path of life in a way that allows us to achieve our maximum potential.**

the pitfalls of spiritual self-deception and egotism, it is necessary to arrive at a real awareness that, because all creation is connected, you cannot be truly free until everything else is too. The open acceptance of the world, and the awareness that the individual's spiritual development benefits everything, everywhere, is known as 'bodhicitta' or 'complete openness of mind'.

Bodhicitta has been fully explored in Buddhist traditions. It is found in the simple awareness of offering kindness to others at every possible opportunity. The Buddhist cosmology is huge, with millions of universes existing for millions of aeons. Within this ungraspable vastness of space and time, individuals are said to have incarnated numberless times. If this is the case then everyone we meet and every being we come across has, at one time or another, been our mother and has looked after, loved and cared for us to the best of their ability. In this context bodhicitta is simply acknowledging these past kindnesses.

▽ **Equilibrium, or balance, is the key to the heart chakra energy. Without it there can be no way for us to adapt to constant change.**

# Chakras of communication

The upper three chakras are at the base of the throat, the centre of the forehead and just above the crown of the head. They are physically close together and regulate our communication with and understanding of the world. The throat chakra focuses on the expression of what we know and feel. The brow chakra brings clarity of perception and intuitive insight, and the crown chakra unites the individual to the greater universe.

# Throat chakra – finding peace

Blue is the colour associated with the throat chakra. It is the colour of communication and information but is also the colour of peacefulness. The human nervous system is 'hard-wired' to respond to the blue of twilight by settling down, becoming quiet and preparing to rest during the hours of darkness. As the body becomes less active, so mental activity is also reduced. An observant detachment becomes more apparent. As physical objects become less visible, so too the mental functions become more imaginative, vague and dreamlike. Peace descends.

## the easy flow of energy

With a balance of energies within the throat chakra, peace is a tangible experience, a familiar relaxed occurrence. Where the throat chakra is stressed or blocked in some way, peace may be longed-for, but difficult, if not impossible to achieve.

Wherever there is a concentration of inappropriate energy, pressure begins to build up. Whatever the cause of the build-up, an outward flow is the only means of restoring balance, with energy flowing from an area of high pressure to one of lower

pressure. This outward flow from the body is achieved through expression and communication, via the activity of the throat chakra. If the expression is blocked in some way, the energy will have to find release through one of the other major chakra functions, for example as aggressive, selfish behaviour via the base chakra or as escapism via the brow chakra.

Singing, chanting or playing a musical instrument, even banging on a drum, will help to restore balance to the throat chakra. Toning can also be useful. This is simply making extended vocal sounds out loud for as long as your breath allows. The sound and note are less important than the quality of the vibration created through your body. Toning can be effective at releasing physical and emotional tensions. Just allow whatever sound occurs to come up, and let it go.

## the need to listen

Communication is not simply about personal expression. It is also necessary to listen to what is being expressed by others. Blocks or excess energy can often distract from the true meaning of what someone else is trying to communicate, for there is a

△ **A true sense of peace arises when there is equilibrium within the chakra system and an easy flow of energy through the body.**

▽ **Drumming quietens the mind while allowing excess energy to be dissipated harmlessly through the physical activity.**

tendency to react to each word or phrase as it is heard, rather than comprehending the meaning of the whole.

Without the appropriate outward flow of energy there can be too much involvement with what is being communicated – everything is taken as being relevant to, or critical of, oneself. A block at the throat centre creates a closed circuit where nothing can escape. Problems also occur if individual expression has been stifled, often by overbearing discipline. When this happens the energy within the body must direct itself in one of two ways – upwards to become locked in a fantasy world of the imagination, or downwards to distort the base, sacral and solar plexus as excessive manipulation and dominance of others in overt or covert aggression.

## creative expression

The resolution of such conditions is found in expressing the energy in an effective but safe manner. Any creative artistic occupation will work – as long as the focus is on the activity itself, rather than on the end product. Such activity is a release of excess energy – if a masterpiece of art is the end product this is a bonus, but it is not the intention. Not to be expressive simply because you believe that you 'can't paint' is just reinforcing the same repressive values that have probably caused the problem in the first place.

There are strategies to help you loosen artistic hang-ups that are well worth trying. One is to draw on pages from magazines or newspapers – a clean white piece of drawing paper can be intimidating. Draw with felt tip pens with broad tips. This prevents you from getting caught up with timid little lines. Alternatively, use very small pieces of paper and very fine pens – it is much easier to see your whole design and make an effective image. Set out to use all parts of the paper right up to the corners.

### RELEASING PHYSICAL AND EMOTIONAL TENSION

Use this exercise to release any block that you become aware of that can be traced back to some feelings that you have not expressed. Perhaps someone has made you feel hurt or angry, and instead of confronting those feelings you have suppressed them. Burning incense of some kind while you carry out this process will help to cleanse the emotional debris from your aura and surroundings. Pungent and sweet-smelling herbs were originally used in this way for purification and to drive away demons.

**1** Write down what you wish to say to the person who has hurt or angered you. As you are doing this, let any anger you are feeling find its way on to the page, allowing the feelings to come. When you have finished do not read what you have written.

**2** Take the piece of paper, fold it up, and burn it in the flame of a candle or on an open fire. Simply destroy it completely. If necessary, repeat the process until you sense that your equilibrium has been restored and you can feel peace returning.

# Throat chakra – getting the message

Language is the evolutionary leap that is often considered to have been the major factor in the success of our species. As a means of communicating complex concepts, planning the unknown future and sharing the experiences of the past, language has enabled us to begin living more in our minds and more in the past and the future than in the present moment. Language has given us the ability to understand what is happening to others around us. The growth of society and civilization are based on cooperation and shared dreams, which are communicated by language.

▽ The throat chakra allows us to communicate how we feel and what we think. In the West it is associated with the colour blue.

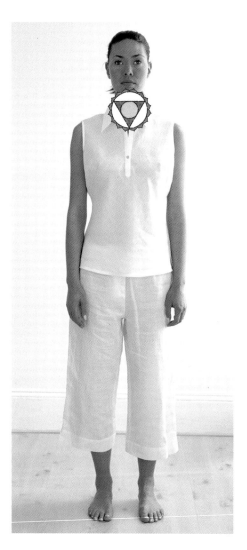

## physical considerations

All the physical organs and structures of the throat have to do with letting energy move through – either inwards or outwards. The mouth, nose and throat are where we first come into contact with the air around us. Even though breathing is initiated in the solar plexus, we feel the air as it passes over the back of the palate and through the upper throat.

The mouth and oesophagus are our first contacts with food – in fact, vital digestive processes are carried out in the mouth. A great deal happens in this small area, and it all has to be carefully regulated – we are able to speak only on the outbreath as air passes over our vocal cords; we have to avoid breathing in at the same time as we swallow, or we choke.

Wrapped around the vital tubes carrying air and food – the trachea and the

△ Every form of expression reveals the emotions and thoughts of the individual, for the acknowledgement of the group.

oesophagus – are the thyroid and parathyroid glands. These major endocrine glands regulate the body's metabolism, ensuring that enough energy is produced

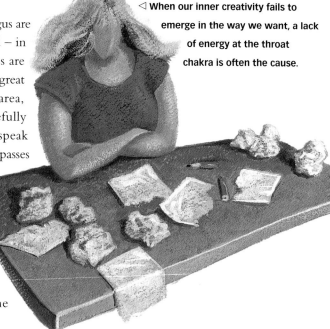

◁ When our inner creativity fails to emerge in the way we want, a lack of energy at the throat chakra is often the cause.

from food for our needs. Lethargy and sluggishness result from an underactive thyroid and hyperactivity is due to an overactive thyroid.

## voice

The voice allows us to express what we are feeling in the heart and mind. Expressing what is going on inside ourselves to those around us gives a shared understanding and a sense of belonging. Blocks in our ability to communicate may not cause an immediate problem, as they would with the physical organs of the throat, but the curtailment of personal expression is nonetheless deeply disturbing to the energy systems as a whole. In fact, lack of expression denies our existence, our individuality and our right to be heard.

Personal expression of ideas and thoughts, and the ability to communicate through spoken language, or the symbolic languages of writing, singing, performing or any of the other arts, help to maintain the healthy flow of energy through the throat chakra. The expression does not have to be perfect, unique or special in any way for it to be of benefit. Criticism and judgment of our expression are detrimental to the wellbeing of the chakra – indeed, if anything restricts the natural outward exuberant flow of expression, problems are likely to arise.

Indications of blocks in this area may be a stiff neck, throat infection or tension in the shoulders. Headaches or problems with swallowing or eating and metabolic disorders also point to underlying throat chakra problems. Some difficulties become obvious when frustration leads to shouting, or to its opposite: a complete withdrawal of communication.

The throat chakra is like a pressure valve. Its function is to allow the energy from the other chakra centres to express themselves so that other people can understand what is going on. If this ability is suppressed, either

### USTRASANA

This exercise encourages good blood supply to the neck, keeping the energy moving through the chakra. It is a simplified version of the yoga pose ustrasana, the camel pose, which opens up the front of the body.

**1** Sit on your heels on a blanket or mat, clasping your hands behind you.

**2** Breathe in, then, as you breathe out, allow your head to drop backwards. At the same time, raise your arms a little behind you. Breathe normally.

**3** When you are ready to release the posture, release your hands on an outbreath and bring yourself back to sitting upright.

**4** Repeat this three or four times.

internally or because of outside influences, problems will inevitably arise. The chakra system works all the time as one continuous flow of energy, like cogs connected together in a machine. If one begins to seize up, all the other chakras will have their function impaired. For example, if there is a problem in a relationship, where feelings are not being acknowledged or talked about, there may be symptoms at the throat but the heart chakra will also be under strain. So if you find you are suffering from a recurrence of neck or throat problems it is always a good idea to take a look at your situation and see what restrictions might be blocking your ability to express yourself, whether they arise from others or whether you are putting unnecessary limitations on yourself.

# Throat chakra – the teacher

Communication and sound are the keys to the throat chakra. Those who use these skills in their work are drawing on the energy of this centre. Through the throat we communicate how we feel inside – our emotional state – and how we think – our mental processes.

## education

How effective and expressive communication is depends upon how we have been taught when still young. Many traditional forms of education pass knowledge from generation to generation through repetition and learning by rote. Very often, however, the content of the information can be misunderstood.

Many of us will be able to remember instances where hymns or prayers that were repeated regularly at home and school were misheard or just misinterpreted for many years, simply because the meaning of the words had never been explained. Communication by simple repetition has a tendency to break down very quickly, as the game known as Chinese whispers graphically illustrates.

If we, or those we talk to, are unable to understand the content of language – if we cannot 'take it to heart', true communication cannot take place. Problems with effective communication demonstrate that the chakra system has to work as an integrated whole. Without the input of the mind (the sixth and seventh chakras), and personal feelings (the heart), the throat chakra has nothing to work with.

△ **Both teaching and learning use the energies of the throat chakra in the flow of communication.**

## teaching

The effective teacher is a person who feels excitement and interest and can express it to their students in a way that allows the knowledge to become their own. This requires an exploration of the views and opinions of others, with the possibility of dissent and disagreement. New information should be integrated with what is already known and believed, not simply asserted as inflexible dogma.

▷ **Learning by doing is often more effective than learning by rote because it actively involves a broader range of chakra energies, making knowledge personal.**

### WHAT DO YOU BELIEVE?

This exercise is one way of looking at beliefs about yourself. Make a list of what you hold to be true beginning with 'I think that...' For example, 'I think that my feet are too big,' 'I think that I am ignored,' 'I think I talk too much,' 'I think nobody really listens to what I say,' and so on. Don't make excuses or try to rationalize or judge your statements. Very quickly, patterns will emerge that help to reveal core beliefs. Opposing views are often held simultaneously. These create internal tensions whatever viewpoint we adopt. Resolving them can free up enormous amounts of personal creativity. Discovering our inner patterns of belief reveals that we ourselves have been our teacher all along.

◁ **Communication is not simply an exchange of words. Over 90 per cent of meaning is transmitted by non-verbal signals. Modern forms of communication very often exclude these important clues.**

experience and what we have been told by adults. As we mature new beliefs are categorized and grouped under the relevant core beliefs. By adulthood the original core beliefs may be completely obscured by their later, more sophisticated, accretions. Still, every experience is understood in terms of the belief systems we have built up for ourselves. What we are able to hear, what we are able to understand and what we are able to express and create, all depend upon the model that we have drawn up telling us how the world works.

The throat chakra is very much the mouthpiece of the other chakras. What it listens to, what it hears and how it responds are all flavoured by the patterns of stress found within each of the other six chakras. For instance, a series of blocks within the second, sacral chakra, which brings about our sense of playful creativity, may prevent real personal creativity from being expressed via the throat chakra – even though the individual may be a wonderful narrator of other people's material.

▽ **We tend to notice things that interest us, and ignore the rest. We recognize our names being spoken by others even in noisy places.**

Unfortunately, when we are young, we have a tendency to believe everything that we are told. Every scrap of information is gathered and memorized in the process of getting to know how the world works. Because their language skills are still forming, children are able to sense when a conflict of information is occurring, but usually cannot express it effectively, or else they are not given the opportunity to clarify what they have been taught.

## absorption

Learning to explore alternative views, even taking up opposite viewpoints in a debate, is a useful way of developing attitudes of flexibility and tolerance. Without these skills there is the danger that whatever is communicated to us will be automatically believed. Personal belief systems gradually build up in complexity as we grow. However, the basic structure is laid down when we are very young and consists of core beliefs based on personal

# Throat chakra – finding your voice

The throat is traditionally associated with the element of space, which is also called ether and, in the original Sanskrit texts, akasha. This fifth element was conceived as the original container, the vessel that held all the other elements.

## sound

In the original Indian texts the first thing to be created, or to emerge out of the primal space, was the vibration we call sound. These waves of sound constituted the whole of creation – all matter, all thought, all energy are in reality the interplay of the sounds or songs of the Creator. The importance of sound and speech as a creative principle is very common among the peoples of the world. Creation myths often combine the moulding of creatures out of inanimate matter with the life-giving

▽ **Places of sacred significance have nearly always been chosen or constructed because of their special acoustic properties.**

## MANTRA CHANTING

△ **Although mantras often have meaning their real value is in the quality of subtle sound they create within the body.**

Chanting and using mantra meditation offer ways of releasing throat chakra problems and experiencing finer levels of speech. Mantras are powerful sequences of sound that enliven deep levels of energy in the body and mind. Traditionally, mantras are chosen by a teacher to be appropriate to the individual. It is important not to use 'any old sound' as a mantra, as this can have a disruptive effect on subtle levels. The primal sound in many traditions is 'AAAH' – the first vowel sound that is made with a completely relaxed throat. Taking a deep breath and simply chanting AAAH for as long as possible creates a clearing in the throat chakra. Begin loud and after a few repetitions, start to chant more softly, until the sound is simply a thought, then a silence in the mind.

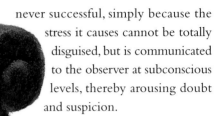

▷ **The soothing sound of storytelling trains the mind to understand many nuances of meaning and language.**

addition of breath or the process of naming. Myths and stories show the magical and spiritual significance of knowing the right names for things.

## truth

Where it is functioning at its highest level the throat chakra should be bringing out our own truth into the world. Truth is not just a matter of correct information. Neither does truth carry any moral weight, though it can be experienced as good or bad, comfortable or uncomfortable, depending on how it interacts with each person's beliefs about what is real. Each of us will dismiss as untrue those things that do not fall within our personal construction of how the universe works.

Speaking from a level of personal truth means that whatever is said carries the conviction of our whole being, sometimes referred to as will. Personal will or truth rarely emerges however, because we are all constrained by the values and concepts we have been taught by others. All our communications are filtered and distorted by the many energy blocks that have arisen from the stresses and traumas of the past. Only with the gradual removal of these stresses can a more honest and open relationship with the world emerge.

## lies, damned lies...

Telling lies has a remarkable effect on the whole body. When a lie is told, conflict in the hemispheres of the brain releases stress hormones that create measurable changes in blood chemistry and skin resistance, and a dip in all the subtle energies of the meridians and subtle bodies. The throat chakra energies become strained and distorted if lying becomes habitual. Lying is

never successful, simply because the stress it causes cannot be totally disguised, but is communicated to the observer at subconscious levels, thereby arousing doubt and suspicion.

Fear, doubt and uncertainty all prevent honest, open communication. We can try to avoid telling lies, but until fear is removed completely all behaviour will be a compromise between what an individual really wants and what they perceive is required by others. By working to clear the throat chakra, these oppressive blocks to creativity and true expression of self can gradually be dissipated.

### TIBETAN MANTRA

The best known mantra is probably OM. It consists of three sounds A-U-M, each of which expresses in seed form the creation of everything in the universe. AAAH is the most natural sound to emerge from the mouth. The O sound begins to shape and control this open flow of energy, symbolizing the creation of form. The M, actually a nasal hum closer to -NG, represents the continuity of the complex vibrations that make up the many levels of reality. The Tibetan mantra OM-AA-HUNG is a variation of this primal sound and can be used as a regular exercise to cleanse the

chakras, open the throat and quieten the mind. It can be done without accompanying visualization, though introducing the other elements adds significantly to the effect.

**1** Take a good breath and sound an OM for as long as you can without straining, rhyming it with 'from'. At the same time visualize white light at the centre of the brow, or the Tibetan character for this sound.
**2** Now take another deep breath and pronounce AA, rhyming it with 'car'. Continue for as long as you can. At the same time see red light at the centre of the throat or the character for this sound, coloured red.
**3** On the third breath, sound HUNG, rhyming it with 'sung'. End the sound by humming with your mouth closed so that your skull bones vibrate. With this sound visualize a blue light at the heart or a blue Tibetan symbol for the sound. Repeat the sequence as many times as you like.

▽ **The formal characters of the Tibetan alphabet spell out the primal sounds OM, AA, HUNG, encapsulating every aspect of creation.**

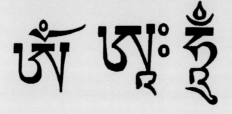

# Brow chakra – seeing the picture

The chakra located in the centre of the forehead is called ajña, meaning to perceive and to command. It is directly related to the senses of sight and hearing, although all three upper chakras – the throat, brow and crown – are physically close together and share many correspondences. Throat chakra influences extend to the mouth and jaw and up to the ears, while the brow has more links with the face, eyes, nose and forehead. The neck and base of the skull can be influenced by both brow and throat energies. Crown chakra energies relate to the cranium, the bones of the top of the head at and above the hairline.

▽ **The brow chakra is the seat of understanding, from where we picture how the world is.**

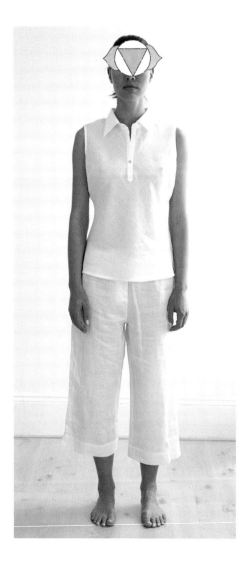

## thoughts

Our everyday awareness is located in the area of the brow chakra, from where our higher sense functions scan the world around us. The consciousness of self, of the unique personality of the mind, is felt to be seated here, like a commander at his control post. We are very much in our heads – more than, say, in our heart or our solar plexus. The physical body belongs to us but we do not think of it as being 'us' in the same way.

We relate to our own thoughts, our interpretations and inner conversations, continually assessing the information that feeds in through the senses. We relate to others by focusing attention on the face – the eyes and the subtle changes of expression, feeling that the 'real person' is somewhere in there. This arises from the awareness that here at the brow chakra we

△ **Perception is understanding how different parts come together to make a whole. It is the job of the brow chakra to interpret clearly.**

begin to make sense of and interpret the world. The brow chakra is all about seeing, not just seeing with the eyes, but seeing with the mind – making sense of and understanding what is being perceived.

## eyesight

We do not see what the eyes see. The eye focuses light through the lens and an upside-down image is thrown on to the retina at the back of the eye. However, only one tiny spot, the fovea, has a concentration of light-sensitive cells great enough to produce a complete focused image; the rest of the eye receives a vaguer, more blurred picture. Rapid movement of the eyes adds more

## CLEAR SEEING

Seeing clearly depends on the coordination between the mind and the eyes. Confusion in understanding (seeing) arises when blocks in the brow chakra disturb the complex relationship between eye movements and nerve impulses as they travel to the centres of visual comprehension in the brain. Getting confused shows that stress is affecting coordination. Practice will re-open these pathways, increasing your ability to focus and understand the world around you. This simple exercise helps both the muscles controlling eye movement and the balance between the left and right hemispheres of the brain.

▽ **Seeing is not simply a sense of perception. We use 'I see' to mean 'I understand'. Seeing relies on the flexibility of the mind as well as the sharpness of the eyes.**

**1** Sit in a relaxed position with an upright head. Gaze forwards with your eyes relaxed.

**2** Turn your eyes upwards and as high as they will go, making sure your head does not move. Now slowly and attentively roll your eyes in a clockwise direction.

**3** When you return to the top again, relax and gaze forward for a moment.

**4** Now repeat the exercise, but this time move your eyes anticlockwise, in the opposite direction to before. Make sure your head remains still and that your eyes move as slowly and evenly as possible.

**5** Repeat each cycle a couple of times unless you feel some strain. If you want to check your eye-brain coordination, do this exercise while you are saying a nursery rhyme or counting numbers.

of memories, the brain organizes the visual information so that we can understand and really 'see'. Perception is the art of creating order from potential chaos, from random impulses. Perception is the main function of the brow chakra.

Balancing this chakra can help physical problems with the eyes, but more than this, it will help remove confusion caused by an inability to distinguish important things from insignificant ones; in visual terms, the foreground from the background. Clear seeing, understanding and perspective are all mental skills that are needed to interpret visual data, as well as the mental pictures that are our thoughts, memories and ideas.

Seeing the picture allows us to move within the orderly, familiar patterns of life. Without the brow chakra making sense of information received by the brain, we would be paralysed by confusion and indecision.

▽ **Pattern-making is essential for the mind to understand what it is being shown by the eyes. Whenever possible a pattern will be seen, even in a random display of colours.**

information, scanning the field of vision to allow us to get a clearer set of images. When these images travel to the brain they are switched, so that information from the left eye travels to the right hemisphere of the brain and vice versa.

## breaking the code

The brain interprets the flurry of electrical nerve impulses and fills in all the gaps itself. Recognizing familiar shapes and relationships between things, creating patterns that mean something from its store

# Brow chakra – creative dreaming

The colour associated with the brow chakra is indigo – the deep blue of a midnight sky. It is the colour of deep silence and stillness, of resonant emptiness and solitude. The brow chakra has a certain degree of detachment from emotional concerns.

## perspective

In order to see clearly, a distance must be maintained between subject and object. It is possible to recognize patterns only when the background, known as the field, is empty. In the same way, the emotions at the brow chakra have to be quiet in order to allow clear images to appear. Because the process of seeing involves so much 'filling in' by the brain, any strong emotional involvement can distort the picture we receive and our eyes can deceive us. If our emotional needs are too strong it is possible to become obsessed with the fine details of the pattern so that nothing else is seen – the 'big picture' is lost in the power of a single idea or dream. Silence and detachment allow the brow chakra to keep its perspective.

▽ **Time and space are laws of physical reality that do not constrain the non-physical worlds of the mind and spirit. All things become possible.**

## detachment

Jumping to conclusions and making assumptions are signs that the brow chakra is becoming confused by too much emotional noise, blurring the clear distinction between 'I want' and 'I see'. Allowing the spaciousness of detached and passive watching increases the possibility that intuition – the flash of knowing that seems to come from nowhere – will arise in the mind. Receptivity and openness to new possibilities allow the necessary clarity in the brow for accurate perception.

Detachment is crucial to the functioning of the brow chakra at all levels, not just at the emotional level. Mental agility requires the ability to step back from the normal waking experiences of time and space. Where the throat chakra uses sound to communicate in language – a linear, time-based experience – the brow chakra uses light to carry messages in the form of visual symbols and pictures. The internal world of dreams, daydreams and the imagination is not limited by the rules of the physical universe. Anything can appear: the impossible alongside the mundane, the fantastic with the ordinary. As in dreams, the logic of time and matter can be ignored.

△ **Making sense of things requires the perspective of distance to see the whole picture. Taking a rest from problems allows the ajña to see new patterns that may give solutions.**

Transformations occur continually, changing scenes and context. Events can happen simultaneously or even run backwards in time. From the perspective of conscious awareness all this is confusing and difficult to understand. From the perspective of the mental functioning of the brow chakra this language of light is a straightforward communication of energy that directly affects the electrical impulses of the brain, and from there, the whole system.

The brow chakra, resting in its state of quiet observation, can build up, interpret and change the very nature of our reality. It is no wonder that its Sanskrit name, ajña, also means 'one who commands'. The new discipline of psychoneuro-immunology is a medical adaptation of the visualization techniques of yogis and mystics who, through experience, knew full well the power of the mind to alter every aspect of the body and the physical world by constructing meaningful images of light within their own minds.

## MATSYASANA

Here are two versions of an exercise that can help to focus energy at the brow chakra. Try both versions and choose whichever is the most comfortable or effective for you.

The name for this posture, the fish, comes from Matsya, the name for the fish incarnation of Vishnu, the Hindu deity who is the source and maintainer of the universe and everything in it.

**1** For the first version (left), begin by kneeling on a blanket or mat. Place the palms of your hands on the floor behind you, fingers pointing forwards, bending your elbows.

**2** Lean back on to your elbows and breathe in. As you breathe out, let your head drop backwards and arch your back slightly. Breathe normally, focusing on your brow chakra.

**3** For the second version (below), sit with your legs out in front of you and your feet together. Place the palms of your hands under your hips, bending your elbows behind you.

**4** Lean back on to your elbows and breathe in. As you breathe out, lean backwards until you are supporting yourself on your arms. Allow your head to drop backwards and arch your back slightly. Breathe normally, again focusing on your brow chakra.

**5** When you are ready to come out of this position, allow your elbows to slide away, lowering yourself to a lying position.

**6** Roll on to your side and sit up.

# Brow chakra – visions

In popular thought the brow chakra is considered to be synonymous with the 'third eye'. In traditional Indian texts the forehead has many interrelated smaller chakras, which extend upwards from the ajña between the eyebrows until they merge with the functions of the crown chakra. Each of these chakras deals with increasingly fine experiences of perception, clarity and realms of subtle energy where deities and other powerful spirits dwell. The sixth and seventh chakras enable consciousness to move beyond the physical universe. To the ardent materialist of the 21st century, reality is objective solidity. What happens in the mind, not being physical or measurable in any way, is illusory, ephemeral, subjective. In fact, normal reality is largely a mind-created construct that can only be experienced subjectively, within ourselves.

## insight and intuition

Intuition is hard to define, but can be understood as a prompting from all the levels of awareness beyond the everyday conscious mind, which some would associate with the unconscious or subconscious mind. Intuition presents a whole picture, an overview and an understanding that goes beyond the simple explanation of its parts. The whole picture given us in a flash of intuition brings a sense of solidity, of usefulness to the mind. Giving ourselves space to notice and act on intuitive insight frees the energy of the brow chakra. Confidence in the subtle signals received from these areas of perception can develop into 'clear seeing' or clairvoyance.

## clairvoyance

The clairvoyant experience is not necessarily only a visual one; it is 'clear seeing' in the sense of receiving clear, penetrating insight. The knowledge that accompanies the act of clairvoyance may include visual data, but these are not necessarily perceived in the same way that we see the everyday world. The information is more akin to dream imagery and memory. The attention travels, or moves beyond time and space, to visualize new information. For many people, it seems difficult to distinguish clairvoyance from imagination, and is usually referred to as 'only my imagination', as if it should be instantly discounted as an unsafe source of information. With experience and an increase in confidence the difference can be felt quite clearly – it is as though different mental muscles have come into play.

How we receive information depends very much on the way we naturally interpret our senses. Psychologists recognize three distinct types of response that we all possess, though we favour one over the others. A visual imagination will find it very easy to see thoughts in terms of pictures, in clear detail and full colour. A kinaesthetic imagination will interpret thoughts and images as feelings, either as moods or as sensations related to the body. An auditory imagination will interpret information as words, phrases or dialogue.

Recognizing which type we are makes it easier to identify the prompting of the brow chakra's intuition for what it is. For example, with a kinaesthetic mind it is no good expecting to see clear images. With a visual mind it is important to learn how the mind employs symbols, whereas with an auditory mind, thoughts pop into the head.

▽ **The brow chakra has the ability to see beyond the obvious, accessing the realms of intuition and clairvoyance to gain insight.**

## PSYCHOMETRY

This exercise provides a way of receiving impressions about an object, its history and owners. It is best carried out with an open curiosity and a sense of fun. Don't worry about getting it right or wrong, just play with the possibilities. Practise with objects from many different people and places, and you will quickly develop your accuracy and the strength of your impressions.

**1** Ask a friend for a piece of jewellery or a watch. If it is old and has had more than one owner, all the better. Sit comfortably and allow your breathing to settle, then turn your attention inwards and allow your senses to still.

**2** Pick up the object, hold it in your hands and focus on it. Begin to process your thoughts, feelings and any sensations or imagery that come to you.

**3** To deepen the process you might find it helpful to place the item against your brow chakra. After a minute or so put the object down. Turn your attention to yourself once again, allowing your breathing to settle. Turn your attention to the soles of your feet for a minute to ground your energy, then relate your impressions.

# Crown chakra – the fountain head

The Sanskrit name for the crown chakra is sahasrara, meaning 'thousandfold'. This refers to the image of the thousand-petalled lotus which, in Hindu thought, represents the epitome of the human condition. The chakra is described as being positioned just above the head.

## the pituitary gland

The gland most often associated with the crown chakra is the pituitary, though some texts do quote the relevant gland as being

▽ **The crown chakra is the main co-ordinating centre of the body and ensures that the individual is also connected to universal sources of energy.**

the pineal. The pituitary gland is located at the base of the brain. It has two sections, the anterior and posterior, which are each responsible for releasing particular hormones. The pituitary is often referred to as the 'master gland' because it affects so many other glands and body functions.

## the brain

The brain is a most complex organ with four main sections and billions of nerves. One section of the brain, the cerebrum, is involved with sensation, reasoning, planning and problem-solving. The diencephalon contains the pineal gland, the thalamus and the hypothalamus, which are referred to collectively as the limbic system. This controls body temperature, water balance, appetite, heart rate, sleep patterns and emotions. The brain stem, midbrain, pons and medulla oblongata control breathing, heart rate and blood pressure. The cerebellum controls posture, balance and the co-ordination of the muscles that are associated with movement.

## co-ordination

From the viewpoint of physical health, the crown chakra is mostly concerned with co-ordination. Co-ordination is needed at all levels. Individual cells within the pituitary gland and the diencephalon have to co-ordinate to ensure the smooth running of the bodily functions. The cerebellum is responsible for helping us to co-ordinate our muscles to achieve balance, posture and movement.

Co-ordination skills are learned at an early age – and reinforced by crawling on all-fours. Research in the last 30 years has shown that children who do not crawl on all-fours in infancy often experience co-ordination difficulties as they grow up. It has been found that returning to this early form of locomotion, even as an adult, can assist the cerebellum in gaining full muscle control. It has also been discovered that

**CROSS CRAWL**
This exercise can be fun if your approach is playful, and especially if you have problems coordinating your arms and legs, or even your thought patterns.

**1** Stand up straight, but relaxed.
**2** Lift up and bend your right knee.
**3** As you do this, bring your left hand to your chin.
**4** Bring your left elbow and right knee into contact or as close as you can.
**5** Lower your right leg, relax your left arm.
**6** Lift up and bend your left knee.

**7** As you do this, bring your right hand to your chin, bending the right elbow.
**8** Bring the right elbow and left knee into contact or as close as you can.
**9** This is one cycle. Repeat fairly quickly 10–30 times.

## ADHO MUKHA SVANASANA

The dog posture helps to balance the energy between the feet and the crown chakra.

**1** Kneel on a non-slip surface on all-fours, making sure your knees are in a straight line under your hips. Make sure your hands are in a straight line under your shoulders and spread your fingers. Tuck your toes under.

**2** Breathe in, lifting your pelvis and straightening your legs, keeping your head low.

**3** Breathe naturally. As you stay in the posture, imagine your bottom is lifting upwards, but your heels are lowering to the floor, stretching your back.

**4** When you decide to release the posture, breathe in, then as you breathe out, lower yourself back on to all-fours.

**5** Slide yourself back until you are sitting on your heels, rest your forehead on the floor and relax for a few moments.

△ **The well-known test of rubbing your stomach while tapping your head is a good example of body-mind co-ordination.**

▽ **Activities such as balancing and juggling require whole-brain co-ordination. Balance in life demands whole-chakra co-ordination.**

many types of learning difficulties can be helped by exercises that utilize opposite parts of the body, confirming that brain co-ordination and function can be improved.

Co-ordination problems can occur on many levels throughout life. Physical difficulties like poor balance or clumsiness are quite obvious manifestations of the problem. Dyslexia often results from poor co-ordination between brain hemispheres, as the eyes move across a page of writing or scan down a text. On a less obvious level, co-ordination with the world as a whole is also a function of the crown chakra. Finding yourself at the right place at the right time, or just happening to meet the one person you were needing to speak to, having lucky coincidences and strange sequences of events that all work out very well, are signs that your crown chakra is feeding you good information.

# Crown chakra – the illusion of detachment

The development of expanded awareness underpins the crown chakra at the emotional level. The opportunity to understand our individual role in the world does not present itself until our teenage years, when we start to move away from the family base.

Growing up in a balanced way, developing adults use the lessons from childhood to create a sense of unity and empathy with people around them. Service to others is often thought to be truly selfless, but there may be hidden motives. We often serve others so we can feel useful and needed, or to create an ideal world where we don't have to see people suffer. We may also see others as more worthy of being cared for than ourselves, diverting attention away from our own needs. Helping those less fortunate can sometimes suppress a sense of our individuality. The loss of personal identity can lead to feeling overwhelmed.

## negative attachment

Many philosophies encourage us to free ourselves from emotional 'attachment' in order to achieve spiritual goals. However, the state of being 'non-attached' sometimes acts as a mask for a refusal to accept personal

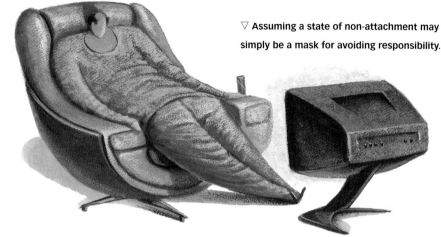

▽ **Assuming a state of non-attachment may simply be a mask for avoiding responsibility.**

▽ **When there is a lack of awareness of personal needs, it is easy for the enthusiastic helper to be a martyr to idealism.**

responsibility. The need to renounce or escape from the responsibility of the family, work or the world in general must be carefully examined for its real motive. Though a change in direction may seem to offer more personal freedom, it could be that working within the current situation could provide a better opportunity for growth. Being emotionally attached to something is sometimes bound up with a fearful unwillingness to allow that thing to change. This closes down other possibilities.

The crown chakra is concerned with openness, and when you get over-attached to a closed way of thinking or feeling, this will tend to prevent you from dealing with reality. The remedy is to be compassionate with yourself and consider all possibilities. Unless this open compassion is first directed towards yourself, allowing healing at the crown chakra, it is impossible to be truly compassionate.

## reality and fantasy

With the upper chakras, particularly the brow and crown chakras, there are a lot of fine or subtle energies coming into play. Because we often feel restricted by the inflexibility of the three-dimensional world (things take time and effort to accomplish, plans go wrong, and so on), there can be a certain attractiveness in the ephemeral quality of these areas of consciousness. The lack of restrictions, the breadth of possibilities, the sense of freedom can work a powerful magic on those dissatisfied with the world of here and now.

For those not drawn to metaphysics and philosophy this might manifest as retreat into a fantasy world of imagination. In a dominant personality where the base chakra is still strong, this imbalance might become a dogmatic idealism or even a megalomania.

An interest in spirituality has the potential to open new awareness of thought and activity that can really help people to break out of old behaviour patterns and become more fulfilled. But equally it can trap us in a web of glamour filled with bright, shiny, amazing things that can never be grasped for long enough to integrate usefully into life. Balance is always achieved where all the chakras are able to perform efficiently. For example, when we are truly grounded, rooted in the secure energies of the base chakra, it will be possible to experience finer, less tangible qualities of reality without losing perspective.

## OPENING UP

Sometimes it can be difficult to imagine how we could continue in life without someone or something. We may have become over-dependent on a person, a way of living or a belief. This exercise will help you to open your life to new possibilities.

**1** Identify a person, situation or belief that you are overly or fearfully attached to.

**2** Sit for a minute or two, allowing your thoughts and emotions to dwell on the issue.

**3** Note down on a sheet of paper all the things you can think of that embody that attachment.

**4** If it is a person: note their qualities, what they give you, what you feel you may lose if they go.

**5** If it is a situation: note what it is you value about it, what status it gives you, why you need it.

**6** If it is a belief, thought or feeling: note what will change if it is no longer with you, and try to include why it is that you fear this.

**7** Look at what you have written. Try to discover the games you have been playing with yourself, or the stories you have been allowing yourself to believe. Sit with this for a few minutes, with your eyes away from your notes, then look again at what you have written.

**8** Close your eyes and imagine all the illusions, untruths or problems you have discovered filling a large bubble in front of you.

**9** When the bubble is full, imagine it floating slowly up into a cloudless sky and dispersing.

# Crown chakra – thought

Thought processes associated with the crown chakra fall into two main categories: how we think the world operates and those thoughts linking us to the universal scheme of things. Our beliefs about the world, our role in it and what we expect from the world form the basis of a behavioural programme that affects all our chakras. We build up a store of beliefs from our experiences in the world. However, thoughts linking us to the wider universe tend to be less easy to identify, and often surface through dreams and meditation. What we expect, especially what we fear, has a knack of being drawn towards us in some way.

## reactions

The way we interpret events and then react to them is the reason why our lives progress or falter in the way they do. For example, suppose you trap your fingers in a door. The possible reactions are:

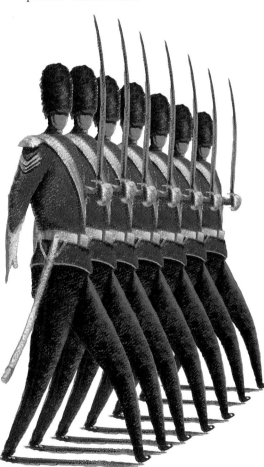

## TUNING IN

The crown chakra enables us to move into realms beyond the physical universe, and this exercise is useful for beginning to co-create a dialogue with an image of a deity or archetype. Sit in a chair, with an empty chair nearby. Imagine an image of a deity or archetype that you strongly relate to, seated in the empty chair. Think of a question or a situation you are encountering where you would appreciate guidance. Pose the question to the image. Close your eyes and sit quietly for a minute or two, then see yourself in the other chair as the image you created. Bearing in mind the question, answer it as spontaneously as you can. If you do not get an answer, don't worry. It is likely that thoughts in the next few hours or dreams overnight will shed some light on your question.

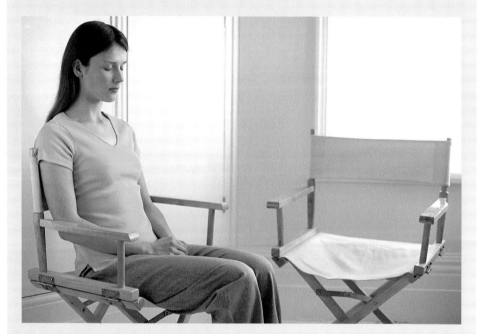

1 No reaction.
2 An exclamation followed by personal thoughts that you should have been more careful.
3 An exclamation followed by berating yourself for always being so stupid.
4 Slamming the door, blaming the person in front of you or behind you.
 5 Hitting the person behind you because it was their fault.

◁ **A society that makes no space for personal revelation runs the risk of becoming repressive and stagnant**.

Each reaction to a stimulus reveals your programming concerning that stimulus, and at the same time reinforces that programming. Your reaction also determines how the world reacts back. In the case of the trapped fingers, options 4 and 5 would be likely to invite a negative riposte, escalating the situation further.

## universal links

The crown chakra is our link to the universal sources of energy and information. In a natural maturing process the adolescent or young adult will begin to look for

△ The desire to expand and grow is inherent in all chakras, from the base right up to the crown, where its connection to universal energy reminds us constantly that more is possible.

answers to questions such as 'Why am I here?' that initiate the search for greater knowledge. Unfortunately this natural progression can be seriously hampered by family, social and religious backgrounds that do not accept individual exploration. In extreme cases, most traditions contain groups or factions whose fundamentalist, sexist or authoritarian practices instil

shame, fear and self-disgust into children who question the status quo. This repression effectively disconnects people from their personal links with spirituality of any type. Children who are experiencing these sorts of restrictions need to break through them or they will find it impossible to develop as individuals and reach their full potential. When the crown chakra is prevented from working normally it is unable to provide all the energy and information required by the other chakras.

A healthy crown chakra is finely balanced on all levels. The thoughts that come and go need to be allowed free passage. It is only when we try to hold on to thoughts, without allowing alternatives or the possibility of change, that disruption of the crown chakra happens.

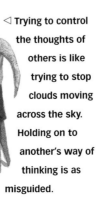

◁ Trying to control the thoughts of others is like trying to stop clouds moving across the sky. Holding on to another's way of thinking is as misguided.

## LITTLE YOGA NIDRA

This exercise, yoga sleep, combines the ability to visualize with the flow of information and energy throughout the body. Sit or lie in a comfortable position and relax for a few minutes, allowing your breathing to slow.

**1** Take your attention down to your left big toe. Don't move it, but be aware of it as a focus for the mind.
**2** Shift the focus in turn to your second, third, fourth and fifth toes. Then to the ball of the foot, instep, top of the foot and left heel.
**3** Carry on to the lower leg, the back of the knee, the top of the knee, top of the thigh, back of the thigh and left buttock.
**4** Take your attention down to your right big toe, second, third, fourth and fifth toes; the ball of the foot, instep, top of the foot and heel; lower leg, back of the knee, top of the knee, top of the thigh, back of the thigh and right buttock.
**5** Take the attention to the left side of your back, the left side from hip to armpit and the left side of the chest. Then to the right side of your back, right side from hip to armpit, right side of the chest.
**6** Take your attention to your left thumb. Then first finger, second, third and fourth; the palm of your hand, back of the hand, wrist, inside of the elbow, outside of the elbow, upper arm, left shoulder.
**7** Then to your right thumb; first, second, third and fourth finger; the palm of your hand, back of the hand, wrist, inside of the elbow, outside of the elbow, upper arm and right shoulder.
**8** On to your head and neck; left side of your face, right side of your face; left ear, right ear; left eye, right eye; mouth, inside the mouth.
**9** At the end you should be feeling totally relaxed. You can repeat it if you are particularly tense or find it hard to relax.

# Crown chakra – unity

△ With the crown chakra cleared of stresses, a sense of lightness, clarity and belonging flows through the whole chakra system.

▽ The series of poses, or asanas, that are undertaken during the practice of hatha yoga are designed to prepare the body for meditation.

The crown chakra focuses on what we experience as well as what we know or understand. If each level of each chakra has been integrated, the crown chakra represents illumination. Unless we truly understand what we see we are unable to apply our creative skills, fulfilling our visions of what is possible. The more we fulfil our visions, the more our consciousness expands, the more we understand what we see, and so on, in ever-increasing awareness.

## yoga

Meditation is a key to the process of increasing awareness. In traditional Hindu philosophies, meditation is undertaken only when the body and mind have been harnessed towards that goal. This is the purpose of yoga, in particular raja yoga, also known as the eight-fold path. The steps or 'limbs' are sequential challenges or tasks:

1 Yama – 'general behaviour'. The student is expected to follow the disciplines that are said to be the foundation of an ethical society: ahimsa (non-violence), satya (speaking the truth), asteya (not envying or stealing), brahmacharya (not wasting

### TRATAK
This is usually practised using a lighted candle as a focus, but you can use anything, like a flower or a stone. Although at first it may cause your eyes to run, it is used to improve eyesight. Place the object at eye level about an arm's length away from you.

Close your eyes and settle your breathing. Open your eyes and look steadily at the item. Try not to strain. After a minute, close your eyes. Visualize the item in your heart chakra or at the brow chakra. When the image fades, open your eyes and repeat.

▷ Many people who think that they cannot meditate, have simply not found a technique that suits them. Traditional techniques include gazing at an object (tratak), use of sound (mantra) and use of shape or geometry (yantra).

resources), aparigraha (not hoarding what you don't need).

**2** Niyama – 'observances'. The student should achieve the following: saucha (purity), santosha (contentment), tapas (effort), svadhyaya (spiritual study), isvara pranidhana (dedication of all activity to higher divine forces).

**3** Asana – 'postures'. Physical exercises prepare the body for sitting in meditation.

**4** Pranayama – 'breath control'. Breathing techniques control and redirect the life-force around the body.

**5** Pratyahara – 'sense control'. This focuses on reaching an understanding of how the mind works so that unwanted tendencies can be weeded out.

**6** Dharana – 'concentration'. This is the preparation of the mind for meditation.

**7** Dhyana – 'meditation': the ultimate goal.

**8** Samadhi – 'union': the fruit of all the preceding practices.

## meditation

Although raja yoga may seem rigid and austere to Westerners, there is logic in it. When all the steps are followed, meditation comes more easily. If you simply decide you are going to meditate and sit down and expect your body, emotions and mind to comply, you will be very lucky if they do so for more than a few minutes, if that.

The mind is a wonderfully restless, inventive faculty and cannot be reined in without great understanding or cunning. Good meditation techniques offer the mind something to do to keep it occupied or active in a tight focus that enables us to experience ourselves in the gaps between thoughts. The more we experience the gap between the thoughts, the more relaxed our bodies become and the more clearly we can see how our thoughts shape our lives.

▷ The crown chakra is the source of all chakra energies in the same way that white light is the source of the rainbow spectrum.

# Keeping the balance

To be effective and long-lasting, chakra healing needs to keep in view a unified picture of the system. The chakras are dynamic energies that represent the whole person, so chakra healing must also deal with the whole person.

# The dynamics of harmony

The chakra system is complex and interrelated – each chakra, both major and minor, can be thought of as a cog in a machine. A change in the movement of one will create changes throughout the whole structure. There will be an efficient flow of energy when all parts are locked together in their activity, working harmoniously together. If one chakra becomes damaged or has its normal range of activity restricted this inevitably puts strain on its closest neighbours, which will also begin to suffer.

A chakra that becomes unbalanced has become stuck at an inappropriate level of activity. It is either working with insufficient energy for its task, or it is working too hard. In either circumstance the other chakras will have to compensate by changing their levels of energy. This means that the system as a whole will be working at one level when it may be more appropriate for it to function at another.

## overall balance

The chakra system, like the rest of the body, responds to the circumstances of its environment. In some circumstances a particular chakra will tend to take a larger role, but it should still operate in a balanced way within the normal working parameters of the system.

Different jobs and lifestyles need special areas of expertise, and the dynamics of the chakras need to adjust accordingly. For example, a singer will naturally need to have an especially active throat chakra to keep the voice healthy. The heart chakra, too, will need to have plenty of energy to foster a depth of feeling,

△ **All parts of the chakra system respond to changes in every other part. Releasing stress from one area will help to relax the whole system, making everything run better.**

empathy and personal involvement in the work. In such a person, an observer who was sensitive to energy fields would see a lot of activity at those two centres. Only if too much energy is focused in one area will problems start to show, beginning in

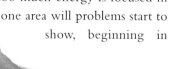

▷ **False equilibrium is where a temporary stability has been achieved. However, even a slight change will bring about a breakdown in order. When this occurs in the chakra system, illness may develop.**

⊲ **Crystals, with their brilliant colour and unique structures are very effective ways to bring balance to the chakra system.**

## considerations

In learning about the symptoms of chakra imbalance presented here and in other books, it is important not to become disheartened about your own state of energetic health. At one time or another most of us will experience extremes of under- and overactivity in all our chakras. It is more important to recognize the common tendencies that are repeated through our lives. Once the most prevalent states are known they can be worked on and necessary alterations can begin to be made.

A physical balancing technique can have a beneficial effect on an emotional chakra stress, and a mental visualization exercise can allow positive change to happen at a physical, everyday level. So use those techniques and exercises that you find most helpful and that fit most comfortably into your everyday life.

Many traditional systems of spiritual development take into account the differences between individuals and their lifestyles, providing different sorts of practices to suit their needs. Today we are lucky in having a wide range of chakra balancing techniques from all around the world. Even the most hectic lifestyle can accommodate sufficient practices to help to reduce the burden of stress that overloads the chakra system and will eventually lead to health problems. The only thing that is needed is for us to set aside a little time dedicated to our own repair. This is largely a process of developing a habit. At first, all sorts of

those places where there are natural weaknesses as a result of past stresses or current overuse.

The chakra system will change gear with a change of activity. Meditation requires a different sort of energy from cooking the dinner; playing a musical instrument requires different skills from listening to an orchestra; escaping from a stressful situation uses different resources from gazing at a serene sunset. Problems arise when, through stress of one sort or another, the chakra system fails to change gear and becomes stuck in a single mode of functioning.

Throughout our lives, stresses of many sorts accumulate in all our systems, from physical to spiritual. These stresses can be like grains of sand or grit that create a little roughness in the workings of our chakra cogs, or they can be like a spanner that seriously throws the whole mechanism out of alignment.

distractions may arise until the routine becomes a natural part of our day. Most balancing practices need a little effort and dedication in the beginning – not only to bring in a new routine, but also because we are beginning to make changes in our energy systems.

Correcting a false equilibrium requires skill and patience. Like a tightrope walker who has been working for years with a pole that has a large weight at one end and nothing on the other end, we adjust to the weight of stress we have accumulated in our lives in order to continue as best we can. Removing all the stress in one go may seem to be the best solution but, like the tightrope walker, we need to familiarize ourselves gradually with the new state of balance at each step. If not, the risk increases that we will feel less secure than we did when we had all the stress.

Like kicking an addictive habit, the biggest problem most of us face is that habitual patterns of behaviour feel comfortable and part of our true personality. Working with a balancing system that focuses on the different levels of body, mind and emotion can be helpful in maintaining an even development of chakra healing. Traditional methods like yoga, Tai Chi and Chi Kung all have outer, physical activities that release stress from the body. They also have mental techniques that involve meditative states, or visualizations that help to clarify the subtle energies of the mind and emotions. It is important to pay attention to all these different levels of practice. For example, it will be of limited value to have a body that is supple and toned if you are still emotionally insecure or stuck in some past trauma.

Contemporary techniques, such as crystal therapy, colour therapy and flower essences, can help to remove specific stresses in chakra centres as well as bringing the whole body into a better state of balance.

# Maintaining harmony

The more our energy systems are brought into harmonious balance, the easier it is to maintain that balance. An old, worn engine is so full of leaks and random rattles it is hard to notice any new disturbing sounds of dysfunction. With a engine that runs smoothly the slightest drop in efficiency is noticed immediately and can be put right.

## exploration

Until some of the stresses can be removed from the chakra system, every one of us will be so busy maintaining our false sense of equilibrium that there will be little spare energy for exploring individual potential. Learning to expand into life is what the evolution of the chakras from base to crown shows us. Getting stuck in any one area narrows our perspective on life. Rather than being able to explore the world with seven different lenses, each with its own special abilities to filter and magnify our experience, we can find ourselves with a single obsessive keyhole through which we squint in an eager attempt to find out what

▽ **When all chakras are free of stress the individual also becomes free to move in whatever direction is of most benefit.**

△ **A balanced and sensitive chakra system will recognize any upset and be able to restore proper functioning automatically.**

▷ **Taking time to balance your chakras is giving time back to your life, so that you will be better able to achieve your goals.**

our life has really been missing. In reality we have all the keys to all the doorways within us at all times. The chakra system is much more than a line of coloured spheres reflecting our bodies' other functions.

## opening doorways

As the ancient yogis of India and Tibet discovered, clearing the chakras of the build-up of debris allows life to be entirely transformed – not by escapist fantasy but by the clear, honest experience of reality as satisfying and nourishing. In this state each chakra becomes a translucent doorway allowing a free flow of universal energies in and out of the body. False boundaries and a frustrating sense of separation dissolve because it was only the stress and imbalance that created them in the first place.

The chakra system always works in two apparently opposite directions. From the base chakra upwards there is an increasing experience of expansion, from the focus and solidity of physical matter, through experience of sensation, personal power, relationship with the rest of the world, communication, understanding and finally integration on all levels at the crown chakra.

Simultaneously there is a flow of energy towards the grounding solidity of physical reality, from the timeless and directionless unity of the crown chakra through

the defining vision of the brow, the form-giving quality of naming, a stabilizing relationship between the self and the world, learning how to control one's power, exploring the senses and finally being able to mould and create the raw material of the world – the practical energy of the base chakra.

In the same way that the individual chakras reflect and balance one another,

▷ **Once you are familiar with the sensation of balanced chakras it becomes easier to enjoy the new freedom it brings.**

each relying on the others in equal measure, the two opposing tides are part of one process, where expansion into the spiritual realms can be effective

only with a reciprocal exploration into the universe of matter.

Whether you consider yourself to be a spiritual or a pragmatic person, whether your goals in life are based on material success or spiritual fulfilment, whether you are a steel-worker or an aromatherapist, a teenager or an octagenarian, learning to heal and work with the chakras is one of the most effective routes to wellbeing.

# Salute to the sun

The salute to the sun is a traditional sequence of exercises from hatha yoga that systematically activates the energies of each chakra. Practised regularly, it can help to energize each chakra and then keep them all in balance. Traditionally this sequence is practised as the sun rises.

**1 Begin by deep breathing for two to five minutes.**

▽ **2 Stand upright and bring your palms together in the traditional 'prayer' position at the centre of your chest. Breathe in and out. Become aware of the distribution of weight on each foot.**

△ **3 On the next inbreath, stretch your arms up above your head and lean back slightly from your waist, looking up towards your hands.**

## YOGA EXPERTISE

Don't worry if when looking at the series of postures in the salute to the sun, you realize you cannot copy them exactly. Just do the best that you can, your chakras will still respond to the sequence, even if your yoga is not advanced.

△ 4 On the outbreath, straighten and bend forward from the hips with the intention of reaching the floor with your hands. (Don't worry if you have to bend your knees.) Place your hands on the floor, your fingertips in line with your toes.

△ 5 On the next inbreath, send your right leg back so that your knee touches the floor and your toes are tucked under. Look upwards. If you have to shuffle your hands and feet around for stability, that is fine.

▽ 6 On the outbreath, lower your head and send your left leg back behind you to join the right leg. Allow your bottom to lift upwards away from the floor. Let your head drop down between your arms. Breathe in.

◁ 7 On the next outbreath, lower yourself, bending your knees so they touch the floor. Continue lowering your chest to the floor, then your chin. (Your hips stay off the floor.)

◁ 8 On the next inbreath, lower your hips, flatten your toes and lift your head and chest up, straightening your arms. Look upwards.

▽ 9 On the next outbreath, tuck your toes back under, pressing on your hands. Lift your hips so they are the highest part of you off the floor, and lower your head.

△ 10 Breathing in (lifting your chin so your knee doesn't catch it), bring your right foot forwards between your hands. (You may have to shuffle your body around a bit to do this.) Look upwards.

▽ 11 Breathing out, bring your left foot up to join your left, creating a forward bend. Keep your head low.

12 The next inbreath takes you upright again, leaning back slightly, with your hands above your head, looking upwards.

△ 13 On the outbreath, lower your arms. Repeat, sending the left leg back first (in step 6). Gradually build up the number of rounds from two to four, then six, and so on. Try to coordinate your breathing as you go. It will eventually come naturally as the postures themselves create an ebbing and flowing of the breath.

# Glossary, suppliers and acknowledgements

## Chakra healing glossary

**Ajña:** 'command', the brow chakra

**Akasha:** pure cosmic sound

**Anahata:** 'unstruck', the heart chakra

**Anandakanda:** the spiritual heart, containing our deepest hopes and wishes

**Asanas:** postures used in the practice of hatha yoga

**Bija mantra:** the sound that stimulates the energy of each chakra

**Bindu:** the cosmic seed, or origin of creation of the universe

**Bodhicitta:** complete openness of mind, acceptance

**Chi:** life-energy in traditional Chinese philosophy, the equivalent of prana

**Chi Kung:** Chinese energizing exercise using breathing control and visualization

**Dharana:** concentration

**Dhyana:** meditation

**Hatha yoga:** the physical aspect of yoga – the practice of a series of postures to aid spiritual development and health

**Ida:** left-hand nadi, carrying lunar energy

**Kundalini:** 'coiled up', the life-force, which resides in the base chakra; when awakened and flowing freely, it brings realization and enlightenment

**Manipura:** 'city of gems', the solar plexus chakra

**Mudras:** positions of the hands designed to balance energy

**Muladhara:** 'foundation' or 'root', the base chakra

**Nada:** the quality of sound

**Nadi:** a channel of energy

**Nadi sodhana:** alternate nostril breathing, an exercise to balance energy

**Niyama:** observances of purity, contentment, effort, spiritual study, dedication to higher forces

**Pingala:** right-hand nadi, carrying solar energy

**Prana:** breath or wind, life-energy

**Pranayama:** breath control

**Pratyahara:** sense control

**Raja yoga:** 'the eight-fold path' that leads to meditation and enlightenment

**Sahasrara:** 'thousand-petalled', the crown chakra

**Samadhi:** 'union', comprehension

**Sushumna:** the central nadi, running parallel to the spine

**Svadistana:** 'sweetness', the sacral chakra

**Tai Chi:** Chinese martial art involving breath control and balanced movement

**Vedas:** body of sacred Hindu texts compiled from c.3000 BC

**Vishuddha:** 'pure', the throat chakra

**Yama:** general behaviour

## Crystal healing suppliers

### UK

Burhouse Ltd, Quarmby Mills
Tanyard Road, Oakes
Huddersfield HD3 4YP
Tel: +44(0)1484 655675
Email: sales@burhouse.com

Charlie's Rock Shop
Unit 14, 1929 Shop,
18 Watermill Way
Merton Abbey Mills,
London SW19 2RD
Tel: +44 (0)208 544 1207

Crystals
25 High Sreet, Glastonbury
Somerset BA6 9DP
Tel: +44(0)1458 835090
Web: www.crystalshop.co.uk

EarthWorks
43 Wessex Trade Centre,
Poole, Bournemouth,
Dorset BH12 3PG
Tel: +44(0)1202 717127
Email: earthworksuk@aol.com

Evolution
117 Fore Street
Exeter, Devon EX4 3JQ
Tel/Fax: +44(0)1392 410759

Simon & Sue Lilly
PO Box 6, Exminster
Exeter, Devon EX6 8YE
Tel/Fax: +44(0)1392 832005
Email: info@greenmanessences.com
Web: www.greenmanessences.com

### USA

Crystal Magic
2978 West Hwy 89A
Sedona AZ86336, Tel: (050) 282-1622

Multistone International
135 South Holliday St, Strasburg,
VA 22657, Tel: (540) 465-8777
Web: www.multistoneintl.com

Rosley's Rocks and Gems
2153 N. Sheffield Ave,
Chicago, IL 60614
(800) 844-1498
Web: www.crystalmaster.com

## AUSTRALIA

CK Minerals Pty Ltd
PO Box 6026, Vermont South
VIC 3133
Tel: 61 3 9872 3886
Email: GYRIL@ckminerals.com.au

Living Energies
Shop B80
Chadstone Shopping Centre
Chadstone VIC 3148
Tel: 61 3 9568 2188
and
Shop 113 Wahringah Mall
Brookvale NSW 2100
Tel: 61 2 9907 1716

Crystal Living
Shop 270, Lower Level
Garden City Shopping Centre
Cnr. Logan and Kessels Rds
Upper Mount Gravatt
QLD 4122
Tel: 61 7 3420 6700

Prosperous Stones
Shop B3 Bay Village
Hastings Street, Noosa
QLD 4567
Tel: 61 7 5445 4622

## Colour healing suppliers
*All products are available internationally.*

Green Man Essences
PO Box 6, Exminster, Exeter
Devon, EX6 8YE, UK
*Suppliers of colour/light essences.*
Email: info@greenmanessences.com
Web: www.greenmanessences.com

AuraLight
'Unicornis', Obi Obi Road
Mapleton QLD 4560, Australia
*Manufacturers of two layers
of colour in bottles*
Email: info@auralight.net
Web: www.auralight.net

Aura-Soma
Dev Aura, Little London
Tetford, Lincs LN9 6QB, UK
*Manufacturers of two layers
of colour in bottles*
Email: info@asict.demon.co.uk

AvaTara
Pitt White, Mill Lane
Uplyme, Devon DT7 3TZ, UK
*Manufacturers of two layers
of colour in bottles*
Email: mail@avataracolour.com
Web: www.avataracolour.com

## Colour healing
## international groups
Light Information for Growth
and Healing Trust
*A charitable trust to promote the use of light, colour
and sound in physical, mental and spiritual health.*
28 Devonshire Road,
Bognor Regis
West Sussex PO21 2SY, UK
Email: dorothye.parker@currantbun.com
Web: www.lighttrust.co.uk

International Association of Colour
*A contact for colour therapy schools worldwide.*
46 Cottenham Road, Histon
Cambridge CB4 9ES, UK

Irlen Institute
*Colour overlays for use in education.*
5380 Village Road, Long Beach
CA 90808, USA
Web: www.irlenuk.com

BeColourWise Courses,
including "Name Colour Courses".
Mary Hykel Hunt
Email: hykel@lineone.net

## Acknowledgements
The publishers would like to thank the
following agencies and photographers for
permission to use their images:
Key: t = top, b = bottom, r = right, l = left, m
= middle

**Crystal healing:** Thanks to Kay Harrison of
'Evolution', Exeter and 'Crystals' of Exeter, and
also to Charlie, at Charlie's Rock Shop,
London, for lending crystals and minerals for
the photography.
   Natural History Photographic Agency: p13t,
Peter Parks; Simon and Sue Lilly p28br.
**Colour healing:** AKG 152t; The Art Archive
121bl; David Noble 158b; Elizabeth Whiting
104bl; 108bl; Robert Harding Picture Library
99tl, 103b, 105tr; The Ronald Grant Archive
127b; Scala 98br, 99br; Sonia Halliday 128ml,
and Laura Lushington 123tl; The Stock Market
97br, 102tr, 103tr, 106bl, 116t, 124ml, 127tl;
Sue and Simon Lilly 160t, 161; Sylvia Corday
p95br; 96br; 128tl.
**Chakra healing:** All artworks created by
Gary Walton, except for the following: Penny
Brown, pp171, 176, 177, 180; Samantha J
Elmhurst, p173.
   Additional images were supplied by the
following libraries: The Artarchive/British
Library, p168 and 172, Attitudes practised by
Hindu devotees in Asanas and Matras 18th
century; Fortean Picture Library, Pair of cosmic
men of traditional Nepalese/Tibetan style
depicting the seven chakras. Private collection,
purchased in Nepal; Werner Forman Archive,
p229, Ceramic tiles from the Alcazar of Seville,
Islamic, 14th century.

# Index